FIGHTING LIKE CATS AND DOGS

By Kyle King

FIGHTING LIKE CATS AND DOGS

By Kyle King

CLEMSON UNIVERSITY PRESS

Revised Edition, 2024

ISBN: 978-1-63804-152-8

Published by Clemson University Press

For information about Clemson University Press,
please visit our website at www.clemson.edu/press.

Typeset by Yana Gudakova
Cover design by Mars O'Keefe

Contents

1977

Charley Pell Leads a Tiger Revival

The raucous delirium of the Tiger players and coaches on the sideline and the joyous pandemonium of the visiting fans in the stands behind their bench suddenly turned to stunned dejection and furious outrage. Winless Clemson had taken a 7–0 lead on the 17th-ranked Bulldogs early in the third quarter and had scratched and clawed to maintain that meager advantage into the final minute of the contest.

Then, without warning, Georgia appeared on the verge of dashing the Tigers' hopes just as Clemson was preparing to celebrate its first win in Athens since 1914, a decade and a half before Sanford Stadium was constructed and the hedges were planted. Vincent Joseph Dooley, outdueled for much of the waterlogged afternoon by Charles Byron Pell, unleashed a bit of trickery in the midst of his desperation…and, with six seconds showing on the game clock, the Dogs did the impossible and scored a touchdown.

The more than 56,000 spectators erupted in exclamations of elated relief and deflated disbelief. An offensive tackle for the Country Gentlemen slammed his helmet down and shouted, "This can't be happening!" In the midst of the cacophony raining down upon the field, Georgia quarterback Jeff Pyburn raised his hands to signal for silence, but, before the crowd could respond, the whistle blew. The Bulldogs were flagged for delay of game. The football, resting nine feet from the goal, was moved back to the eight yard line, the same spot from which Pyburn had found tight end Ulysses Norris for the touchdown.

The penalty changed the percentages, but not the Georgia head coach's decision. Vince Dooley, like Charley Pell, was playing for the win.

Dooley's election to go for two drew its share of criticism; as *The Atlanta Journal-Constitution's* Norman Arey noted, "at best it was more of a hope than a real chance." Once the outcome had been determined, the Bulldog headmaster offered in his own defense a word of explanation: "I thought that since we had an opportunity to win the game, we would go ahead and try. I didn't feel we deserved to win in the first place, so I thought I'd stretch out luck to see if we could win it."

The teams lined up for the conversion attempt. Linebacker Randy Scott, the Clemson captain, spotted a problem. Scott would be named the ACC defensive player of the week following an outing against the Red and Black in which he made 14 tackles, intercepted a pass, and forced a fumble. As a native of Waycross, Ga., Scott badly wanted the win over the Bulldogs, and he realized why the victory was now in dire peril, despite the five-yard setback there were only 10 Tigers on the field.

Georgia had overloaded one side of the formation, stationing Norris, flanker Jesse Murray, and running back Kevin McLee to the right. With Clemson a man down, defensive end Steve Gibbs would be forced to cover multiple receivers when the Bulldogs flooded his area of the field.

Scott yelled for a time out, but, like Pyburn trying to quiet the crowd, he was late. The ball snapped. The blocking broke down and defensive tackle Archie Reese chased the Georgia quarterback from the pocket. Pyburn rolled to his right, toward the sideline. Gibbs had dropped back in an effort to blanket both Murray and Norris. The sophomore signal caller spotted the junior tight end and saw that he was open. Pyburn had to hurry his throw, but he got the pass away before being sacked. Gibbs and Norris went up after the airborne pigskin.

No one outside of the Clemson program ever expected the 46th installment of the border rivalry to come down to a do-or-die two-point try. No less an expert than Jimmy the Greek dubbed the Dogs an 11-point favorite over the Country Gentlemen. The preseason consensus among various media outlets had been that, while the Tigers might improve incrementally in Pell's first season, they would not be markedly better than they had been in Red Parker's final couple of campaigns.

**Charley Pell claimed his first victory as Clemson's head coach
against the bulldogs in Athens**

For every positive the Fort Hill Felines had to offer, there seemed to be a corresponding negative. Quarterback Steve Fuller would be back under center for his junior year after amassing 835 passing yards and 503 rushing yards in a sophomore season in which he had started nine games. The Clemson receiving corps was anchored by split end Jerry Butler and the flanker position would be manned by Dwight Clark, although Willie Jordan was pressing for playing time at the latter spot after spending 1975 as a quarterback and 1976 as a free safety. Butler, Clark, and Jordan all were juniors.

The Tigers also returned Ken Callicutt and Warren Ratchford in the backfield, but the Jungaleer offense was apt to be hampered by the shift to a new system and a rash of injuries. Guard Billy Hudson, fullback Tracy Perry, and tackles Lacy Brumley and Jimmy Weeks all spent time on the sick list as their healthy teammates made the switch from Parker's veer attack to Pell's power I formation.

On the other side of the ball, Clemson brought back eight start-ers, but Pell's "50" defense had its weak points, as well. Three of the returning first-teamers were to be found among the five linemen while a secondary that featured four men deep had to be shaken up due to the lack of depth that put junior college transfer Bubba Rollins in the running for the strong safety spot. The only 1976 starter in the sec-ondary who was back at his previous position in 1977 was cornerback Rex Varn, who was benched due to an emergency appendectomy after being named conference defensive back of the week for his opening performance against Maryland.

With all these challenges confronting the beleaguered Tigers, Clemson began the Charley Pell era at home on September 10 against the 10th-ranked defending ACC champion Terrapins. The Orange and Purple put up a valiant fight against a Maryland club that would end the autumn with a Hall of Fame Bowl win, but the Country Gentlemen came up short in a 21-14 decision.

The loss was familiar territory for the Tigers. In the team's previ-ous 27 outings, Clemson had taken part in 14 games settled by sin-gle-digit margins (including ties) and had won only four of them. The moral victory of a narrow defeat was nothing new for the Jungaleers, but Pell persuaded his players that the closeness of the contest had proven their ability to compete. The South Carolinians went back to work in preparation for their September 17 trek to play defending SEC champion Georgia.

The Bulldogs had begun the autumn with a 27-16 home win over first-year head coach Rich Brooks's Oregon Ducks. The Red and Black appeared sound at most potions, boasting a solid offensive line, six senior starters returning on defense, and the "Mac Backs" – junior Willie McClendon and senior Kevin McLee – lining up at running back. The questions about the quarterback spot appeared to have been answered by the addition of sophomore Jeff Pyburn to the starting lineup.

As Vince Dooley got his team geared up for the game against Clemson that was expected to give him his 100th head coaching vic-tory, the only real concern about the visiting Tigers was one Erk Rus-sell had expressed in that year's summer manual: "During the past two years, we have faced 13 Veer or split-back teams, six Wishbone teams, and five I-formation teams. Our record over the past two years is 19-5. Three of our losses have been to I teams. Our defense has been geared more to play against the Veer and Wishbone (with stop-

Junior quarterback Steve Fuller completed just four passes for 57 yards against Georgia, but he led the Tigers to the upset in Athens that changed the course of the rivalry.

ping the option a must) because we see these offenses so much. The I is coming back on our schedule and, frankly, it scares me to death."

Clemson and Georgia renewed hostilities at 1:30 on a Saturday afternoon for which the weather was variously characterized by the *Journal-Constitution* as "soggy" and shifting "in intensity from a drizzle to a downpour" (Furman Bisher), "gray, overcast, rainy" and "wet from the steady drizzle which fell throughout the game" (Norman Arey), and "a monsoon" (Lewis Grizzard). In the visitors' locker room prior to kickoff, Pell gave the floor to Clebe McClary, a highly-decorated Marine who had been wounded in Vietnam, for the combat veteran to deliver an inspirational pregame pep talk.

There were mix-ups and miscues from the start. Bulldog place-kicker Cary Long sent the opening kickoff into the end zone, where it was fielded by Tiger tailback Lester "Rubber Duck" Brown. The sophomore safety man made the mistake of bringing the ball out and the Classic City Canines swarmed over him at his own eight yard line.

Due to such mistakes in the sloppy conditions, neither team mounted a serious scoring threat in the first half. The closest Clemson came to putting points on the board was a 54-yard field goal attempt by place-kicker Obed Ariri that came up just short. One early Georgia series included a false start, a busted play, and a pass overthrown by 20 yards.

That error-riddled Bulldog possession was one of two first-half drives by the Red and Black to end in Jeff Pyburn interceptions. The sophomore quarterback later described the soaked Sanford Stadium turf as "probably the most slippery field I've ever played on in my life." Randy Scott and freshman defensive back Eddie Geathers both picked off Pyburn passes prior to intermission, with one of their grabs snuffing out a Georgia march at the Clemson 25 yard line in the second period. Although Steve Fuller would not throw an interception all afternoon, his one completion in six first-half attempts contributed to a scoreless opening 30 minutes. There had not been a series meeting in which neither team notched a point before the break since 1919.

After such a lackluster first half, it did not take long for the fireworks to begin in the third quarter. The Tigers kicked off and the Bulldogs punted the pigskin back to give the South Carolinians possession at their own 10 yard line. Clemson could not move the ball, so freshman David Sims was sent in to boot the ball away. Sim's punt proved to be the start of the Country Gentlemen's lone scoring drive.

Cornerback Billy Woods awaited the punt at midfield but the senior defensive starter could not hold onto the oblong in the slippery conditions. Jeff Soowal and Rick Wyatt were on hand for the Jungaleers and Clemson came away with the football. The Tigers retook custody of the oval and advanced it 49 yards in nine plays.

Fuller found Butler over the middle for 15 yards, then the Orange-and-Purple signal caller connected with Clark on third and 10 to carry the Clemsonians to the Bulldog six yard line. A personal foul penalty against the Red and Black set up a three-yard run by Brown that ended with the sophomore tailback diving into the end zone with 6:24 left to play in the third period. Place-kicker Jimmy Russell's extra point gave the Tigers a 7-0 lead.

From that point, the Clemson defense took charge, often bending but never breaking. The Fort Hill Felines kicked off and the Dogs started from their own 32. A 10-play march covering 56 yards was halted at the Tiger 12 yard line when the Clemson defensive front stonewalled Pyburn on fourth and one, stopping him for no gain on a quarterback sneak late in the quarter.

Three plays after turning the ball over on downs, the Classic City Canines caught a break when Fuller fumbled at his own 20 yard line and sophomore defensive end Gordon Terry made the recovery for Georgia. The Bulldogs netted five yards in their next two snaps before Scott burst through the right side of the line from his linebacker spot on third down and knocked the ball loose from Pyburn's possession. The spheroid came to rest on the 17 yard line with Clemson's Brian Kier on top of it early in the final stanza.

Later in the fourth quarter, Sims again was called upon to punt and the Georgia safety man looked to field the short kick at the Tiger 42. The Tigers were penalized for interfering with his fair catch, however, so the Bulldogs began their drive from the visitors' 27 yard line.

Pyburn and McLee combined to carry the Red and Black to within seven yards of pay dirt, but, after the sophomore quarterback was thrown for a loss on third down, Dooley elected to rely upon the foot of freshman Noble Rexford "Rex" Robinson. The first-year place-kicker had split the uprights on an extra point and a pair of field goals (one of them from 47 yards out) against Oregon, but Robinson's 30-yard three-point try against the Jungaleers arced to the left and sailed just outside the post.

Three times since Clemson had scored the contest's only touchdown thus far, Georgia had ventured within 15 yards of tallying the tying score, yet each time the Tigers had denied the Dogs so much as a single point. Pell's Country Gentlemen were beating the Red and Black using the Dooley blueprint of unyielding defense and ball-control offense, leading no less impassioned a Bulldog partisan than Lewis Grizzard to admit that, "had Clemson been beaten in those last six seconds, justice would not have been served."

The Orange and Purple, though, had no intentions of affording Georgia even six seconds within which to attempt a comeback. Following Robinson's missed field goal attempt, the Tigers took over at their own 20 yard line with 6:02 showing on the clock. The Country Gentlemen covered 40 yards in 10 plays without throwing a pass, but, after picking up three first downs in succession, Clemson gambled on fourth and one.

Pell knew the Bulldogs had no time outs left, so he left his offense on the field and Fuller fumbled the snap from center to turn the ball over on downs with 25 ticks remaining in the game. The line of scrimmage was the Georgia 42 yard line. The Tigers went into a prevent defense.

Pyburn pitched a lateral to Norris, who unleashed an aerial 50 yards downfield to Murray. The senior flanker, making his first start for the Red and Black at the end of an injury-hampered collegiate career, made the most of his opportunity with six catches for 112 yards, but none was bigger than the one he brought in with the game on the line. As many as five Clemson defenders were in the receiver's vicinity—Pell would say later, "It looked like we had 12 guys around Jesse Murray when he caught the ball"—but he made the grab at the eight yard line.

After a Pyburn pass was batted down to stop the clock with 12 seconds to go, the Georgia quarterback rolled right on second down, spied Norris in the right corner of the end zone, and completed his only touchdown toss of the game to the Bulldog tight end. Norris's catch made it a 7–6 ballgame and set up the two-point conversion try on which Pyburn rolled out to the right once more and sent the pigskin hurtling towards Norris in the end zone.

Clemson defensive end Jonathan Brooks told the press, "We knew we had to pressure Pyburn. It was what we tried to do all afternoon." Reese's pursuit of the Bulldog signal caller forced him to release a high pass. He overthrew both Murray and Norris, but the tight end went up for it.

Pyburn's memory of the event was as uncertain as the field conditions. In response to a reporter's question, the quarterback could only admit, "I can't remember really what happened. I was being rushed hard, and I just tried to get the ball up. I saw some of our people over there, but I don't really know." Norris, however, was clear: "I was open on the play."

Gibbs broke up the play, the football sailed over Norris's outstretched fingertips and continued out of the end zone, and the Tigers held on for the victory between the hedges that gave the visitors the first one-point win in series history.

The result was bedlam. The Clemson band stayed and played continuously as the Tiger players and coaches celebrated in the locker room for 45 minutes before marching back out onto the soggy sod to be regaled by the Jungaleer musicians with choruses of "Tiger Rag" and "We Don't Give a Damn About the Whole State of Georgia." Charley Pell sat down on the floor and wept. "He didn't sob," Grizzard explained when describing the scene. "He cried like a man cries when he sits back down in the pew after giving his only daughter away in marriage."

Pell, who had been a graduate assistant for Bear Bryant on the day Vince Dooley began his career as a head coach with a loss in Tuscaloosa, had his first victory as the Clemson skipper on what proved to be a bad day for the SEC. On the same Saturday that 17th-ranked Georgia fell to the winless Tigers, the Southeast saw No. 4 Alabama lose to un-ranked Nebraska, Kentucky suffer its only regular-season setback to a Baylor squad that would finish with a losing record, Sun Bowl-bound LSU drop a three-point decision to Lee Corso's Indiana Hoosiers, and Auburn come up short against Southern Miss. Only Ole Miss's upset of third-ranked Notre Dame redeemed the day for the league.

In many respects, the game was as close as the score indicated. Clemson and Georgia gained 14 first downs apiece. Warren Ratch-ford's game-leading 77 yards on 12 carries helped the Tigers amass 179 yards on the ground while the Dogs tallied 161 rushing yards on the strength of a performance by Kevin McLee that tied him with Glynn Harrison for second place all-time on the Red and Black rushing list (behind Frank Sinkwich). The home team punted five times to the visi-tors' seven.

In other ways, though, the numbers were misleading. Geor-gia's 120 passing yards more than doubled the Clemson total; in fact, the Bulldogs gained more yards through the air on their final drive (58) than the Tigers did all afternoon (57). However, Jeff Pyburn had thrown two interceptions and the Classic City Canines had lost a pair of fumbles, with three of the Athenians' turnovers coming on the Fort Hill Felines' side of the field.

The Country Gentlemen fell on all but one of their four fumbles and none of Steve Fuller's 11 pass attempts found their way into the clutches of anyone wearing a red jersey. Turnovers, though, told only part of the story; Clemson won, and deserved to win, because the Tiger defense slowed down the Bulldogs' outside veer play, forced ev-erything up the middle, and made the big stop every time it counted.

Pell recognized the magnitude of the victory. "I've been in foot-ball a pretty good while," he told the press. "I've been in some big ones, but I've never been around a group of men that worked harder and paid more for the price to get what they've got today." In ac-knowledgment of the importance of the event, the Clemson head coach started one team tradition, furthered another, and revived a third.

The first was introduced on the way home from Athens, when Pell stopped the team buses in Commerce, Ga., and sent the manag-ers into a drug store to buy victory cigars, which he passed out to the players. The second was accomplished after the Tigers' return to Fort Hill, when the Orange and Purple's first road win over a ranked opponent since 1959 was enshrined in the "Graveyard" at the entrance to the practice fields behind the Jervey Athletic Center, where victories over top 25 teams away from Memorial Stadium are commemorated.

The third tradition was *winning*.

Vince Dooley, admitting that Clemson simply "whipped" Georgia up front, concluded his postgame comments with a weary admission: "We are going to have a very difficult year...Clemson was supposed to be one of the easier teams on our schedule." Only the first half of that statement turned out to be accurate.

1977 proved to be an outstanding year for Tiger athletics. The men's basketball team carded a record-setting 22 wins, achieved a No. 1 ranking in the course of the season, and produced an All-American and a first-round draft pick in Tree Rollins. The baseball team advanced to Omaha for the College World Series, the women's volleyball program was established, and the school even had discussions with the Greenville Zoo about obtaining a live tiger mascot for Clemson.

Added to those accomplishments was the resurgence of Fort Hill football under the guidance of Charley Pell, who was not even assigned his own state trooper as a bodyguard until after the loss to Maryland. The first-year skipper had taken over a program that had posted eight losing seasons in the previous nine years, and, just two games into his tenure, he had a signature victory and a 1–1 record that matched the one Vince Dooley had owned at the same point in his career in the Classic City.

One week later, Pell reached another milestone by giving the Country Gentlemen their first two-game winning streak since 1974. A 66-yard touchdown strike from Fuller to Butler dropped the Yellow Jackets to 0–2 all-time by the shores of Lake Hartwell and allowed the Tigers to triumph over Georgia Tech by the largest margin they had claimed over the Engineers since 1903, when John Heisman still resided in the Palmetto State.

The Jungaleers' 31–14 win over Georgia Tech was followed up by a 31–13 victory at Virginia Tech and a 31–0 blanking of Virginia. A second-half comeback in Durham gave the South Carolinians their first triumph over Duke in three years, and that 17–11 outcome earned Clemson its first ranking since 1959. The Tigers checked in at No. 19 in the UPI poll and No. 20 in the AP poll as the Tangerine, Peach, and even Orange Bowls began expressing interest in the revived Fort Hill Felines.

N.C. State, which would wind up capturing the Peach Bowl berth and a top 20 spot in the final coaches' poll, arrived in Death Valley as an ACC contender yet left on the short end of a 7–3 score after Willie Jordan's 75-yard punt return set up a 19-yard touch- down pass from Steve Fuller to Jerry Butler. The next week's 26–0 beating of Wake Forest extended the Clemson winning streak to seven games, marking the longest string of consecutive victories since a nine-game skein covering parts of the 1950 and 1951 campaigns.

The Tigers tied favored North Carolina in Chapel Hill in what amounted to a conference championship game. The 13–13 deadlock enabled Bill Dooley's final Tar Heel squad to claim the ACC title and advance to the Liberty Bowl, after which UNC would be ranked as high as 14th in the postseason polls. Clemson came away from the draw with North Carolina sporting a 7-1-1 ledger and a No. 15 AP ranking as the Orange and Purple prepared to host fifth-ranked Notre Dame at Memorial Stadium.

Representatives from eight different bowls were on hand to see Death Valley invaded by the Fighting Irish, who had not allowed a rushing touchdown all year. The game featured a wealth of future NFL talent, as more than 35 players from the rosters of the opposing squads went on to play at the next level…including Notre Dame quarterback Joe Montana and Clemson receiver Dwight Clark, who would hook up for a memorable touchdown pass that allowed the San Francisco 49ers to defeat the Dallas Cowboys in the NFC championship game at the end of the 1981 season.

The Irish got all they bargained for from the Tigers, who held a 17–7 lead and had possession of the ball when disaster struck. A Jungaleer fumble at the Golden Domers' 16 yard line opened the door for Montana to lead a comeback and Notre Dame escaped the Palmetto State with a 21–17 win. The narrow victory marked the closest contest in the season's last 10 games for the Fighting Irish, whose Cotton Bowl shellacking of top-ranked Texas clinched the national championship for Notre Dame.

Due to the closeness of the loss, the Country Gentlemen did not drop in the national rankings and the inspired Tigers leapt out to a 24–0 lead over the Gamecocks in the first Clemson-South Carolina game to be televised on ABC. The Palmetto State Poultry overcame that sizeable deficit and went out in front by a 27–24 score with just under two minutes to play in the game.

Steve Fuller responded by guiding the Fort Hill Felines on a 67-yard march that ended with Jerry Butler leaping into the air after the football and falling backward into the Williams-Brice Stadium end zone for the game-winning touchdown with 49 seconds showing on the clock. Butler's reception, which continues to live in Clemson lore as "The Catch," later was selected by ESPN's Ivan Maisel as one of the 100 defining plays in college football history.

Across the border in Athens, the Bulldogs were making history of another sort as they posted their only losing season in the 25-year Vince Dooley era. Georgia followed up the loss to Clemson by doing what the Tigers would later do; namely, winning a night game in Columbia. The Red and Black did not have Jerry Butler, even though the Dogs had recruited him heavily out of high school, but they nevertheless managed to secure a 15–13 victory over South Carolina to give Dooley the 100th win of his career.

The following Saturday, at Tuscaloosa, Sugar Bowl-bound Alabama exacted its revenge for the Crimson Tide's shutout loss in Athens the year before, as well as for the 1965 flea flicker for which every Bama fan insisted Pat Hodgson's knees were down. In this instance, a fourth-quarter catch by a Georgia receiver was mistakenly ruled out of bounds, allowing the Tide to get away with an 18–10 win.

After a one-point win over Ole Miss and an 11-point win at Vanderbilt, the Dogs hosted Kentucky for a game attended by England's Prince Charles and suffered the most one-sided regular-season setback of Dooley's tenure on the Georgia sideline. The Wildcats mauled the Red and Black by a 33–0 margin. The Classic City Canines improved to 5–3 with a homecoming win over Richmond, but it was all downhill from there.

Jeff Pyburn aggravated a knee injury on the first play of the second quarter in a nationally-televised loss to Florida. The Gators' halftime adjustments allowed them to shut down the Dogs after intermission and the Saurians departed Jacksonville with a 22–17 win. Auburn's 33–14 triumph between the hedges gave the Plainsmen their largest margin of victory over the Red and Black in nearly a quarter of a century and the rash of quarter- back injuries continued in Atlanta, where Georgia would start a fourth-string signal caller against the Yellow Jackets and conclude the 16–7 loss to Georgia Tech with the Bulldogs' sixth-string QB on the field.

At 5–6, Georgia was completely out of the bowl picture, but the Tigers were headed for postseason play for the first time in 18 years. 11th-ranked Clemson was extended a Gator Bowl invitation to face 10th-ranked defending national champion Pittsburgh. The Panthers, like the Country Gentlemen, came into the game with an 8–2–1 record that included a loss to Notre Dame. Both teams had first-year head coaches who previously had played for Bear Bryant at Alabama: Clemson's Charley Pell and Pitt's Jackie Sherrill.

The Orange-and-Purple faithful could not have been more enthusiastic about the bowl bid. One Clemson student even went so far as to cut out a two-foot-high stencil of the Tiger paw and spray-paint the famous logo at five-mile intervals on the road between Fort Hill and Jacksonville. Unfortunately, what awaited the Jungaleers in the Gator Bowl was a disappointing end to a fine campaign, as the Panthers prevailed by a 34–3 margin.

The loss took away little of the luster of the season, though. All three of Clemson's losses had been to teams ranked in the top 10 at the time of the contest and the Tigers were ranked 19th in the final AP poll. The Country Gentlemen had come within an extra point of a conference championship and several individual players were singled out for special recognition.

Right guard Joe Bostic was named All-American and a record-setting seven Tigers made All-ACC. Steve Fuller established a new school mark with 1,655 passing yards, received a National Football Foundation scholar-athlete award, and captured conference player of the year honors. ACC coach of the year Charley Pell was correct when he said after the Gator Bowl, "We came a million miles from last January. This has been a Cinderella ballclub. It's done what no one said it could do."

That storybook season began with a one-point win on a soggy afternoon between the hedges...and Clemson had done it with a team top heavy with juniors. Joe Bostic, Jonathan Brooks, Jerry Butler, Dwight Clark, Steve Fuller, Steve Kenney, Anthony King, Bubba Rollins, Steve Ryan, Randy Scott, and Rich Tuten all would be back for an even more special season in 1978.

1978

Upstart Underdogs Prevent Pell From Achieving Perfection

**Though expectations for the Bulldogs were low in 1978,
Vince Dooley guided the Red and Black to a nine-win season
that included a victory over an outstanding Clemson club.**

S eldom has a one-point win by a bowl-bound conference runner-
up over a squad that finished with a losing record represented a
sea change in any rivalry as stark as that marked by the Tigers'
1977 triumph over the Bulldogs, but the fact that times had changed
for the Fort Hill Felines was attested to by a forthright admission
made by Vince Dooley on the eve of Georgia's 1978 showdown with

the Country Gentlemen: "This is the first time Clemson has ever been favored against us and rightfully so. It will take a super effort to defeat the Tigers' greatest team ever."

The Red-and-Black head coach was not alone in holding that opinion. On the morning of the September 23 contest, *The Atlanta Journal-Constitution's* Jesse Outlar acknowledged that "Dooley may be right" about the quality of the Clemson club just before the newspaper editor picked the Tigers to defeat the Dogs.

The consensus among sportswriters on both sides of the Savannah River was that the Country Gentlemen would claim their second straight victory over the Classic City Canines. "The forecasters all agree," proclaimed *The Greenville News*, "Clemson will have little trouble with Georgia." While *The Tiger's* Richard Brooks conceded that the Bulldogs "could quite possibly spoil some unsuspecting team's perfect season," he concluded that the Red and Black would finish 4–7.

This was not mere *hubris* on the part of the Palmetto State media. Georgia, operating from the I formation and fielding at tight end offensive captain and Spartanburg native Mark Hodge (who had been a teammate of Clemson quarterback Steve Fuller in high school), promised to launch a potent attack, but the Dogs were not expected to accomplish much defensively.

The Red and Black returned only three starters on that side of the ball after losing every first-stringer in the linebacker corps and in the secondary, prompting Brooks to note that "opponents should run through Georgia defenders like beer through a freshman coed." The Bulldogs, tabbed in the preseason as favorites against just three of their 11 slated opponents, were picked to finish eighth in the 10-team SEC.

Clemson, by contrast, was the favorite to win the ACC championship. The Tigers' first-team offensive unit featured seven seniors who would each start at least nine games for the Fort Hill Felines, including such familiar stars as guard Joe Bostic, split end Jerry Butler, flanker Dwight Clark, tight end Anthony King, and Fuller. The Jungaleer quarterback entered his final collegiate campaign as the school's all-time leader in total offense.

Although depth was something of an issue for an "Orange Crush" defense that had experienced several fourth-quarter letdowns the year before, the Tiger D (commonly called "Charley's Angels" in honor of former defensive coordinator and second-year head coach Charley Pell) lost only three 1977 starters to graduation and brought back three of five regulars on the line, with the departed Mark Heniford's defensive end spot being filled by capable senior Steve Gibbs, an experienced backup who had proven himself in Athens the prior autumn.

Bubba Brown and Randy Scott, who had started 12 games apiece at linebacker for Clemson in 1977, each would start 12 games at linebacker for Clemson in 1978. Even though returning cornerback Rex Varn would lose the early part of his junior season to a collarbone injury, versatile senior Willie Jordan was moved over from strong safety to fill in for him.

The 18th-ranked Country Gentlemen, entering the autumn sporting an AP top 20 spot for the first time since 1960, did nothing in their opening outing to disabuse the experts of their faith in the Orange and Purple. Clemson claimed its historic 100th win in Death Valley by delivering a 58–3 demolition of The Citadel to delight the hometown fans as Fuller set a school record with nine consecutive completions. On the same day the Tigers were thrashing one set of Bulldogs on the banks of Lake Hartwell, however, a different breed of Bulldog was surprising some pundits between the hedges.

Favored Baylor, expected to make some noise in the Southwest Conference, took a 7–0 lead in Sanford Stadium before a pair of fourth-quarter fumble recoveries and a trio of Rex Robinson field goals enabled the Red and Black to notch a 16–14 victory over the Bears. Georgia played nearly mistake-free football in the regionally-televised upset, as the Dogs never fumbled, were flagged only for two minor infractions, and went without an interception until starting quarterback Jeff Pyburn was spelled by freshman Benjamin Franklin "Buck" Belue and the rookie signal caller's first collegiate pass was picked off by the visiting Texans.

The 60,000 fans sitting in the stands (and the up to 10,000 more stationed on the bridge and the railroad tracks) for the 1:30 kickoff between Clemson and Georgia the following Saturday afternoon therefore had reason to believe that, while the Bulldogs might be better than expected, the Tigers certainly were as good as advertised. Four out of six prognosticators who picked the game for *The Red and Black* predicted a Jungaleer victory and one of the two homers who sided with the Dogs for the University of Georgia student newspaper, executive editor Tom Cotney, spent the day at the campus infirmary with a 102-degree fever and missed the game he had called correctly.

Due to a new scheduling contract between the longstanding nonconference rivals, Clemson came to the Classic City to play a second consecutive game between the hedges. Not since Vince Dooley's first

**Willie McClendon rushed for 1,312 yards in 1978,
setting a Georgia record for rushing yards by a senior
that still stands.**

two seasons at Georgia had the Tigers made back-to-back trips to Athens, where the Fort Hill Felines were just 1-16 since 1914. The game also represented another significant milestone in the history of the series, as the 1978 contest marked the first time since 1916 that Clemson and Georgia had squared off for six seasons in a row.

The hometown Bulldogs kicked off and the visiting Tigers began their opening drive at the 18 yard line. Seven plays and four minutes later, Orange-and-Purple senior tailback Warren Ratchford bulled his way up to the middle on third and one from the Georgia 48 and the pigskin popped loose from his grasp. Cornerback Scott Woerner made the recovery for the Red and Black. It was an early indicator of the sort of day the Orange and Purple had in store for them.

The Dogs swiftly moved 39 yards in the opposite direction, reaching the Clemson 12 yard line before the celebrated Jungaleer D bowed up and denied the host squad any additional advancement. Georgia's sophomore placekicker, who had been named the offensive player of the game by ABC and awarded the game ball by Dooley the week before, came onto the field and Robinson booted a 29-yard field goal to give the Classic City Canines a 3–0 edge with just over eight and a half minutes to go in the opening period.

The Tigers responded by going on the march early in the second stanza. Clemson moved the oval from the Country Gentlemen's 29 yard line to the Georgians' 28 before fullback Tracy Perry fumbled for the South Carolinians and right end Gordon Terry scooped up the free football for the Athenians, as he had done against the Tigers the year before.

The Bulldogs carted the pigskin back the way it had come, driving from their own 23 yard line to the Tiger 22 on an 11-play possession highlighted by tailback Willie McClendon's 22-yard dash. The senior running back would finish his afternoon with 120 yards on 24 carries. The 55-yard trek ended with Robinson's 39-yard field goal to move the Red and Black out in front by a 6–0 tally with a little more than seven minutes remaining before intermission.

Clemson continued to struggle offensively, as the Tigers' next possession ended in another Ratchford fumble inside Bulldog territory. The senior halfback was beside himself after an error-prone first half in which he twice coughed up the ball and also mishandled a kickoff to give the South Carolinians poor starting field position. In the locker room following the outing, Ratchford called his performance against Georgia "the worst game I've ever played" and vowed: "I won't get over this until I redeem myself."

It wasn't all Ratchford's fault, however. After the Bears connected on 15 of 24 pass attempts against the Bulldogs in the season opener, changes were made in the Red-and-Black secondary. Sophomore Bob Kelly was shifted to cornerback and classmate Jeff Hipp, a Palmetto State native, took over for Kelly at safety. The other corner continued to be manned by fellow sophomore Woerner, who would end the day with a fumble recovery, a trio of pass breakups (including a pass batted from Ratchford's grasp), three unassisted tackles and a pair of assists (among them a stop of Ratchford on a pitchout to prevent Clemson from picking up a first down on the Bulldogs' side of the field), and a game-sealing second-half interception.

The Georgia underclassmen assembled in the reshuffled defensive backfield covered the Tiger receivers so effectively that Fuller was forced to scramble after dropping back to throw on 15 separate plays. The South Carolinians' senior signal caller finished the afternoon as the Country Gentlemen's leading rusher, but the 77 yards Fuller gained on the ground came primarily because his 22 attempts over the top resulted in a mere 10 completions for 137 yards. Dooley would insist in the wake of the contest that it was "one of the best defensive games I've seen a Georgia team play."

The Fort Hill Felines' inability to sustain a drive without surrendering possession forced Pell into a desperate gamble late in the second quarter. In spite of a new rule giving the opposing team custody of the football at the line of scrimmage following a missed field goal attempt, Clemson assigned to Nigerian place-kicker Obed Ariri the task of kicking a 49-yard three-pointer. The try was unsuccessful and the underdog Bulldogs went to the locker room holding a six-point lead on their favored guests.

Fittingly, Georgia's 1968 SEC championship team was honored at midfield during the halftime festivities. The Red and Black certainly looked like a championship-caliber club during the opening 30 minutes, in which the Dogs committed no penalties and no turnovers. Dooley, incidentally, indicated afterwards that he did not care for the latter term; as the Classic City Canines' coach explained, "I would like to call them takeovers instead of turnovers. I think we were causing Clemson to lose the ball."

Pell concurred, admitting: "We gave a good solid Georgia team a chance to whip us. They executed their game plan better than we executed our game plan – and I'm convinced that was the difference." Fuller, however, assigned more blame to the Tigers than credit to the Bulldogs, telling the press, "I'm not upset over Georgia beating us, because I don't feel like they did. I feel like we beat ourselves. They were a well-prepared football team, and they took advantage of what we gave 'em."

The second half began with Clemson kicking off and the Athenians took possession with the line of scrimmage at the home team's 20 yard line. The Dogs proceeded to hold the ball for 18 plays and run almost eight minutes off of the game clock in the course of a methodical 80-yard march that gave the Red and Black their second touchdown in as many games that fall.

The drive was capped off with a third-down play from the Tiger 11. Pyburn took the snap and looked to his right while Scott came bearing down on him. Feeling the pressure from the Clemson linebacker, the Georgia quarterback threw off-balance and released a wobbling pass as he was hit. Flanker Carmon Prince, who was a step ahead of the defender, managed to make the reception for the only touchdown of the day.

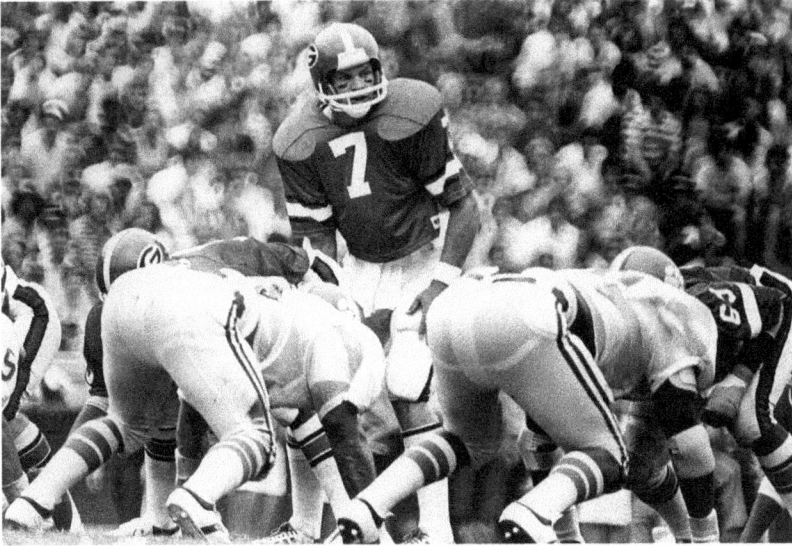

Georgia quarterback Jeff Pyburn passed for just 82 yards against Clemson in 1978, but, unlike the Tigers' Steve Fuller, he did not throw an interception.

Under circumstances much less desperate than those of a year before, the Bulldogs went for two and Pyburn's pass was dropped at the goal line by tight end Ulysses Norris. The incomplete conversion attempt kept the Georgia lead at 12 points, but the long march to paydirt effectively ended all hope for the visiting Jungaleers.

Nevertheless, the Tigers continued to fight. A Fuller run to the Bulldog 19 yard line ended in a fumble, which Kelly recovered for the Red and Black with about 10 minutes remaining in the game. The next Clemson possession reached the Georgia 34 with roughly seven minutes left to play when Fuller sailed a pass to slot end Perry Tuttle in the end zone, only to have Woerner leap in front of the freshman receiver, snatch the airborne pigskin from his hands, and return the interception to the Jungaleer 41 yard line. Even though a penalty for piling on pushed the Dogs back to their own 44, Dooley called the Georgia defensive back's pick "the biggest play of the game."

The Tigers' frustrating day between the hedges ended in the only way it could, with Kelly intercepting a Fuller pass in the Bulldog end zone on the final play of the game to clinch the 12–0 Georgia victory. The final statistics indicated that it had been a remarkably even game;

each team earned 16 first downs, both squads punted four times apiece, and Clemson narrowly led in total offensive yards (293–287).

However, the Red and Black defense had been superb in the clutch. The Country Gentlemen committed all six of their turnovers— or, as Vince Dooley would have put it, the Classic City Canines committed all six of their takeovers—on Georgia's side of the field. Clemson encroached as far as the Athenians' 28 yard line four times, only to punt once and have the ball taken away thrice.

Likewise, although the Bulldog offense had been relatively ineffectual on third down, Georgia had been able to control the ball (and, hence, the clock) from the second quarter forward. The Red and Black may not have managed many outstanding offensive plays— Jeff Pyburn's longest completion was for 21 yards—but neither were they guilty of many mistakes. On a day on which the Georgia defense shut down celebrated Clemson receiver Jerry Butler (who had two catches for 27 yards), the 12 points were more than enough.

The glaring goose egg put up by a Tiger offense that would average 32 points per game over the course of the campaign marked the Bulldogs' fifth shutout of Clemson in the last nine clashes in the rivalry. Another 25 years and 15 series meetings would pass before the Red and Black would again hold the Orange and Purple scoreless, but the Classic City Canines' 19th shutout of the Fort Hill Felines was arguably the most shocking, as only one other regular-season opponent would hold the Country Gentlemen under 28 points.

Although the locker rooms remained the same and many of the key players involved were unchanged, the moods of the respective teams had been reversed in the space of a year. In 1977, Clemson had taken the field after receiving a pregame pep talk from a decorated veteran; in 1978, Georgia had taken the field after being presented with custom-made military dog tags by an Army ROTC professor at the University as part of a publicity program whose slogan was, "Every dog should have a tag." Likewise, in 1977, the Tigers had been jubilant in the visitors' dressing room after their stunning victory between the hedges, but, in 1978, a *Red and Black* headline proclaimed: "Clemson troops solemn after loss to Bulldogs."

Vince Dooley, on the other hand, was almost ebullient, saying, "I'm happy to win any game where our team is the underdog....We beat a team that is supposed to be better than we are." *The Tiger's* Cobb Oxford, despite maintaining that "Clemson led in every statistic except the score," concluded that the South Carolinians "made more errors than the Atlanta Braves" and that being favored to win "spelled their doom." Pointing to the Bulldogs' 32–12–3 record in the series and noting that eight of the Jungaleers' dozen wins in the rivalry came before 1910, Oxford stated with considerable exaggeration that "Georgia losing to Clemson is like the Tigers being defeated by The Citadel."

The sportswriter for the Fort Hill student newspaper did, however, echo the sentiment expressed by Frank Howard years before, when the Baron of Barlow Bend decided to drop Presbyterian from the Orange and Purple's schedule. "Last year," Oxford wrote, "the opener with Maryland was a hard-fought seven-point defeat, [and] the Tigers were prepared for the game 'between the hedges.'" Dooley concurred, commenting, "I wonder if beating The Citadel as easy as they did hurt them. It couldn't have helped them prepare for us."

Nevertheless, all was not lost for Clemson. Steve Fuller put the result into perspective when he observed, "There are too many games left in the season for us to let one tough loss get us down." The postgame report written by Dan Foster of *The Greenville News* put it best: "It was an opportunity that was lost, not a whole season."

The Tigers rebounded from their four-fumble, two-interception afternoon in Athens to batter Villanova, Virginia Tech, Virginia, and Duke by a cumulative tally of 127–29. The Fort Hill Felines' improvement to 5–1 enabled Clemson to climb back into the top 20 in both polls before the Tigers traveled to Raleigh for their October 28 date with N.C. State. The Wolfpack, also sporting a 5–1 ledger, became victims not only of the Orange and Purple, but also of the Browns.

Clemson tailback Lester Brown, who would finish fourth in the country in scoring despite starting only eight games, turned in a 117-yard, two-touchdown performance, while Tiger linebacker Bubba Brown earned *Sports Illustrated* national defensive player of the week honors with 18 tackles against N.C. State. Together, they guided the South Carolinians to a 33–10 triumph over a Wolfpack squad that would end the autumn with a 9–3 record, a Tangerine Bowl win, and a No. 18 final ranking in the sportswriters' poll.

The Country Gentlemen worked their way up in the standings with a 51–6 thumping of Wake Forest and a 13–9 escape against North Carolina to set up another critical conference clash on the road. This time, the 12th-ranked Tigers made the trek to the Old Line State to face 11th-ranked Maryland in a battle for ACC supremacy.

Although Clemson employed a balanced attack that generated 226 yards on the ground and 216 through the air, Steve Fuller's touchdown passes of 87 yards to Jerry Butler and 62 yards to Dwight Clark allowed the Fort Hill Felines to overcome three separate seven-point deficits and claim a 28–24 victory over the Terrapins. Maryland went on to post a nine-win regular season, receive a Sun Bowl bid, and finish in the AP top 20.

The win clinched Clemson's first Atlantic Coast Conference championship since 1967, prompting representatives of the Gator Bowl to extend a second consecutive invitation to the Tigers in the locker room after the victory over the Terps. The team was met by 8,000 supporters at the Greenville-Spartanburg Airport upon its return from College Park and Monday's rankings saw the Fort Hill Felines catapulted into the top 10.

The Jungaleers wrapped up the regular season in their home finale against the rival Gamecocks. In the first game played in Death Valley after the addition of the upper deck to the south stands of Memorial Stadium, a record crowd of 78,000 fans saw the Orange and Purple produce three 100-yard rushers in a single outing for the first time since 1950. Clemson held a 14–0 lead before South Carolina had taken its first offensive snap and the home team dealt the Palmetto State Poultry a 41–23 defeat.

To the victors went the spoils. The 10–1 Tigers moved up to seventh in the November 27 polls, marking the highest ranking ever held by a Clemson squad at the end of a regular season. Charley Pell again was named ACC coach of the year. Joe Bostic again was named first-team All-American. Steve Fuller again was named ACC player of the year, made academic All-ACC for the third time, and eventually became the second Tiger athlete to have his jersey number retired.

Lester Brown's top four finish in scoring was not the only national distinction earned by a Clemson player, either. Jerry Butler was among the top 10 players in the country in receiving. Willie Jordan was the fourth-best punt returner in college football (ahead of, among others, eighth-place Scott Woerner). As a team, the Tigers ranked fourth in total offense, fifth in scoring offense, sixth in rushing offense, eighth in pass defense, fifth in scoring defense, and fourth in turnover margin. Four of Clemson's 15 lost fumbles, and two of the Tigers' five interceptions, in the course of their 1978 campaign came in Athens.

The 1978 Orange-and-Purple squad produced two players who finished among the top 10 vote-getters in that year's Heisman Trophy balloting (including sixth-place finisher Fuller, who received 19 first-place votes) and six first-round NFL draft picks (including Butler, who became the highest Clemson player taken in the professional football draft since Banks McFadden nearly 40 years before, and Dwight Clark, who was selected by the San Francisco 49ers' Bill Walsh).

Clemson had come a long way since the loss to Georgia that dropped the Tigers from the No. 18 spot in the UPI rankings and allowed the Bulldogs to ascend to a No. 19 placement in the AP poll. The Red and Black also had made great strides, although the Athenians stumbled in a night game in Columbia one week after upending the Jungaleers in Sanford Stadium. A favored South Carolina squad led by George Rogers (and aided by first-year Gamecock assistant coach Ray Goff) collared the Dogs by a 27–10 margin.

After that setback, Georgia again demonstrated the penchant for comeback victories the team had exhibited against Baylor. Ole Miss took an early 3–0 lead on the Classic City Ca nines before Vince Dooley's club reeled off 42 unanswered points. A favored LSU unit went up 14–0 on the Bulldogs in a night game in Baton Rouge before Georgia came back (thanks partly to a 99-yard kickoff return by freshman split end Lindsay Scott) to claim a 24–17 victory over a Bayou Bengal outfit that finished 8–4 and attended the Liberty Bowl.

Following the Red and Black's 31–10 win over Vanderbilt, Kentucky went out in front of the Dogs by 16 points in an evening contest in Lexington, yet Georgia again roared back to hand the Wildcats a 17–16 setback on a last-second Rex Robinson field goal. The Classic City Canines, dubbed the "Wonderdogs" due to their ability to come from behind and find a way to win, took care of VMI at home in a 41–3 laugher before traveling to Jacksonville to face the Florida Gators and their imperiled coach, Doug Dickey.

The Sunshine State Saurians became the first team to hold Willie McClendon under 100 yards in an autumn in which the senior tailback would break Frank Sinkwich's 37-year-old school rushing record. Even so, an early 3–0 Florida lead failed to hold up as, for the third time in six years, a fourth-quarter two-point conversion attempt settled the outcome. Georgia emerged from the Cocktail Party a 24–22 winner over Florida, signaling the end of Dickey's days as the head coach in Gainesville and earning the Bulldogs a No. 8 poll position…in the country, not (as the experts had forecast) in the conference.

Auburn managed to tie Georgia and deprive the Dogs (with a 5–0–1 SEC ledger) of the conference championship that instead went to Alabama (at 6–0 in league play), but the Red and Black achieved redemption in their final home game against a Peach Bowl-bound Yellow

Jacket squad that had won seven of its last eight outings. When Georgia Tech built up a 20–0 lead between the hedges, Dooley benched Jeff Pyburn and sent in Buck Belue, who brought the Bulldogs back to beat the Engineers in a nationally-televised 29–28 thriller.

Georgia finished its scheduled slate with a 9–1–1 record and a No. 7 spot in the UPI poll after coming from behind in six of the club's nine wins, but the Wonderdogs' luck finally ran out in another night game on New Year's Eve. The Red and Black traveled to Houston for the Bluebonnet Bowl and jumped out to a 22–0 halftime lead on a Stanford squad coached by the selfsame Bill Walsh who would later draft Dwight Clark after becoming an innovative NFL skipper. The Cardinal turned the tables on the Dogs, staging a comeback of their own to hand the Athenians the 25–22 loss that dropped Georgia to 15th in the final coaches' poll and 16th in the sportswriters' season-ending rankings.

Clemson had been back in action two days earlier, in the Gator Bowl on December 29, and that fact rankled Charley Pell. The Tigers had posted their first 10-win season since 1948, captured their conference championship, earned numerous accolades, and finished in the top 10, yet they had been denied a New Year's Day bowl bid. This led Pell to conclude that he would never be able to win a national championship at Fort Hill, and this conviction set into motion a stunning and sudden series of events.

On Saturday, December 2, the Florida Gators lost for the seventh time in the 1978 season and the 43rd time in the nine-year tenure of Doug Dickey, whose service as the head coach in Gainesville was at an end. The following Monday, December 4, the president of the University of Florida met with Pell at the very same Greenville-Spartanburg Airport at which the Clemson Tigers had been greeted by their fans upon their return from claiming the ACC championship. As a result of that early morning meeting, Pell was hired to succeed Dickey at the Gator helm.

Later that same day, Pell returned to Fort Hill and submitted his resignation as the head coach of the Tigers. He took part in a conference call with most of the members of the University's Board of Trustees that afternoon and contacted his assistant coaches, who were on the road recruiting. Pell met with his staff at 4:00 on Monday afternoon before briefly addressing the team at 5:00. The players later reported that their former coach's short speech did not include an express statement that he was leaving, but they understood the import of what he had to say.

Pell left immediately for the Sunshine State, where he was scheduled to appear before the Jacksonville Beach Quarterback Club at 7:00. A press conference had been arranged for 9:00 on Tuesday morning in Gainesville and the new Gator skipper would remain in Florida for the rest of the week. Clemson athletic director Bill McLellan, despite being caught completely off guard by this unexpected turn of events, met with assistant head coach Danny Ford after Pell left for his speaking engagement.

The departing head coach hired a pair of Clemson defensive assistants to follow him to Florida and Pell was interested in taking Ford with him, as well, but he recommended that the young offensive line coach be allowed to succeed him at the Tiger helm. McLellan likewise indicated that he would endorse Ford's candidacy to be the new Clemson head coach.

At 9:30 on the morning of Tuesday, December 5, the Student Affairs Committee of the Board of Trustees convened to decide upon Pell's successor. A petition supporting Ford for the post was signed by almost every Tiger football player and delivered to the committee, which met with the assistant head coach at 10:00. Ford was the only candidate considered and his appointment was recommended unanimously to the full board.

Danny Ford was informed at 1:00 on Tuesday afternoon that he had been chosen and his hiring was announced by the chairman of the Board of Trustees at a news conference a little over two hours later. The new coach went to work immediately without worrying about the formality of a written contract. "There have been too many other things to do, like recruiting and practicing for the Gator Bowl, to sit down and sign a contract," Ford explained. "I decided we could do all that later... If I can't trust the people I work for, then I'm in the wrong business."

It was intended originally that Ford would take over recruiting but that Pell would remain in charge through the bowl game. This initial decision was unpopular with Clemson fans, many of whom were angry over their former head coach's betrayal and wanted their new headmaster installed in his post without delay. Pell did not help matters by making such ill-considered comments as, "I'm splitting, and I may never come back."

The backlash was swift. A banner was unfurled on a building in downtown Clemson announcing: "Pell is a traitor." A still-embittered Red Parker, who now was running a car dealership in Arkansas, emerged from seclusion to tell the media he was not surprised at what he saw as his former defensive coordinator's latest act of disloyalty. All 73 Tiger players signed a new petition, this time asking that Ford be allowed to coach the Gator Bowl. Pell returned from Florida on Saturday, and, on Sunday night, another press conference was convened to announce that all head coaching duties, including bowl preparations, had been turned over to Ford, effective immediately.

Because he departed in a way that left the Clemson faithful justifiably feeling shocked and offended, Charley Pell forfeited the affections of the fan base to whom he had delivered an 18–4–1 record that was exceeded in school history only by John Heisman's 19–3–2 career ledger. Following an 0–1 start, Pell had gone 10–0–1 in ACC play.

In his place now stood Danny Ford, who, at just 30 years of age, was the youngest head coach in Division I college football. He was, however, in good company, as both Heisman and Howard had been hired as Clemson head coaches as 30-year-olds. Likewise, Ford was the fourth Alabama alum among the last five skippers to have served at Fort Hill and his promotion from within was in keeping with the Tiger tradition that had seen Howard and Pell elevated from among the existing assistants when a vacancy at the top occurred.

Ford now faced the daunting challenge of preparing his team for the Gator Bowl. He had less than three weeks within which to get ready, he was shorthanded due to his predecessor's having taken two members of the Clemson staff with him to Gainesville, and he would be matching wits in Jacksonville with Wayne Woodrow "Woody" Hayes, who had been coaching longer than Ford had been alive. Ford took his assigned task in stride, remarking that "I know more about Woody Hayes than he does about me."

The game began with a good omen for the Jungaleers when Clemson was assigned the same locker room in which victorious Pittsburgh had celebrated after the previous year's postseason tilt by the St. John's River. The Tigers took on 20th-ranked Ohio State in the building in which the rival Bulldogs had claimed a two-point triumph over the Florida club that now was coached by Charley Pell, and Danny Ford began his head coaching career with a win in the Gator Bowl by the identical margin.

The Tigers waged a back-and-forth battle with the Buckeyes. Steve Gibbs blocked a critical Ohio State extra point attempt in the second quarter. After Tiger tackle Jim Stuckey stopped OSU quarterback Art Schlichter on a two-point conversion try, Clemson clung to a late 17–15 lead. The Buckeyes were given one last chance when Gator

Bowl MVP Steve Fuller was hit while pitching out to Warren Ratchford and Ohio State recovered the fumbled football.

On third down deep in Tiger territory, Schlichter went to the air and his pass was picked off by second-string middle guard Charlie Bauman, who returned the only interception of his four-year collegiate career for 12 yards before going out of bounds by the Buckeye bench. Hayes, whose contentious relationship with the press caused him to be given a pair of boxing gloves as a gift at the pregame coaches' luncheon, punched Bauman and drew two 15-yard unsportsmanlike conduct penalties for his behavior. Hayes was fired the next day after 28 seasons on the Ohio State sideline.

Clemson finished at No. 6 in both major polls, giving the Tigers their highest final ranking in school history and making 1978 the first season since 1959 in which both the Fort Hill Felines and the Classic City Canines finished in the top 20. The Jungaleers had won 11 games in a single campaign for the first time in three decades and their 19 triumphs in 1977 and '78 marked the best two-year victory tally in school history. Clemson boasted the nation's longest winning streak after taking 10 in a row following the loss to Georgia and the Tigers entered the offseason having begun a new era under the guidance of the country's only undefeated head football coach, Danny Ford.

1979

Marvin Up the Middle

Changes at the top rocked people throughout the world in 1979. The Shah of Iran fled the country and the Ayatollah Khomeini returned to rule in his place. Ugandan president Idi Amin was driven from office, while Anastasio Somoza resigned as the leader of Nicaragua and went into exile. A more peaceful transfer of power took place when Margaret Thatcher became the first female prime minister of Great Britain.

Meanwhile, in upstate South Carolina, the Clemson faithful were preparing for the first full season of the Danny Ford era.

Tiger fans had high hopes for their new coach after he steadied the program in the wake of Charley Pell's abrupt defection and guided the Country Gentlemen to a dramatic bowl win over Ohio State. Expanded Memorial Stadium would open that autumn with new scoreboards, a new sound system, and nearly 9,000 new seats. Tailback Lester Brown would be back for his senior season after becoming the second 1,000-yard rusher in Clemson history in 1978. These were good times for the defending ACC champion Tigers.

Ford knew, though, that his team, while talented, was inexperienced. The Fort Hill Felines had to replace seven starters from the league's leading offense, including Steve Fuller, Jerry Butler, and three of five first-team offensive linemen. Doubts about the depth of the defensive line underscored the uncertainty concerning an Orange-and-Purple squad that lost 15 starters, including eight first-team All-ACC players, from the previous year's club.

**Danny Ford guided the Tigers to eight winds and a
Peach Bowl bid in his first full season as Clemson's head
coach.**

Because the Tigers had to replace so many key figures, Clemson was nowhere to be found in the Associated Press preseason poll. Georgia, however, made the grade as the squad the sportswriters identified as the No. 11 team in the land heading into the fall. The Bulldogs were projected once again to be Alabama's chief challenger for the SEC title. This prediction turned out to be true, but not in the way any of the pundits expected.

The Red and Black had problems of their own. Vince Dooley's Dogs returned 41 letter- men and 15 starters, but Willie McClendon was not to be found among them. Dooley had to choose between sophomore Buck Belue and senior Jeff Pyburn in selecting his first-string quarterback, and, against what was expected to be a difficult schedule, the Classic City Canines would lack the element of surprise that had aided the "Wonderdogs" the year before.

The questions facing Clemson were answered one week earlier than those confronting Georgia, and the Tigers were a good deal more pleased with the results. On September 8, the Country Gentle-men kicked off the campaign in Death Valley against Division I-AA Furman. Although Brown would be taken from the game due to a fe-ver, the Orange-and- Purple tailback tallied 101 yards and two touch-downs in just a dozen first-half carries as the Fort Hill Felines cruised to a 21–0 win. The triumph over the Paladins marked the Jungaleers' first season-opening shutout in seven years.

The Clemson victory was highlighted by the performance of Jesup, Ga.'s Billy Lott, who had succeeded Fuller under center. Lott proved to be a capable replacement for the highly-decorated quar-terback, as the Tigers'new signal caller completed eight of 13 passes for 163 yards, including an 81-yard completion to flanker Perry Tuttle.

The autumn got off to a much rockier start in the Classic City on September 15. The heavily favored Bulldogs were hosting John Mackovic's Wake Forest Demon Deacons, who had not posted a win-ning season since 1971 and had gone 1-10 three times in the previous five years.

In a contest that earned the Wonderdogs the nickname "Blunder-dogs," the Red and Black threw four interceptions and lost three fum-bles, fielded by a running game described by Pyburn as "nonexistent," and surrendered a whopping 570 yards of total offense. Place-kicker Rex Robinson's last-ditch 58-yard field goal try fell only a couple of feet short of the crossbar on the final play of Georgia's stunning 22-21 loss to Wake Forest. The shocking upset springboarded an eight-win regular season and a Tangerine Bowl berth for the Demon Deacons, whose most recent previous foray into postseason play had come in the 1949 Dixie Bowl.

The Bulldogs' next opponent, the Tigers, did not get the opportu-nity to revel in their border rivals' misfortune, however. The same day, Clemson hosted Maryland in the Fort Hill Felines' conference opener. Much about the contest went right for the Tigers, who tallied 22 tackles for loss (including eight sacks) against a Terrapin team that fumbled six times versus the Jungaleers.

Nevertheless, Maryland's Charlie Wysocki rushed for 125 first-half yards against the Orange and Purple while his teammate, Dale Castro, connected on four field goals in the Terps' 19–0 win alongside Lake Hartwell. The result snapped Clemson's 11-game winning streak since the previous year's loss to Georgia, as well as marking the Tigers' first setback in eight home games and 12 conference games. Not since the Bulldogs' 1976 victory in Death

Valley had the South Carolinians been held scoreless in Memorial Stadium. The Terrapins would end the autumn with seven wins, but a four-game midseason losing streak made 1979 one of only two seasons between 1973 and 1985 in which Maryland remained home for the holidays.

Clearly, both Clemson and Georgia needed to make some changes, and quickly. After describing the loss to Wake Forest as the most embarrassing of his career, Dooley offered an unvarnished assessment of his team: "I think the real question here is how badly have we been overrated. I know we are overrated. The question is to what extent we are overrated." On the Thursday night before their trip to the Palmetto State, 36 Georgia players shaved their heads as a show of dedication. Even a team trainer got into the act, leaving enough hair on the back of his skull to spell out "Go Dogs."

Clemson opted to prepare for the showdown by more conventional means. Early in the week, Ford indicated that he intended to simplify the Tigers' offense, and the young coach ultimately decided to concentrate on establishing an inside running game by pounding the fullback up the middle. It was a gutsy move for a team whose fullback, Marvin Sims, had chalked up just 31 yards on seven carries in the South Carolinians' first two games.

In 1979, the Bulldogs prepared to take on the Tigers by shaving their heads before the game.

The grass in Memorial Stadium was soaked from 24 hours' worth of rain prior to the early afternoon contest, yet 63,500 fans were in attendance for the September 22 clash. Both offenses got off to somewhat sluggish starts on a muggy 85-degree day that produced a scoreless first half.

The Bulldogs, who held the ball for 14 minutes and 14 seconds before intermission, gained just 82 offensive yards in the first two quarters. The Tigers, who were in possession of the pigskin for just under 16 of the first 30 minutes of the contest, punted five times in the first half and did not get production from the fullback spot, as Ford had hoped. Sims, whom the Georgians halted for a loss for the first time in the senior back's collegiate career, nearly matched his production from the two previous contests, yet still he had only seven rushes for 29 yards by halftime. Clemson's attempts to run to the outside regularly were stymied by the Bulldogs.

Despite the scoreless deadlock at the break, the opening half had offered an early inkling of the way the wind was blowing. The Tigers lost a Lester Brown fumble at the visitors' 29 yard line in the first quarter and the Jungaleers made it as far as the Bulldog 31 before Billy Lott threw an interception in the second quarter. A Marvin Sims fumble in the final minute before intermission snuffed out another Clemson drive, moving Ford to remark: "If it hadn't been for those turnovers, I think we might have had 21 points in the first half."

The Bulldogs' I-formation attack was struggling. Not only was 1978 senior stand-out Willie McClendon no longer in school, but many players remaining on the Georgia roster had been sidelined. Tailback Matt Simon and fullback Jimmy Womack were out for the Clemson game, and Dooley pointed out afterwards that two tackles and two tight ends had been lost, as well. In McClendon's and Simon's stead, backup tailbacks Melvin Dorsey, Ed Guthrie, and Steve Kelly between them ran the ball 20 times for just 57 yards against the Country Gentlemen.

To the Classic City Canines' growing sick list was added defensive guard Tim Parks, who suffered strained knee ligaments in the second quarter and was replaced in the second half by Eddie Weaver. To make matters worse, cornerback and punt returner Scott Woerner suffered a freak injury in the third quarter, spraining his ankle on a non-contact play.

Clemson kicked off to begin the second half and Georgia could not move the ball, so the Jungaleers began their first possession of the penultimate period at their own 30 yard line. The Country Gentlemen promptly went on the march in the manner their head coach preferred. On the second snap of the Tiger drive, backup fullback Tracy Perry scampered up the middle for 23 yards. The inside ground game belatedly but emphatically had been established by the home team.

In four- and five-yard increments, the Orange and Purple powered their way down the field in 14 plays. Clemson did not attempt a single pass in the course of the possession, but Sims showed his mettle by blasting ahead for 27 yards on six carries during the 70-yard march. On third and goal from the one yard line, Brown went off right tackle and dived into the end zone. Place-kicker Obed Ariri split the uprights and, with 6:51 to play in the third quarter, the Tigers were on the board with a 7–0 advantage.

Marvin Sims was well on his way to a career-high 146 yards, thanks to a 15-carry, 117- yard second half. Clemson's efforts to skirt the ends had failed in the first 30 minutes, but pushing the pile by driving through the middle proved unstoppable in the final two periods. All five starters on the Orange-and-Purple offensive line played the whole game with- out being spelled by any second-stringers, and Sims gave the credit to the Tigers' forward wall. "All I had to do was get the ball and go straight ahead," the fullback explained simply.

Following the touchdown, the South Carolinians kicked off and the visiting Athenians proceeded to move the ball from their own 20 yard line to the opposite 20. Three consecutive completions covering 55 yards moved the Bulldogs inside the Tiger 25 yard line, where Dooley decided to give the ball to Guthrie on three straight snaps. When asked afterwards about his play-calling, the Georgia head coach said, "It didn't work, so I guess you could say it wasn't a good decision...I guess in other years we could have gotten 10 yards in four running plays."

Instead, Guthrie gained five yards on three running plays, so Robinson was sent in for his second field goal attempt of the game. The Bulldog place-kicker had missed a 52- yard try earlier in the outing and his latest three-point effort sailed wide right from 37 yards away to keep the Red and Black off the scoreboard and give the Tigers custody of the football at their own 20.

Two of Lott's five completions of the afternoon came on Clemson's ensuing drive, but the bulk of the work was done by Brown, Perry, and Sims as the Fort Hill Felines covered 79 yards of real estate. A three-yard scamper by Brown on fourth and one gave the Tigers a first down inside the Georgia 10 and a personal foul penalty against the Dogs moved the Country Gentlemen to within nine feet of paydirt.

Three more plays got the South Carolinians only as far as the one yard line and Ford elected to go for it on fourth down for the second time in the drive. As with Dooley's decision to feed the football to Guthrie, the choice caused a head coach to second-guess himself. "I knew better, I knew better, I knew better," Ford later lamented, adding: "I sat back there and listened to some 18-year-olds against my better judgment."

The pigskin went to the tailback on fourth down and the result may well have been the finest collision of nicknames in the history of the Clemson-Georgia rivalry as Eddie "Meat Cleaver" Weaver stopped Lester "Rubber Duck" Brown inches short of the goal line with 9:42 remaining in the game.

The Classic City Canines took over with their offensive backfield lined up in its own end zone. On first down, split end Lindsay Scott ran a fly pattern down the left sideline, but Jeff Pyburn's pass was incomplete. On second down, the snap from center Ray Donaldson was bobbled by Pyburn and the Bulldog quarterback was sacked behind the goal line by cornerback Eddie Geathers and defensive end Bob Goldberg.

Just 13 seconds after their offensive teammates failed to convert on fourth down, Clemson defenders were seen leaping into the air with their arms raised to celebrate the Tigers' 9–0 lead. Such plays as the safety that staked the South Carolinians to a two-score advantage caused Ford to comment, "Our players were good enough today to overcome their coaching."

The home team took the resulting free kick at the Clemson 42 yard line and began the Tigers' third sustained drive of the second half. The Country Gentlemen tallied 36 of the 51 yards they would gain on that possession with a run up the middle by Sims. The play demonstrated the effectiveness of Ford's game plan, which had taken a while to work but which proved devastating after halftime. Clemson held the ball for nearly 22 of the last 30 minutes of the contest and finished the day with over 300 rushing yards to its credit.

Sparked by Sims's latest long run, the Tigers moved inside the Georgia 10 yard line to set up the 24-yard Ariri field goal that made it 12–0 for the Fort Hill Felines with under six minutes to play. As the clock wound down, the fans in the stands must have thought they were

After being stynied on outside runs in the first half, Clemson fullback Marvin Sims broke free for 117 second-half rushing yards against Georgia, most of which came on runs up the middle.

watching a replay of the previous year's game with the teams reversed. In 1979, as in 1978, the winning team had scored a touchdown on its opening drive in the third quarter, and, late in the fourth period, it appeared that the prevailing squad would pocket a 12–0 victory.

As it turned out, though, the 1979 clash between the old rivals had a bit of 1977 in it, as well. Two years before, the two teams also had battled to a scoreless tie at the half, and, once again, a last-second Georgia score produced the Bulldogs' first and only points of the contest. This time, a Clemson punt had the Red and Black starting their final drive inside their own 10 yard line, but Belue soon had the visitors on the move.

The Valdosta sophomore went to the air, as he had done all afternoon. Belue finished the day with 11 completions and 165 yards on 18 passes, but three of his throws had ended up in the arms of Geathers, linebacker Jeff Davis, and defensive back Anthony Rose...all of whom were wearing orange jerseys rather than red britches.

The Classic City Canines' final drive took all of five plays. Belue began by finding Scott over the middle for a 37-yard pickup. Flanker Anthony "Amp" Arnold out-leaped a pair of Clemson defenders to haul in a pass from the Georgia quarterback for a 28-yard gain. In a flash, the Dogs were knocking on the door at the Tigers' 27 yard line.

That distance was virtually halved on a 14-yard reception brought in by flanker Jay Russell, but Belue lost eight yards when he dropped back to pass on the next snap. On the final play of the drive, the Red-and-Black signal caller again found himself under pressure and scampered 21 yards on an impromptu scramble. Belue's dash to the corner of the end zone marked the only Bulldog running play of the day to cover more than seven yards of real estate. Georgia finished with 102 rushing yards on 35 carries.

Robinson's extra point concluded the scoring and the game, as Belue's touchdown run had come with nine seconds showing on the clock. The contest had not been as close as the 12–7 final margin indicated and the series had come curiously close to producing five straight shutouts in the preceding half-decade.

In 1975, the Tigers managed just one big play when Willie Jordan's 62-yard touch- down pass—his lone completion of the first half—gave Clemson its only points of the contest. The Jungaleers were held scoreless in 1976 and 1978, with Georgia narrowly avoiding being kept off the board entirely thanks to touchdowns inside the final 10 seconds in 1977 and 1979. Just three plays separated the series from its longest string of showdowns in which one team or the other was limited to a goose egg since the 1920s.

Nevertheless, the result was historic for both teams. The victory over the Red and Black gave the Country Gentlemen the 400th win in Clemson history, while the second straight setback dropped the Dogs to 0–2 for the first time since 1961. Each coach reacted appropriately to the occasion, with Vince Dooley repeating what he had said before the game: "We're much overrated."

Danny Ford, on the other hand, noted, "We're back on the right track now – hopefully on our way to a good season." The young coach added that he and "mama are going out tonight." Ford had reason to be in a mood to celebrate; in the course of his Clemson career, he would card 21 wins over coaches who had been enshrined in the College Football Hall of Fame by 2008, and he had one of those victories over Dooley, a 1994 inductee into the Hall.

The Tigers enjoyed an open date the following Saturday before returning to action against ACC foe Virginia in the season's fourth straight home game. Clemson handled the Cavaliers in a 17–7 contest before traveling to Blacksburg for Danny Ford's first trip to the Virginia Tech campus since leaving the Hokie staff two years earlier. VPI was in the second year of its re building effort under Bill Dooley and the Jungaleers defeated the Gobblers by a 21–0 margin.

Freshman Chuck McSwain, substituting for the injured Lester Brown, ran for 120 yards and a couple of touchdowns in a 28–10 triumph over Duke in Durham to run the Tigers' record to 5–1 heading into a date in Death Valley with preseason league favorite N.C. State. Clemson trailed the Wolfpack by 10 points at the break before knotting the score in the third quarter on a 38–yard Ariri field goal and an 18–yard McSwain touchdown run.

N.C. State moved back out in front on a field goal following a 53–yard punt return and the Country Gentlemen answered with a drive that produced a first down at the Wolfpack four yard line. Perry ran into the line four times but could not break the plane separating him from the end zone, so the North Carolinians took over on downs at the one yard line to preserve a 16–13 victory over Clemson. N.C. State ultimately won the conference championship with a 5–1 ACC mark but remained home for the holidays with an overall 7–4 record.

The Tigers had no time to lick their wounds, though, because the next Saturday would see Wake Forest invading Fort Hill sporting a 7–1 ledger and a No. 14 national ranking. Clemson's opening drive yielded a 47-yard Ariri field goal, then, after the Orange and Purple kicked off, the Tiger linebackers came through on the first play of the Demon Deacons' ensuing possession. A Bubba Brown deflection produced a Jeff Davis interception which was run back for the touchdown that gave the Country Gentlemen 10 points in a 16-second span. Clemson built up a 24-point halftime lead on the way to a 31–0 whitewashing of Wake Forest.

The triumph catapulted the Fort Hill Felines into the top 20. The Jungaleers clung to a two-point lead in Chapel Hill before Lott scored on a fourth-quarter sneak to salt away a 19–10 win over a Gator Bowl-bound North Carolina outfit that would secure a top 15 ranking at season's end. Yet another big game followed when Clemson traveled to South Bend to take on Notre Dame.

The Fighting Irish built up a 10-point cushion in the first half but the Tigers clawed their way back on a 26-yard touchdown run by Lott and a trio of field goals by Ariri. The Nigerian place-kicker finished his gridiron career as Clemson's leading scorer, and, one day after his heroic efforts against Notre Dame, Ariri booted the only goal for the championship game-bound Tiger soccer team in an NCAA tournament victory over South Carolina.

In the football clash with the Irish, however, the Country Gentlemen were not out of danger after taking a 16–10 lead. Notre Dame went on the march, twice crossing midfield only to have redshirt freshman free safety Terry Kinard halt both drives with key interceptions.

The victory was a significant one for Clemson. The Tigers' 8–2 record boosted them to 13th in both polls and earned them a Peach Bowl invitation, which Ford announced on the plane ride home had been accepted. The bid marked the first time in school history that the Orange and Purple would attend bowl games in three straight seasons.

For the Country Gentlemen's head coach, it meant yet another win over a Hall of Fame-bound coach, Dan Devine. (The two eventual inductees into the Hall who Ford bested in 1979 would square off against one another the following year, when Devine's Domers and Dooley's Dogs met in the Sugar Bowl.) Appropriately, Clemson cemented the win through the efforts of a future Hall of Fame player in Kinard.

Despite a 13–9 loss at South Carolina in a finale in which 15 of the 22 points scored came on field goals, the Tigers had enjoyed the good season Ford had hoped for after the win over Georgia. Clemson took second place in the ACC and fielded a first-rate defense that finished third nationally in points permitted, seventh in yards allowed, and 10th against the run.

The 18th-ranked Jungaleers met 19th-ranked Baylor on a cold blustery New Year's Eve in Atlanta. As the wind chill factor made the fans feel like they were sitting in 23-degree weather, the Tigers took an early lead on a 66-yard march featuring a 27-yard completion from Billy Lott to Lester Brown. By the final period, though, the Bears had gone out in front by two touchdowns.

Clemson continued to fight, reaching the Baylor 24 yard line before an interception ended a possession and again advancing to the Texans' 19, only to have Lott taken down 11 yards behind the line of scrimmage. In the closing seconds, Tiger bandit end Andy Headen blocked a punt, setting up the touchdown and the two-point conversion that pulled the South Carolinians within six points of the Bears.

Headen again came through on special teams by recovering Ariri's onside kick and Lott hit Tuttle for 30 yards to carry the Tigers inside the Baylor 25. A delay of game penalty killed the momentum, though, and a Lott interception allowed the Southwest Conference club to run out the clock and pocket a 24–18 win over Clemson. The back-to-back losses were the first consecutive setbacks suffered by the Orange and Purple since the waning days of the Red Parker era and the Peach Bowl disappointment did not detract from the fact that the Tigers had won 27 games in a three-year stretch.

Certainly, Vince Dooley gladly would have taken such a record, as matters swiftly went from bad to worse in Athens. An 0–2 start after the loss to Clemson became an 0–3 start when the Bulldogs hosted Hall of Fame Bowl-bound South Carolina and suffered a seven-point setback at the hands of the Gamecocks.

Suddenly, though, it was as if a switch had been flipped for Georgia. After going winless against three current and former members of the ACC, the Red and Black went on a tear through their SEC brethren. Georgia proceeded to whip Ole Miss, Tangerine Bowl-bound LSU, Vanderbilt, and Kentucky by a combined 96–51 margin.

In a dismal homecoming game between the hedges, the Dogs fell to a mediocre Virginia club by an embarrassing 31–0 score that was identical to the margin by which the Cavaliers hammered Richmond in Charlottesville. The Classic City Canines fell to 4–4 overall but remained perfect in conference play.

The Bulldogs' league mark improved to 5–0 in Jacksonville, where Buck Belue went down with an ankle injury in the third quarter of a regionally-televised contest against Charley Pell's inaugural Florida outfit. Many among the Clemson faithful undoubtedly were enjoying their former coach's struggles in Gainesville, where season-ending injuries suffered by several Gator starters produced a disastrous campaign. The Dogs administered a 33–10 thrashing to the Saurians in the Gateway City and Pell's Floridians limped to an 0–10–1 finish.

Georgia welcomed 15th-ranked Auburn to Athens on November 17 with an improbable SEC championship and an unbelievable Sugar Bowl bid on the line. The injury-hampered Belue broke his ankle on the first play of the game against the Plainsmen, but the Bulldogs held a 10–9 halftime lead on their oldest rivals before the Tigers came back to secure their eighth win of the season by a 33–13 margin in Sanford Stadium.

Despite the loss, the Red and Black still had a shot at spending the holidays in New Orleans, but they needed Auburn to upend top-ranked Alabama. The Plainsmen did their best, holding an 18–17 fourth-quarter lead on the Crimson Tide, but Bear Bryant's last national championship-winning club came back to capture a 25–18 victory in the Iron Bowl.

Georgia nevertheless managed to end the autumn on a high note against Georgia Tech in Atlanta. A regional television audience watched as Jeff Pyburn started at quarterback for the first time in six weeks and the Bulldogs won a defensive struggle over the favored Yellow Jackets when Red-and-Black safety Jeff Hipp intercepted three passes and forced a fumble. The Dogs emerged triumphant by a 16–3 margin…the very same final score by which they had beaten the Ramblin' Wreck in 1958, the last time Georgia had begun the season in an 0–3 slump.

Although the Classic City Canines finished as the runner-up to Alabama in the SEC standings for the second straight year, their overall 6–5 record left them without a bowl bid for the second time in a three-season span. Before the Bulldogs could begin looking forward to the following football campaign, though, there were recruiting wars to be fought, including the pitched battle between finalists Clemson and Georgia to secure the services of a promising running back from Wrightsville, Ga.

The Dogs would emerge victorious from that fight and would learn just how quickly the right set of players and the proper pair of pants could transform a team from a 6–5 also-ran into a 12–0 national champion. That lesson would be learned in the Classic City the very next year, and history would repeat itself by the shores of Lake Hartwell one season thereafter.

1980

"We're No. 1!" (Part One)

The year 1980 was a good year for Clemson athletics. The various teams of Tigers received their first bid to the NCAA men's basketball tournament, won their first ACC title in outdoor track, reached the final eight in the NCAA men's tennis tournament, appeared in their first NCAA golf tournament, and made it to Omaha for the College World Series. However, despite the successes of the Fort Hill Felines in several sports, 1980 unmistakably was the year of the Dog.

Prior to the start of the season, though, the pollsters were uncertain what to make of Georgia. The Red and Black brought back 43 lettermen from the previous year's club, but that squad had managed only a 6–5 record. The Bulldogs had signed a strong recruiting class the previous spring, yet the Classic City Canines fielded few experienced players at the most important position in Vince Dooley's I-formation attack. Senior Donnie McMickens would start the season opener at tailback, but behind the upperclassman on the depth chart were sophomore Carnie Norris and freshmen Barry Tourge and Herschel Walker.

Nevertheless, thanks to the heralded potential of the hotly-pursued Walker, Georgia was seen as having solid prospects for the autumn. As *The Tiger* noted in its season preview of the Athenians, "The 'Dogs of 1979 fell flat on their faces and turned out to be one of the biggest disappointments in college football. But, the fall of 1980 will be a different story for the red and black as the 'Dogs will howl for a possible SEC crown." The pre-season polls had Georgia ranked 16th by the sportswriters and 20th by the coaches.

What could not be anticipated by the voters was the impact upon the Bulldogs of what became known as "the hog incident."

Each year, at the end of spring practice, the Georgia players hosted a party, called "Seagraves" after the owner of the lake at which the combination picnic and freshman initiation took place. Although the event typically went off without a hitch, Dooley was concerned that it was only a matter of time before matters got out of hand, so the head coach decreed that the Seagraves party be cancelled. The local suppliers of food for the shindig knew not to provide the players with refreshments for their soiree.

The team's senior leaders decided to host the party surreptitiously, but they faced the problem of having to obtain the requisite meal from an alternative source. They elected to swipe a pig from the University's experimental farm and barbecue it. A late-night bow-hunting expedition by the organizers of the event resulted in the procurement of a 400-pound hog and the story got out that the players had stolen a research animal belonging to the school.

An infuriated Dooley had to settle upon a suitable punishment for some of the senior mainstays of his club, right tackle and offensive captain Nat Hudson, center Hugh Nall, middle linebacker and team captain Frank Ros, rover Chris Welton, and left cornerback Scott Woerner. He decided to make them pay for the replacement of the pig and work off their debt by performing humiliating and wearying manual labor such as painting the practice field fence during the heat of the summer.

Something interesting happened as a result of the hog incident, though. One by one, the other players on the team came to Ros and his co-conspirators, offering to chip in to help pay for the pilfered animal. The penalty handed down to the five upperclassmen served as a rallying point for the entire squad, producing a unified bunch of Bulldogs heading into the fall.

The season began with a night game in Knoxville against a Tennessee team coming off of a Bluebonnet Bowl campaign the year before. The Volunteers leapt out to a 15–0 lead before Walker came into the game. In his first collegiate action, the true freshman tailback rushed for 84 yards and two touchdowns, including an initial scoring scamper on which he flattened the Big Orange's Bill Bates *en route* to the end zone. Walker provided the spark that lifted the Dogs to a 16–15 victory and elevated the Red and Black to rankings of No. 12 (AP) and No. 15 (UPI).

Georgia played its first home game of the season the following Saturday against Texas A&M. A nearly flawless performance by the Bulldogs was highlighted by Walker's 145-yard, three-touchdown day as the Classic City Canines cruised to an easy 42–0 triumph. What made the contest particularly noteworthy, though, was the fact that the Red and Black came onto the field wearing their traditional silver britches for the first time since Dooley redesigned the Georgia uniform in 1964.

The return to the Bulldogs' historic pants proved lucky and the Athenians found themselves ranked in the top 10 in both polls as they prepared to host Clemson between the hedges on September 20. Prior to the game, *The Red and Black* cautioned against over-confidence when facing a rival that had beaten Georgia three times in the last six series meetings. "A win," warned the Classic City student newspaper, "won't be easy."

Danny Ford, like Vince Dooley, wasn't altogether certain what kind of team he had on his hands heading into the 1980 campaign. Even with the loss of defensive end Bill Smith to a knee injury, the Tigers had defensive depth, especially in a secondary that returned nine lettermen. The Clemson head coach was confident heading into the outing in Athens that the Country Gentlemen were "in the best shape we've been in physically in a long time."

The question marks, though, abounded on the other side of the ball. The tight end position had been decimated by injuries and graduation had claimed the entire offensive backfield and the interior of the line. The presence of ACC rookie of the year Chuck McSwain at the tailback spot provided the Tigers with a much-needed boost, but the South Carolinians would be breaking in a new signal caller in sophomore Homer Jordan. The rookie starting quarterback had won the job in a battle with classmate Andy Headen, who had spent the previous season in the defensive secondary.

The absence of any senior starters from the unit charged with gaining yards and scoring points prompted *The Tiger* to note, "This may be a growing year for the Tigers offensively." Nevertheless, Clemson started the season on the right note on September 13, when the Orange and Purple chalked up 416 yards of total offense in a 19–3 victory over visiting Rice. No sooner had the Owls been dispatched than the Jungaleers began turning their attention to the Bulldogs.

**Freshman Herschel Walker strapping up for
action at Sanford Stadium.**

For such Tigers as Homer Jordan, an Athens native, and punter David Sims, an Atlantan, the visit to Sanford Stadium was a homecoming. For their teammates, the game represented an opportunity to convince Herschel Walker that, in selecting Georgia over fellow finalist Clemson in the recruiting process, the emerging star had made a poor decision.

Tiger linebacker Jeff Davis made his feelings upon the subject known in no uncertain terms. "Herschel Walker is going to see a defensive team Saturday like he hasn't seen yet," the standout junior promised, adding: "I'd like to show him that he made the wrong choice by not coming to Clemson. And I think everybody else feels that way too."

Davis, who had cemented his reputation as one of the top linebackers in the ACC with an 18-tackle performance against Rice, had a more personal incentive for wanting to perform well between the hedges. The year before, his missed tackle in the closing seconds of the game had allowed Georgia quarterback Buck Belue to score. "I want that goose egg Saturday," said Davis of the shutout he had let get away and hoped now to reclaim.

The contest commenced at 1:30 on a sweltering afternoon on which 61,800 dedicated football enthusiasts braved the 97 per cent humidity. Following the unveiling and unfurling of the first official University of Georgia flag, the Bulldogs kicked off and the Tigers took possession of the pigskin.

Onto the gridiron trotted the Clemson offense, led by Jordan. From the opposite sideline, the Georgia defense entered the field, but something was missing. For the first time in his collegiate career, Scott Woerner was not a part of the Classic City Canines' starting lineup. After being beaten on a touchdown pass against Tennessee and being outplayed by backup Greg Bell against the Aggies, the first-string cornerback was benched and replaced by his understudy. Bell took Woerner's place in the secondary throughout the Country Gentlemen's opening series, on which the Dogs quickly forced a punt.

Consequently, Woerner's first foray onto the field came when Sims was sent in to boot the ball over to the home team. The senior punter's kick was a good one, covering 44 yards on a high arc, and the return man brought it in at the 33 yard line. The demoted defender evaded the first would-be tackler, scooted to the right sideline, and zipped past the Clemson bench accompanied by a group of blockers in scarlet shirts and silver britches. When only Sims stood between him and the goal line, Woerner raised the ball above his head and cruised into the end zone.

Place-kicker Rex Robinson followed up Woerner's 67-yard punt return with a successful extra point to give Georgia a 7–0 lead after just 92 seconds had elapsed in the contest. The Bulldogs kicked off a second time and the Tigers mounted a drive that carried them inside their hosts' 30 yard line. The South Carolinians were unable to advance past that point, so Obed Ariri was brought in to attempt a 47-yard field goal.

The senior place-kicker's three-point try came up short, snapping a string of 13 straight successful field goals by the Nigerian soccer star. The miss ended the second Tiger possession and allowed the Red-and-Black offense to take the field for the first time with 7:11 to play in the first quarter. The initial Georgia series was as quick as it was unimpressive; the Dogs lost four yards in three plays before punting.

The Country Gentlemen began the ensuing drive at their own 40 yard line and marched 49 yards to the Georgia 11. Wide receiver Perry Tuttle ran a slant route and broke toward the middle of the field. Wo-

Scott Woerner celebrates after his 67-yard punt return.

erner was back in at corner, and, because the man he was assigned to cover opted to block on the play, he was free to go after the ball.

Greenville News sports editor Dan Foster groused afterwards that Tuttle "got a shoulder massage from a Georgia defensive back that would cost $10 in a health club," but, despite the Clemson receiver's protestation that the ball was in the air at the time, no flag was thrown. It would not be the last time Woerner would be involved in a play on which pass interference was alleged under eyebrow-raising circumstances that day.

The Bulldog secondary maintained tight coverage of the Tigers all afternoon—some- times too tight, in the view of the officiating crew—but the result was that 14 of the 27 aerials attempted by Orange-and-Purple signal callers ended either in incompletions or in interceptions. Jordan's pass to Tuttle fell into the latter category.

Woerner came in from the right and snatched the oval out of the air near the goal line. He confessed later that he was uncertain whether he was in the end zone when he picked off the pass, so he brought the ball out, took advantage of a block thrown by Welton, and took off down the field. It appeared that Woerner was bound for his second touchdown return of the day, but the combination of the humidity and the fatigue from his previous run caused the cornerback to cramp up, allowing McSwain to drag him down from behind at the two yard line. Officially, Woerner's interception runback covered 98 yards.

There began the Bulldogs' longest touchdown drive of the day. Georgia halved the distance to the goal line on first down before Belue's one-yard dive and Robinson's point after gave the Red and Black a two-touchdown edge with 12 seconds remaining in the opening stanza. The first quarter ended with the Dogs up 14–0 despite having run just five offensive plays and netted minus- two yards.

The home team kicked off for the third time and Jordan promptly fumbled to give Georgia custody of the football 25 yards from paydirt. The Dogs covered 24 of those yards in a single pass—the Athenians' only completion of the first half, in fact—from Belue to flanker Amp Arnold, but the senior receiver was hit near the goal line and coughed up the oblong. In the midst of a scramble for possession, the pigskin rolled into and out of the back of the end zone for a touchback to set the Jungaleers up at their own 20 yard line.

Ford decided to bench Jordan, explaining later that his starting quarterback "was up-tight and anxious playing in front of the home crowd," so Mike Gasque was sent in under center in his stead. Aided by a trio of Georgia penalties, the Fort Hill Felines marched 80 yards downfield in 15 plays, taking nearly seven minutes off the clock in the process.

The drive initially stalled as the Tigers neared the 30 yard line and Ariri divided the uprights from 48 yards away, but an offside penalty on the Dogs prompted Ford to take the Country Gentlemen's first points off the board in order to obtain a first down just short of the 25 yard line.

After freshman fullback Edgar Pickett scampered 21 yards on a run up the middle, the second pass interference penalty of the possession put the South Carolinians three feet from the goal line. The football was fed to tailback Cliff Austin and the Scottsdale, GA., product surged up the middle into the teeth of a Georgia defense that forced the sophomore ballcarrier to fumble. Thinking quickly, Gasque snatched up the loose oval and squirted into the end zone. Ariri converted to cut the Bulldog lead to a touchdown with 6:44 remaining until intermission.

Later in the second quarter, Clemson covered 59 yards on an 11-play drive that made it as far as the Georgia four yard line before Ariri again was called upon to kick a field goal. The senior place-kicker's 21-yard effort was good with 34 seconds showing on the game clock and the contestants headed to the locker room with the Red and Black clinging to a 14–10 advantage.

The Georgia lead was wildly improbable in light of the halftime statistics. In the opening 30 minutes of play, the Tigers had run 57 plays to the Bulldogs' 11, picked up 16 first downs to the Red and Black's *zero,* and held the ball for a whopping 25:10 to the Athenians' minuscule 4:50.

Although both teams had completed passes at the same rate, Clemson had gone eight of 16 for 98 yards, while the Dogs had managed a lone completion on two attempts for a meager 24 yards. The Fort Hill Felines' 41 rushing attempts had generated 141 yards, whereas the Classic City Canines' nine running plays had garnered nine measly yards. All told, the Jungaleers held a commanding 206-yard edge in total offense. It was no wonder that, when some papers fell from a band member's pocket late in the second quarter, disgruntled Georgia fans wondered whether the discarded documents had been the game plan.

However, the Tigers had thrown one interception (to the Bulldogs' none) and Georgia had racked up 165 return yards (to Clemson's none), so, when the visitors kicked off to start the second half, the home team held the only lead that mattered. The Red and Black promptly added to that lead with an offense that finally began to show signs of life.

The Country Gentlemen had backed up Jeff Davis's pregame comments by holding Herschel Walker to a paltry 12 yards in the first two quarters, marking arguably the most effective first-half containment of a gamebreaking Georgia back by a Clemson club since Bob Williams's Tigers similarly limited Bob McWhorter in 1913. As the third quarter got underway, however, the Dogs began to control the ball and Walker started picking up yardage, first downs, and momentum on sweeps out of the I formation.

Georgia's opening drive began at the host squad's 23 yard line and spanned 52 yards in 10 snaps. The possession stalled 25 yards from the Clemson end zone, but Robinson's 42- yard field goal upped the Bulldog lead to 17–10 with just over 11 minutes to play in the period. The home team kicked off to the visitors, but the Tigers did not keep the ball for long.

A Gasque pass intended for wide receiver Jerry Gaillard was picked off at the Clemson 31 yard line by Red-and-Black left end Robert Miles. The senior defender, whose manhood jokingly would be questioned on a weekly basis throughout the season in a mock telegram read to the team by Erk Russell that purportedly had been sent by the upcoming opponent's head coach, returned the pick 18 yards to set up the 27-yard Robinson three-pointer that staked the Dogs to a 10-point lead moments after the third quarter passed the halfway mark.

Shortly before the close of the penultimate period, Sims took the hit that knocked him from the game with a hyperextended knee and drew the roughing penalty that sustained a Tiger drive covering 52 yards. The Orange and Purple's 10-play march culminated in a 45-yard Ariri field goal to cut the lead to a touchdown. Some 17 minutes and 17 seconds remained in the game.

That 20–13 score stayed the same for much of the final period as the two teams traded possessions without tallying additional points. That state of affairs changed when Clemson penetrated to the Georgia eight yard line on a 73-yard drive ending in a 25-yard Ariri field goal. With almost seven minutes left to go, the Bulldog lead was back down to four points.

The Classic City Canines responded, making it as far as the Tiger 42 before being thrown for losses on consecutive plays. Dooley sent Jim Broadway onto the field for what would have been the Bulldogs' fifth punt of the day, but Broadway mishandled a good snap and Clemson was given new life when Davis recovered the fumble at the Georgia 41 yard line.

A first-down run picked up a couple of yards, then Gasque looked to Gaillard for a big gain. Both the junior receiver and the defensive back shadowing him went up after the ball. Woerner, who was covering Gaillard, believed his feet got tangled up with those of the intended target, but the official saw it differently and threw a flag for pass interference. The debatable call drew boos from the home crowd and gave the Tigers a 29-yard gain inside the three-minute mark.

On first down from the 10 yard line, the Country Gentlemen made no headway. On second down, Gasque was to sprint out to the left corner with the option of passing or running. When Welton came up and shut off the corner, the Clemson quarterback pulled up and threw over the middle in Gaillard's direction under heavy pressure. "I never saw what happened to it," Gasque confessed to the press following the game. "I got hit and I was on the ground."

What happened to the ball was that it was tipped...then tipped again...then caught. Linebacker Nate Taylor made the initial deflection for the Dogs and the next two pairs of hands to touch the pigskin belonged to Palmetto State natives. Frank Ros of Greenville knocked the oval a second time to keep the football in the air long enough for it to be brought in by Jeff Hipp, a senior safety who hailed from Columbia.

Hipp's pick at the Georgia one yard line gave the Bulldogs their third interception of the afternoon, but, with two minutes left to play, the game was not over yet. Once all was said and done, Dooley admitted that he considered "giving them a safety, but I kept thinking about Tuttle, and about Ariri kicking another field goal." Instead, the Red-and- Black coach sent his offense onto the field and watched in horror as, for the first time in the opening 68 carries of his collegiate career, Herschel Walker fumbled the football.

The freshman sensation promptly picked up the bobbled pigskin and kept his legs moving forward to escape immediate danger, then, on third down from his own seven yard line, Walker plowed ahead for a 20-yard pickup. It was the standout tailback's longest run of the day, giving him his fourth jaunt of more than 10 yards and his fifth first down scamper of the afternoon. Walker's closing carry enabled Belue to run out the clock and put a wild 20–16 victory in the books.

Vince Dooley could only laugh at the head-scratching nature of the outcome and remark, "I was hoping that their offense had worn itself out running up and down the field." Danny Ford, who was in no mood to be jocular, stated his case plainly: "We played the pants off of 'em."

It was hard to argue with the Clemson coach's contention. The Bulldogs had punted twice as often as the Tigers, had drawn 97 yards in penalties on seven flags, and had gained only 157 yards, trailing by nearly two football fields the 351 yards amassed by the Country Gentlemen. Pickett, who had played most of the second half on account of starting fullback Jeff McCall's bruised shoulder, rushed for 77 yards on a dozen carries, while the Red and Black netted just five rushing yards on runs by players other than Walker while managing two completions for 31 passing yards.

Nevertheless, the Dogs had done what they needed to do to win. Georgia offset its two giveaways with four takeaways and did much to even the numbers in the second half. Although Clemson held an overall 26–10 lead in first downs, the two teams had moved the chains 10 times apiece after the break. Likewise, the Tigers' game-long 204–126 advantage in rushing yards disguised the fact that the Red and Black outrushed the South Carolinians by a 117–63 margin in the final 30 minutes. Herschel Walker finished with 121 yards on 23 carries, Georgia notched 183 return yards (against Clemson's one), and Scott Woerner was named *Sports Illustrated's* national defensive player of the week.

The march to the national championship had begun. The No. 10 Bulldogs clobbered Texas Christian by a 34–3 margin to improve to 4-0 and eighth in both polls heading into a bye week. Losses by No. 2 Ohio State and No. 3 Nebraska allowed Georgia to inch up to sixth while idle, and the Red and Black earned advancement to the No. 5 spot with a 28–21 win over Ole Miss and a 41–0 throttling of Vanderbilt. Against the Commodores, Walker galloped for 283 yards and three scores.

A 27–0 triumph over Kentucky got the Red and Black up to No. 4 in time for their first televised game of the season, against 14th-ranked South Carolina on November 1. The clash with the Gamecocks showcased the talents of the nation's top two tailbacks, Herschel Walker and George Rogers. Although the South Carolina senior would win the Heisman Trophy, the regular-season race between the two contenders was statistically a dead heat.

Over the course of the campaign, Rogers gained 6.0 yards per carry to Walker's 5.9 average. The Bulldog freshman tallied 1,805 all-purpose yards and 15 touchdowns, just ahead of the Gamecock upperclassman's 1,804 yards and 14 scores. In the head-to-head battle between the two, Walker ran for 219 yards and a touchdown in Georgia's 13–10 win over South Carolina. Rogers gained 168 yards against the Red-and-Black defense and lost the ball on a critical late fumble.

While the Dogs were edging the Gator Bowl-bound Palmetto State Poultry between the hedges, No. 1 Alabama and No. 2 UCLA were losing close contests to unranked opponents, so the top two spots in the polls the following week were occupied by No. 1 Notre Dame and No. 2 Georgia. On November 8, the perfect scenario unfolded for the Classic City Canines, although it appeared that fate would not be so kind to the Red and Black.

In Jacksonville, 20th-ranked Florida held a 21–20 lead on the Dogs with 63 seconds remaining in the game. Georgia faced third and 11 from its own seven yard line and Gator coach Charley Pell seemed to be on the verge of doing what he had done as the Clemson skipper in 1977; namely, dealing the Athenians a one-point defeat in an earth-shaking upset.

Instead, Buck Belue connected with split end Lindsay Scott on the 93-yard touchdown pass that preserved the Bulldogs' undefeated season by giving Georgia a 26–21 win over a Saurian squad that would emerge victorious from the Tangerine Bowl at season's end. Meanwhile, in Atlanta, lowly Georgia Tech tied the top-rated Fighting Irish to topple Notre Dame from its poll position and allow the Red and Black to ascend to the No. 1 ranking for the first time since November 1942.

At Auburn a week later, Greg Bell blocked a punt and Freddie Gilbert returned it for a touchdown in a 31–21 victory over the Plainsmen. The Dogs got a week off before hosting the Yellow Jackets in the season finale. Georgia Tech was in its first season under new coach Bill Curry and the Engineers fought hard against their in-state rivals, but a Ramblin' Wreck end zone celebration following the visitors' first touchdown infuriated Scott Woerner, who had been beaten on the play.

An unsportsmanlike conduct penalty was assessed on the kickoff and the outraged Woerner responded with a 71-yard return to set up a one-play Georgia touchdown drive. The Bulldogs completed an undefeated regular season with a 38–20 triumph over Georgia Tech. Following a brief flirtation between Vince Dooley and Auburn that reportedly involved a million-dollar offer for the Red-and-Black head coach to take over his *alma mater's* beleaguered football program, the Dogs lit out for New Orleans for their Sugar Bowl date with seventh-ranked Notre Dame.

With the national championship on the line, freshman Terry Hoage blocked a first- quarter Fighting Irish field goal attempt, Herschel Walker rushed for 150 yards and two touchdowns while taking 34 snaps with a dislocated shoulder, and Scott Woerner intercepted a Notre Dame pass at the Bulldogs' 34 yard line to seal the 17–10 win that left Georgia the only undefeated squad in major college football and the undisputed No. 1 team in the land.

The accolades showered upon the Red and Black went beyond capturing the national championship, however. Vince Dooley was named the NCAA national coach of the year and Herschel Walker was declared the UPI national back of the year. Nine Bulldogs made All-SEC and three made All-American. Scott Woerner finished first in the country in punt returns and Jeff Hipp finished first in the country in interceptions...two categories in which the Clemson Tigers could attest to the Georgians' effectiveness. The men in silver britches led the nation in turnover margin and ended up in the top 10 in scoring defense.

While the unlikely victory over the Jungaleers springboarded a triumphant season in the Classic City, the Fort Hill Felines returned home to Lake Hartwell and struggled through the remainder of a diffi-

cult season. A lackluster 17–10 win over Division I-AA Western Carolina the next Saturday was followed by a similarly close shave against
Virginia Tech to open Clemson's October slate.

The Tigers held a 13–7 fourth-quarter lead on VPI when a first-
and-goal play carried the Hokies inside the Orange-and-Purple one
yard line. The Country Gentlemen turned back the Gobblers twice,
forcing a field goal, and Clemson hung on to win by a 13–10 margin
over a Virginia Tech squad headed for a Peach Bowl date.

From there, it was on to Charlottesville for the Tigers. The Fort
Hill Felines trailed the Cavaliers by two touchdowns entering the final period but Clemson staged the largest fourth-quarter comeback in
school history, capping off a 27–24 victory over Virginia with a 52-yard
Obed Ariri field goal with six seconds showing on the clock.

Danny Ford's club stood at 4–1 and, like the Bulldogs who had
dealt the Tigers their only setback, Clemson had shown a penchant for
winning close contests. The worst, however, was yet to come. On October 18, a Duke unit sporting an 0–5 record came into Death Valley
and dropped a 34–17 whipping on the Country Gentlemen. The Blue
Devils would win only one other game all year, a five-point decision
over 1-9-1 Georgia Tech.

Clemson suffered a second straight setback at N.C. State, falling
24–20 to Monte Kiffin's Wolfpack in the Textile Bowl before escaping
Winston-Salem with a 35–33 victory over Wake Forest. Next No. 14
North Carolina came calling and Jeff Davis responded with a school-
record 24 tackles against the Tar Heels in Memorial Stadium.

In the game in which Ariri became the NCAA's field goal leader,
the Tigers held the ball inside the visitors' five yard line when UNC's
Lawrence Taylor sacked Homer Jordan to preserve a 24–19 triumph
for the Bluebonnet Bowl-bound Tar Heels. North Carolina would end
the year ranked in the top 10 and Clemson would not lose another
home game for the next four years.

For the moment, though, the Jungaleers' struggles continued
with a 34–7 drubbing administered by Maryland in College Park. The
27-point margin made the loss the most lopsided of Ford's 11-year career as the head coach at Fort Hill. The Terrapins finished the regular
season ranked in the UPI top 20 and attended the Tangerine Bowl.

Ford knew there were rumblings among Clemson fans not anxious to return to the losing ways of Hootie Ingram and Red Parker. The
young head coach recognized that something special would have to
be done if the 5-5 Tigers were to salvage their season against a South

Carolina outfit ranked in the top 15. Fortunately for Ford, he knew just what to do.

Before the season, the coach had gotten equipment manager Len Gough to order orange pants for the team, which would be kept concealed and broken out on a special occasion. This was it. Just prior to the annual battle with the Gamecocks, while the Tigers were warming up on the field wearing their usual white uniform pants, the managers were putting the special trousers in the players' lockers.

Just as the return of the silver britches energized the Georgia team, the introduction of the orange pants just before the South Carolina game had its intended effect on the Clemson squad…and the Tiger faithful. Jeff Davis later described the scene as the uniquely outfitted Country Gentlemen made their traditional entrance into Memorial Stadium: "When we got to the top of the hill there was a roar like I had never heard before. It had been kept a complete surprise from the players and the fans."

Bill Smith concurred. "The fans went ballistic," said the junior defensive end. "We had orange shirts, orange pants, and orange helmets on, we were decked out from head to toe." Possibly alluding to the footgear the Jungaleers had worn for their 1967 clash with N.C. State, Smith added, "It was amazing we didn't have orange shoes on." What the Tigers did have was Danny Ford's assurance that Clemson did not lose when wearing orange britches.

Ford was right. The Orange and Purple once again kept George Rogers out of the end zone, forcing the Heisman Trophy winner to conclude his college career without ever having scored against the Tigers. The Clemson defense forced four turnovers and strong safety Willie Underwood earned *Sports Illustrated* national defensive player of the week recognition with a Scott Woerner-like performance against the Palmetto State Poultry. Underwood turned two second-half interceptions into a 37-yard touchdown return and a 64-yard runback to set up another score.

Although South Carolina would be ranked 18th in the final regular-season poll and end the autumn in a late December bowl, the Gamecocks absorbed a 27-6 beating from their upstate rivals. The Tigers' 21-point margin of victory was their largest over USC in 14 years and the win gave Clemson momentum heading into what otherwise might have been a long and dreary offseason.

Danny Ford had weathered the storm of four losses in a five-week span and had learned a thing or two about coaching in the process. The young skipper confessed later, "I overreacted to losing. I didn't give the players enough credit for what they overcame. Every time you walk on the football field, you don't expect them to be perfect, but I was impatient."

Ford had decided to make some changes in the way his program would be run, in the hope of restoring the Tigers to their recently re-established place among the nation's elite. The team would have to re-bound from a mediocre season, but there was hope. After all, if a pair of silver britches could transform a 6–5 Georgia squad into a 12–0 na-tional champion, why couldn't a pair of orange pants do the same for 6–5 Clemson?

1981

"We're No. 1!" (Part Two)

In the first week of January 1981, as the Georgia Bulldogs continued to celebrate the national championship they had won on New Year's Day, the Clemson Tigers began preparing for the fall campaign that still was eight months in the future. Acting from their own initiative, the players started showing up in the weight room to work out or at the practice field to jog.

Danny Ford knew how precarious his position had been before his masterful introduction of the orange pants fired up the Tigers and led them to the season-ending victory that salvaged a 6–5 record and subdued, if not silenced, the grumbling alumni who wondered whether the young head coach had been promoted before he was ready to lead the Clemson program.

Ford saw the flaws in his own guidance of his team and moved immediately to correct them. In 1980, he had insisted upon pregame silence on the bus and in the locker room so his coaches and players could concentrate on preparing themselves for the contest; because this approach only added to the tension, Ford resolved to ease up on everyone.

The head coach also eased up on himself, delegating more duties to his assistants, and made some critical staff decisions. Ford was able to retain the services of Curley Hallman, who had replaced Mickey Andrews as the Country Gentlemen's secondary coach. Hallman had been offered the opportunity to serve as an assistant on Vince Dooley's staff at Georgia, but he decided to stay put and continue directing a Clemson defensive backfield that would snag 23 interceptions while surrendering just six touchdown passes in 1981.

Ford also brought in an elder statesman from Bill Dooley's staff at Virginia Tech. Tom Harper, who was more than 15 years older than the man under whom he would serve at Fort Hill, relocated to upstate South Carolina to become the Tigers' defensive line coach, defensive coordinator, and assistant head coach. The move by Ford had a stabilizing influence on the program.

These changes infused the Clemson Tigers with a revived sense of dedication and produced a sharp spring scrimmage game. The team boasted 53 returning lettermen and brought back all 11 offensive starters. Although Obed Ariri, the Nigerian soccer player turned Tiger field goal specialist, was gone, another Nigerian soccer player was available to replace him, in the form of freshman place-kicker Donald Igwebuike.

To those within the program, it appeared that something special was on the horizon. Hallman told a reporter that he turned down the Georgia offer because he felt Clemson returned a nucleus of players capable of claiming a national championship. Wide receiver Perry Tuttle was among the many who were optimistic about the upcoming season. In June, strength coach George Dostal hung a sign in the weight room that read, "Believe: Clemson Tigers 11–0. In the Orange Bowl vs. Nebraska." No one on the outside looking in saw much cause for confidence, though, so the Jungaleers began the season unranked and did not receive even a single vote for inclusion in the AP top 20.

On the other side of the Savannah River, Vince Dooley's Georgia Bulldogs did not have to worry about such slights. The defending national champion Dogs were a pre-season top 10 team. The Red and Black inched their way up to sixth by beginning the season with a 44–0 manhandling of Garden State Bowl-bound Tennessee, then the Classic City Canines crept up to No. 4 by beating California by two touchdowns.

Two games into the young autumn, Georgia owned a 15-game winning streak, was averaging almost 459 yards per game, and had surrendered a total of only 70 rushing yards and just 13 points. Senior quarterback Buck Belue had completed 19 of 32 passes for 253 yards, three touchdowns, and no interceptions through the season's first eight quarters, while sophomore tailback Herschel Walker had tallied 328 yards in 65 carries during that same span despite a bruised hand that had been troubling him since the Tennessee game.

The Bulldogs appeared to be hitting on all cylinders as the Tigers prepared to host them in Death Valley and the Clemson coaching staff was outwardly deferential to the defending champs on the eve of their September 19 showdown. Harper called Walker "probably the finest running back in the history of the game" and announced: "I don't know how to stop him." The Orange-and-Purple defensive coordinator continued, "Quite honestly, I don't know if we can stay toe to toe with them." Offensive line coach Larry Van Der Heyden echoed his colleague's sentiments, saying: "Our practices this week have kind of concerned us. They've been pretty low key...I really wonder if we're ready to play."

Yet again, this appeared perfectly reasonable to those outside the Tiger program. When the Jungaleers' scheduled season-opening opponent, Villanova, opted to drop its football program in April 1981, Clemson had to scramble to line up a replacement date against tiny Wofford of the NAIA. The Terriers took a 3–0 lead on their opening drive, were tied with the Tigers after 15 minutes of play, and had gained 201 yards by halftime. The game was more than 20 minutes old before quarterback Homer Jordan hooked up with Tuttle on the 80-yard touchdown pass that set the stage for the Fort Hill Felines' 45–10 victory.

One week later, the Tigers traveled to Tulane for their first night game in five years and the first indoor game in Clemson football history. (The evening kickoff threw off Jungaleer center Tony Berryhill's eating schedule, causing him to vomit repeatedly during the game. He used that to his advantage, however, making certain to throw up in the area he wanted the nose guard to vacate.) The Green Wave were riding a three-game losing streak that would stretch to six straight setbacks before being snapped, yet Tulane was up on the Tigers by a 5–0 count at the end of the first quarter.

The South Carolinians came back to win a hard-fought defensive struggle by a 13–5 final margin in a game in which the Green Wave was held to 40 rushing yards and the Country Gentlemen forced seven turnovers. Each of the five Clemson defensive backs registered at least one interception and the Tigers were off to a 2–0 start for the first time in more than a decade, but nothing in the Jungaleers' first two victories impressed the pollsters enough to earn Clemson a spot in the top 20. The Fort Hill Felines' case was not helped by the fact that, even with Berryhill's unique method for securing an advantage against the defense, they gained a mere 177 yards in the confrontation with Tulane.

In spite of the public poor-mouthing by Harper and Van Der Heyden, though, the Tigers were ready to knock helmets with the Dogs. In fact, they had spent the past year preparing for their grudge match with the Red and Black. The South Carolinians had dominated the Georgians statistically between the hedges in their last meeting, and they took the view that the loss in Athens had started the downward spiral that did not end until the upset of the Gamecocks that began their current winning streak. As *The Charlotte Observer's* Ken Tysiac would later write, "One remarkable quarter for Scott Woerner created a whole year of angst for Clemson's players."

The significance of the game to the Tigers was attested to by the fact that the traditional "First Friday" parade and pep rally were delayed until the week of the clash with the Bulldogs, even though Memorial Stadium already had played host to the season's initial home game. A banner reading "Curb the Dawg" was unfurled over Main Street.

Although older alumni and 72-year-old Frank Howard continued to maintain that South Carolina remained Clemson's principal rival, younger Tiger fans seemed to disagree. *The Atlanta Constitution's* Ivan Maisel reported that several students from the campus bordering Lake Hartwell placed greater importance on the Georgia game.

"This has been the one," said freshman Frank Lucius. "It's a personal vendetta," said sophomore Kenneth Conner. "This is it, this is everything," said senior Chris Patterson, confirming *Greenville Piedmont* sports editor Abe Hardesty's description of the Dogs as the Country Gentlemen's "arch rival."

Clemson defensive tackle Jeff Bryant, an Atlanta native, agreed with his fellow under graduates, as did Athens product Homer Jordan. The Tiger signal caller stated, "It's getting bigger than the South Carolina game." Bryant was even more unequivocal: "For me it's bigger. I been looking forward to this all year."

It came as no surprise to Ford, then, when his seniors came to him at midweek and asked to wear the orange britches against the Dogs. The Clemson head coach refused, saying he wanted to save them for the season-ender against the Gamecocks. "I don't want to embarrass the orange pants," Ford explained to his players. "I don't want to take the glow off them. I don't want to take the chance. I want to wear them again when I know we can win." The athletes responded: "Well, we can wear them this week." Finally, Ford agreed to grant their request.

The move did not catch Dooley unawares, either. "We expect them to wear orange," the Georgia head coach told the press. "It won't be a surprise if they do. Now, wouldn't it be something if we wore our red pants?" Dooley was joking about the Bulldogs' red road britches, but he was not kidding when he said: "All the motivation should be in Clemson's corner....The percentages have to be against us winning."

Ford scoffed at his Bulldog counterpart's comments, chiding, "That's just Dooley talking." Georgia had been installed as a four-point favorite, but *Atlanta Constitution* sports editor Jesse Outlar foresaw a Tiger victory over the opponent that he acknowledged had "replaced South Carolina as Clemson football enemy No. 1." The 50th series meeting between the old rivals would not be televised, so a packed house of 63,500 was foreseen, and only about 6,700 of those would be cheering for the Red and Black.

The visitors understood the difficulty that would accompany the trip to Death Valley. "Theirs is the kind of defense that can panic you if an offensive line doesn't hold together," Georgia center Joe Happe observed before the game. Added Happe, "We can't scatter and run." Clearly, the Bulldogs comprehended the challenge they would face in the Palmetto State.

Thus, the stage was set for an upset. *The Greenville News* summed up the stakes on the day of the game: "Clemson, winner of two straight games and seeking a return to self- and peer- respect, sees this as a once-in-a-lifetime opportunity. What better way of rocketing back into national prominence than by bumping off the fourth-ranked, defending national champions?"

The combatants convened in Memorial Stadium at 1:00 on a 69-degree Saturday afternoon with both rosters stocked with healthy bodies, as each team was without only one of its starters. Tiger wide receiver Jerry Gaillard and Bulldog defensive end Freddie Gilbert were the only first-stringers who would be watching the game from the sidelines, although at least one of the coaches wouldn't have minded being a spectator himself. "I'd like to sit up in the stands and watch it," said Dooley beforehand. "Yes, I'd pay the price to see this one."

The initial indication in the first quarter was that Dooley would have enjoyed himself had he been seated in the bleachers. Georgia mounted a drive that carried the visitors into Clemson territory and gave them a first down at the home team's 17 yard line. On the next play, however, Walker uncharacteristically fumbled and strong safety Jeff Suttle recovered the loose oval for the Tigers. The turnover was an early indication of the course the contest would take.

Nevertheless, some of the Country Gentlemen became apprehensive as the game proceeded to the second period with neither team having scored. Tuttle later recalled that "everybody was panicking, going crazy" before Jordan "walked into the huddle and yelled, 'Shut the hell up!'" The junior quarterback was taking charge of his football team, and his maturity and leadership very shortly would pay dividends.

Even though the game remained scoreless, the Bulldog offense already was self-destructing under the relentless pressure of the Jungaleer defense. To Walker's fumble was added a pair of Belue interceptions in a three-minute span. The second of those errant throws by the Georgia signal caller was picked off by strong safety Tim Childers to give Clemson custody of the pigskin at the Athenians' 18 yard line.

Jordan kept the ball on one scamper and two other carries went to fullback Kevin Mack. The second rush by the sophomore ballcarrier gave the South Carolinians a first down at the eight yard line and Tuttle ran a quick out on the next snap for the first, and biggest, of his five catches on the day.

The senior standout was on his way out of bounds when he made a diving catch in the right side of the end zone, keeping his feet in the field of play for the grab that made him the second-leading receiver in Clemson history. Place-kicker Bob Paulling's extra point put the Fort Hill Felines out in front by a 7–0 margin with just over seven minutes left to play before intermission.

Later in the first half, Walker again put the ball on the ground and the fumble was retrieved by middle guard William Perry at the Georgia 34 yard line. The 6'3", 295-pound Perry would attain later fame as the Chicago Bears' "Refrigerator," but, at the moment, the 18-year-old rookie was in the act of becoming for Clemson what Walker had been for Georgia: Perry, like the stellar tailback from whom he had wrested possession of the oval, was a freshman who would make his presence felt in a national championship season as a first-year collegian. Perry, also like Walker, would become his school's first three-time All-American.

The fumble recovery came with just 29 seconds left in the second quarter, so the Tigers had to move swiftly in order to capitalize on the Classic City Canines' latest turnover. A pair of running plays picked up 11 yards and a first down to set up a 39-yard Igwebuike field goal with 11 seconds showing on the clock. Much to the delight of the hometown crowd, Clemson went to the locker room holding a 10-point halftime lead on the defending national champions.

While the home team was surging and the visitors were imploding, both defenses were acquitting themselves admirably. To the casual observer the Bulldogs might merely have appeared unlucky. Herschel Walker, ordinarily an extremely reliable ballcarrier, coughed up the pigskin three times against Clemson and the Athenians lost possession on two of those fumbles.

Likewise, Buck Belue, who had thrown just nine regular-season interceptions as a junior, tossed two picks in the first 30 minutes of play against the Tigers. As if that were not bad enough, the Bulldogs' senior signal caller was guiding a Georgia drive early in the second period when he dropped back to pass and saw the football slip from his grasp. Naturally, Clemson pounced upon the fumble.

This was not, however, simply ill fortune for the Red and Black. As senior linebacker Jeff Davis later explained, the Tigers' strategy was to make Walker run from sideline to sideline rather than turning upfield, thereby forcing the Bulldogs to rely on Belue's arm. By applying pressure with the defensive line and using multiple zones in the secondary rather than the man coverage Clemson had employed against Tulane, the Country Gentlemen planned to make the Georgia quarterback throw under duress and commit costly mistakes.

This approach had its intended impact, as two of Belue's attempts to throw to senior flanker Lindsay Scott in double coverage resulted in interceptions. Childers remarked after the game, "The pass that I caught was right to me."

While Clemson clearly was getting the better of the exchange, though, the home team was not the only contestant to have offered an impressive defensive effort before intermission. The South Carolinians had run 10 offensive series in the first half and nine of those had begun with running plays which went for an average gain of fewer than three yards. Half of the Tigers' possessions had started at or on the Bulldogs' side of the 50 yard line, yet those five drives produced one touchdown, one field goal, a missed field goal attempt, a bad snap on another would-be three-point try, and a punt (one of seven Jungaleer punts that afternoon). Three second-quarter trips inside the Athenians' 25 yard line yielded no points.

The second half commenced with a Clemson kickoff and Georgia started a 10-play march from its own 20 yard line. In the course of the Bulldogs' most successful series of the day, Walker finally broke free for the 21-yard gain that was to be his longest run of the afternoon. The sophomore tailback appeared certain to score, as cornerback Anthony

Herschel Walker lost two of his three fumbles in Death Valley in 1981, including one recovered by freshman middle guard William Perry.

Rose was the lone Tiger between Walker and the end zone. However, Rose positioned himself perfectly, forced the ballcarrier back towards the middle of the field, and made a textbook touchdown-saving tackle at the 30 yard line.

Undeterred, Belue at last found Scott for the senior receiver's longest catch of the day, a 14-yard completion that gave the Dogs a first down at the Clemson 16. There the Tigers once again rose up, halting Walker for no gain on the next snap, but Belue looked like he was about to atone for his first-half miscues when he sent a sure touchdown pass to tight end Norris Brown at the three yard line...yet the ball was dropped when it arrived.

The Georgia quarterback was sacked on third down, so freshman place-kicker Kevin Butler came into the contest and connected on a 40-yard field goal attempt to cut the lead to seven points with 11:24 remaining in the third quarter. The scoring drive left the Bulldogs newly energized, and the Red and Black proceeded to hold their hosts following the ensuing kickoff.

When the Athenians got the ball back, they advanced 26 yards, but the Georgia penetration into Tiger territory came to an abrupt close when Walker took the handoff on third and two, only to be stonewalled at the line of scrimmage. As was the case all afternoon, the Bulldog running back was gang-tackled, but end Danny Triplett led the way.

Triplett would tally 10 other tackles in the 60-minute slugfest, but he was not alone. Davis also notched 11 stops over the course of the contest and a Clemson defense which featured eight future NFL players registered six sacks, in addition to forcing at least eight of the Bulldogs' nine turnovers.

Just 10 snaps after Triplett's momentum-reclaiming tackle forced a Georgia punt, the Classic City Canines faced another third-and-two situation, this time at their own 17 yard line. Again the ball went to Walker and again the standout tailback failed to move the chains, as the middle was bottled up and left tackle Dan Benish dropped Walker for a one-yard loss when he tried to go wide. "There are some games that are hard-hitting," the sophomore running back subsequently observed in a notable understatement, "and I'd say this was a real hard-hitting one."

Late in the third quarter, Bulldog punter Jim Broadway got off a 36-yard kick which was returned eight yards by free safety Billy Davis. The Tigers went on the move from the Georgia 45, with Jordan twice finding Tuttle for third-down completions to sustain a drive that reached the 12 yard line before stalling. On the third play of the fourth period, Igwebuike drilled a 29-yard field goal to extend the Clemson lead to 10 points with 14 minutes to go.

As the Dogs tried desperately to rally from their 13–3 deficit, Georgia took to the air. Buck Belue threw three more interceptions in the final 10 minutes. The senior signal caller at one point had passes picked off on consecutive attempts, with Billy Davis snagging one and Anthony Rose hauling in another. The latter grab set up a 41-yard three-point try on which Igwebuike came up short. Davis and Rose joined Childers and free safety Terry Kinard among the Tiger defensive backs who had hauled in aerials from the Red-and-Black quarterback that afternoon.

Prior to the game, Vince Dooley had told the press that "Clemson's team this year is as good as the one that went 11–1 in 1978." His assessment proved correct, but what the Georgia head coach could not have known at the time was that his Dogs would suffer in Death Valley the same fate that awaited the 1978 Tigers between the hedges, when too many turnovers would doom the efforts of the visiting team.

A tenacious Clemson defense, led by senior tackle Jeff Bryant, harassed Georgia quarterback Buck Belue all afternoon.

The comparison between the two games was made complete on the Athenians' final drive. After guiding the Bulldogs from their own 24 to the Clemson 25, Belue threw his final pass of the afternoon into the end zone, only to see his day end the way Steve Fuller's had three years before: with an interception.

Cornerback Rod McSwain became the fifth Tiger defensive back to pick off the Georgia signal caller, bringing to an unbelievable *nine* the total number of turnovers the Red and Black had committed. Never before had Clemson tallied so many takeaways and never before had the Country Gentlemen knocked off a top-four team in Memorial Stadium.

When McSwain brought in Belue's errant throw with a little over a minute remaining in the game, the celebration began. The squad in orange pants would take possession at the 20 and run out the clock to close out its 13-3 victory over the team in silver britches. McSwain and his fellow Clemson defenders left the field with their index fingers held aloft as the hometown fans stood and applauded for the last of many times that day.

The Tiger faithful continued to clap throughout the final minute of the contest as Herschel Walker, concerned about being caught in a crowd with his bruised hand, headed for the locker room with an escort. The Clemson players sarcastically asked, "How 'bout them Dogs?" and sang a chorus of "We Don't Give a Damn About the Whole State of Georgia."

The Country Gentlemen had a right to crow after expunging their demons from a year before. Joe Happe had stated beforehand that it was important not to panic, but the Dogs had failed to retain their composure when the going got rough. Vince Dooley, who flatly acknowledged that his team had gotten "whipped," noted that "we were simply intimidated by their defense" and "we were just plain rattled."

Walker admitted that he "didn't concentrate as well" due to the crowd noise in Memorial Stadium, but Jeff Davis had a simpler explanation for the Bulldog tailback's lack of focus: "I was looking for Herschel the first half. He was looking for me the second half." Jeff Bryant and Tim Childers both commented on Georgia's lack of aggressiveness, with the senior defensive tackle adding, "I think that we must have wanted it more."

In one sense, the significance of the result was immediately apparent. Noting that "[o]nly a super effort by the Bulldog defenders averted a rout," Jesse Outlar reported that "[t]he Tigers should have assured themselves a bowl bid with this impressive triumph." In the Clemson locker room, though, the players were aiming a bit higher. "Right now," Perry Tuttle told the press, "I feel great about what we can do the rest of the season." Co-captain and tailback Cliff Austin concurred, comparing the 1981 Tigers to the 1980 Bulldogs and opining that the victory over Georgia "may just be the thing that could get us on our way."

In another sense, though, the full magnitude of Clemson's achievement on what *The Atlanta Journal-Constitution* called a "Day of Infamy" could not be appreciated adequately until the season was done. Buck Belue would finish his senior year with a 60.6 per cent completion rate (better than that of Pittsburgh's Dan Marino) and only nine interceptions. Belue's nine picks were the second-fewest of any quarterback among the top seven NCAA signal callers in pass efficiency rating, but he was picked off five times by the Tigers.

Likewise, Herschel Walker's day in Death Valley was the worst regular-season outing of his sophomore season. Against Clemson, Walker tallied the second-fewest carries (28), the fewest rushing yards (111), the fewest first-down runs (5), and the fewest runs over 10 yards (4) of any single-game effort that autumn.

The Jungaleer D had limited to three points a Georgia offense that would average 32 points a game and finish ranked seventh in the nation in scoring. The year-end statistics had the Red and Black among the top five teams in the land in rushing offense and in total offense, yet Clemson held the visiting squad well below its season averages.

Nevertheless, the 1981 clash between the longtime rivals mirrored their 1980 showdown, with the loser coming out ahead statistically. The Dogs led in first downs (16-15), total yards (255-236), and rushing yards (122-101), with the Tigers holding only a six-foot edge in passing yardage despite the fact that Home Jordan had a much better day (59 yards on 25 rushing attempts, 135 yards and a touchdown on 11-of-18 passing) than his Red-and-Black counterpart (-6 yards on 7 rushing attempts, 133 yards and 5 interceptions on 12-of-26 passing).

Although the Bulldog defense was on the field for nine minutes more than the Athenian offense, the Tigers were held to 13 points—three fewer than they had scored in Sanford Stadium the year before—

Tiger defenders picked off five of Buck Belue's passes in the course of claiming nine takeaways against Georgia in 1981.

and the Classic City Canines recovered fumbles by Jordan and wide receiver Frank Magwood in Georgia territory. In light of those facts, it was not hard to understand why Lindsay Scott insisted that "Clemson didn't beat us, we beat ourselves."

The senior receiver's head coach knew better, though. Vince Dooley commented afterwards, "The game was won by the Clemson defense. They were aggressive, harassed us, intimidated us, and they deserved to win the football game." "Georgia wanted to go toe to toe and jaw to jaw," remarked Danny Ford, "and I think our guys accepted it real well." Ford, who would be named the UPI national coach of the week following his team's stellar effort, was putting it mildly.

When asked where the Red and Black would go from there, full-back Ronnie Stewart quipped, "Back to Athens." Though bloody, the Bulldogs were unbowed. "I don't plan to lose no more," promised determined cornerback Dale Williams. Walker agreed: "It hurt a great deal, but I think we're a winner, and I don't think we'll let this get us down."

The immediate impact of the outcome in Death Valley was a shakeup in the top 20. Georgia dropped to 16th in the coaches' rankings and 17th in the sportwriters' poll, whereas Clemson appeared at No. 18 (UPI) and No. 19 (AP). The Dogs gradually clawed their way back up into the top four with wins over South Carolina (24–0), Ole Miss (37–7), Vanderbilt (53–21), Kentucky (21–0), and Temple (49–3).

Next up for the Red and Black was their trek to Jacksonville to face Peach Bowl-bound Florida. Charley Pell, taking note of the fact that his former assistant Danny Ford was the only opposing coach to have bested the Bulldogs in their last 21 games, decided that imitation was the sincerest form of flattery. Drawing his inspiration from Clemson, Pell outfitted his Gators with brand-new orange pants (which the Sunshine State Saurians had not worn in over 30 years) and directed his defense to throw everything it had at Herschel Walker.

Neither tactic worked. Although Florida leapt out to an early 14–0 lead, Walker responded by racking up 192 rushing yards on 47 carries, 55 receiving yards on four catches, and 32 return yards on a pair of kickoff runbacks. All told, the sophomore sensation scored four touchdowns—two through the air and two on the ground—to pace Georgia's second straight 26–21 conquest of the Gators.

The win pushed the Red and Black's record to 8–1 and the Dogs followed that up with a 24–13 triumph over former Georgia guard Pat Dye's inaugural Auburn club. The Athenians inched up to No. 3 in both polls and capped off their regular season with a nationally-televised romp over Georgia Tech at Grant Field. The Classic City Canines scored on their first six possessions to take a 34-point halftime lead along the way to a 44–7 rout of the Yellow Jackets.

At 10-1, the SEC champion Bulldogs had earned an automatic bid to the Sugar Bowl, where Georgia would have an outside chance at claiming a second consecutive national title. The Red and Black arrived in New Orleans as the No. 2 team in the land, and, with a little help, they could defend their 1980 final ranking. In the Superdome against a Pittsburgh squad that had spent four weeks during November as the nation's consensus No. 1 team, Georgia held a late 20–17 lead, only to see Dan Marino complete a 33-yard touchdown pass on fourth down with 35 seconds left to play. The Sugar Bowl thriller featured six lead changes.

Although the disappointing postseason loss dropped the Dogs to 10–2, the setback was inconsequential where the national championship was concerned, for the help the Classic City Canines would have needed to retake the top poll position was not forthcoming. The Clemson players who held their index fingers up in the air while leaving the field after clinching their win over Georgia proved prophetic in a wild season of college football.

Preseason No. 1 Michigan had opened the autumn with a loss to unranked Wisconsin on the same day that No. 2 Alabama fell to a Georgia Tech outfit headed for a 1–10 campaign. Newly-anointed No. 1 Notre Dame was then upended by the Wolverines on the same afternoon that the Tigers defeated the Dogs in Death Valley, allowing Southern California to ascend to the top spot in both polls.

Clemson had a bye week after its win over Georgia gave the Country Gentlemen their first 3–0 start in a third of a century, during which the Jungaleers crept up to No. 14 in both sets of rankings. In a regionally-televised October 3 date with Kentucky, the Tigers once again failed to hold the lead after 15 minutes of play, as the Wildcats were up 3–0 at the break. After gaining just 65 yards and four first downs in the first half, Clemson roared back to score 21 unanswered points and the increased exposure provided by the broadcast allowed the Fort Hill Felines to vault into the top 10.

The Tigers began ACC play with a shutout of winless Virginia while a Peach Bowl representative watched from the press box, but the Orange and Purple's rise to loftier heights continued when three teams ranked ahead of them (including the top-rated Trojans) either lost to or were tied by opponents appearing nowhere in the top 20.

Clemson moved up to No. 6 in the sportswriters' poll and No. 7 in the coaches' poll.

The South Carolinians rolled up 563 yards of total offense against Duke on the strength of Cliff Austin's 19-carry, 178-yard performance and Homer Jordan's 198-yard passing day. With their 38–10 win over the Blue Devils (and a loss to unranked Arkansas by No. 1 Texas), the Tigers took over the fourth and fifth spots, respectively, in the AP and UPI polls.

Against N.C. State, the Clemson defense gave up the first rushing touchdown it had allowed all season and was down 7–0 early, but the Fort Hill Felines gained 304 yards on the ground to overcome their three interceptions and two lost fumbles in a 17–7 victory. Up to No. 3 (AP) and No. 4 (UPI) moved the Orange and Purple.

On Halloween, while No. 1 Penn State was being beaten by un-ranked Miami (Florida), Clemson set 21 school, stadium, and confer-ence records in an epic throttling of first-year head coach Al Groh's Wake Forest unit by the shores of Lake Hartwell. 81 Tigers took the field against the Demon Deacons and nine of them scored as the South Carolinians generated 756 yards of total offense, converted 12 out of 12 third downs, and never punted, fumbled, or threw an interception.

The Jungaleers scored five touchdowns in the second quarter alone and they kept up the barrage after intermission, as Jordan con-nected with Tuttle for a 75- yard touchdown pass on the first play from scrimmage of the second half. Ford emptied the bench as the game got out of hand, but the Country Gentlemen continued to play hard. In the fourth quarter, defensive end Steve Berlin registered a sack on his first snap as a Clemson player and fifth-string running back Craig Crawford scampered 72 yards to score the last of the Tigers' 12 touch-downs on his first career carry.

The unbelievable 82–24 outburst over Wake Forest was rewarded with a No. 2 ranking bestowed by the sportswriters and a No. 3 poll position awarded by the coaches. This set up a showdown with eighth-ranked North Carolina in Chapel Hill. Representatives from eight dif-ferent bowl games were on hand for the first meeting between top 10 teams in Atlantic Coast Conference history.

The Tar Heels twice ventured inside the Clemson 10 yard line but were held to field goals each time. Although UNC completed a 30-yard pass for the longest play from scrimmage recorded against the Tigers that fall, Jeff Bryant countered by recovering a fumble on a backwards pass that no other player on the field realized was a lateral.

The defensive tackle's heads-up play preserved a two-point win in a defensive struggle, leading *The Greenville News* to commemorate the historic score with the headline, "Tigers are 10-8-cious."

Clemson was the nation's consensus No. 2 team after besting a North Carolina squad that would conclude the campaign with a 10–2 ledger, a Gator Bowl victory, and a top 10 final ranking. For the first time since the Georgia game, the Tigers broke out the orange pants and wore them against Maryland with the conference title—and perhaps more—at stake.

Jordan set a school record with his 270-yard, three-touchdown passing performance versus the Terrapins, as his 20 completions were the most ever by a Clemson quarterback in an Orange-and-Purple victory, and senior Jerry Gaillard caught his first career touchdown pass in his last home game. The 21–7 triumph secured the Tigers' seventh ACC championship.

The Country Gentlemen closed out their regular-season slate in Columbia on November 21. Although the Gamecocks staked themselves to an early 7–0 advantage, the Tigers delivered a 29–13 victory over South Carolina that prompted the Clemson faithful to throw oranges onto the field when the Jungaleers scored. What the fans already knew to be true was confirmed immediately after the game, when Orange Bowl officials called the Clemson locker room to extend a formal invitation for the Fort Hill Felines to spend New Year's Day in Miami. It would be the Tigers' first January bowl game since the 1958 season and the occasion marked the team's fourth bowl game in a five-year stretch.

Danny Ford gave his players the week off before beginning preparations to face Big Eight champion Nebraska in the Orange Bowl. The Clemson head coach traveled to Birmingham to attend the Alabama-Auburn game on November 28. Ford watched as his mentor, Bear Bryant, earned his record-setting 315th career victory with an Iron Bowl triumph, then he received an even better bit of news: No. 1 Pitt had taken a 14–0 first- quarter lead on No. 11 Penn State when the Panthers' Dan Marino threw the crucial interception that began the Nittany Lions' run of 48 unanswered points in an earthshaking upset of the country's top team.

In the final regular-season AP poll released on November 30, the Panthers plummeted to No. 10, the Sugar Bowl-bound Bulldogs moved up from No. 3 to No. 2, and second-ranked Clemson ascended to the top spot in the sportswriters' rankings. The coaches concurred, bestowing the first No. 1 ranking in school history upon the

Tigers and placing the team they had beaten on September 19 one notch behind them.

The fourth-ranked Cornhuskers were dubbed a six-point favorite by the oddsmakers, but Ford and his charges were undeterred. The South Carolinians journeyed to South Florida early and took part in tough workouts to acclimate themselves to the heat. Although the Orange Bowl would be played at night, the temperature would be in the high 70s and the humidity would hover near 75 per cent.

The Tigers' trip to Miami was not without its trials—on the day of the game, Cliff Austin was stuck in an elevator for over two hours—but the Country Gentlemen were ready. The Rose Bowl, which aired immediately before the Orange Bowl, ran long, so kickoff of the Clemson-Nebraska tilt was delayed.

Sensing that the wait was heightening his team's pregame tension, Ford gestured towards the boom box beside Terry Kinard and asked, "Does that thing work?" The defensive back told the coach that it did. "Well," Ford replied, "turn it on." Music, dancing, and laughter followed. The Tigers relaxed.

Nebraska went out in front by a 7–3 score early—for the eighth time in 12 games, Clemson did not hold the lead at the end of the first quarter—but the Tigers were in their orange pants once again and they would not be denied, not even by a Cornhusker club featuring a two-time Outland Trophy winner and a future Heisman Trophy winner.

Both teams were given additional incentive while the game was being played. Earlier in the day, No. 6 Texas had beaten No. 3 Alabama in a 14–12 Cotton Bowl upset. In the middle of the fourth quarter in Miami, word arrived from New Orleans that No. 10 Pittsburgh had dealt No. 2 Georgia a 24–20 defeat in the Sugar Bowl. The winner of the battle between No. 1 Clemson and No. 4 Nebraska would be crowned the national champion.

The Country Gentlemen had many heroes in the Orange Bowl. Frank Magwood brought in a tipped pass for a 42-yard gain. Billy Davis contributed a 47-yard punt return. Jeff Davis carded 14 tackles. Cliff Austin scored a critical third-quarter touchdown. At the conclusion of the contest, though, there was no doubt which Tiger was the MVP. Homer Jordan completed 11 of his 22 aerial attempts, generated 180 yards of total offense, and delivered a crucial run to pick up a first down late in the game and deny Nebraska possession of the pigskin.

Ford's intense conditioning regimen paid dividends in Miami. Dan Benish lost 13 pounds in the national championship game and Homer Jordan had to be given glucose and water intravenously in both arms to combat his postgame dehydration. Nevertheless, the Tigers were better prepared for the heat and humidity than their opponents, allowing Clemson to prevail by a 22–15 final margin.

The Orange-and-Purple head coach was paid two high compliments after the contest. The first came from his own players, who hoisted Ford onto their shoulders once their victory was won. The second came from the opposing coach when Nebraska skipper Tom Osborne told the Clemson staff that he had never seen his Cornhuskers affected by a hostile crowd…until that night.

As the only undefeated major college team, the Tigers unanimously were proclaimed the national champions. The Jungaleers' 12–0 run included victories over Georgia, North Carolina, and Nebraska squads ranked fifth, eighth, and ninth, respectively, in the final UPI poll. The Bulldogs' lone losses were to Clemson and Pittsburgh, the clubs the coaches had ranked No. 1 and No. 2.

The Fort Hill Felines did more than just claim Clemson's first national title in any sport. Jeff Davis was named the conference's most valuable player. Danny Ford was named the ACC coach of the year and recognized as the national coach of the year by five different organizations after becoming the youngest man (at 33, four months younger than previous record-holder Bud Wilkinson of Oklahoma) ever to win a college football national championship. Eight Tigers made All-ACC and five made All-American. Perry Tuttle became the first Clemson athlete to appear on the cover of *Sports Illustrated* while still enrolled as a student.

The Tiger defense that had forced Nebraska to go three and out nine times in the Orange Bowl set a school mark with 41 forced turnovers in 1981. The Country Gentlemen ended up seventh in the nation in turnover margin and ranked eighth overall in total defense. The titanic nature of the September 19 struggle between the Bulldogs and the Tigers was reaffirmed in the final NCAA numbers, as well: Clemson finished second in scoring defense and seventh in rushing defense, while Georgia wound up second in rushing defense and third in scoring defense.

Just as the Clemson-Georgia game in Death Valley had been a virtual replay of the previous year's outing between the hedges, so too had history repeated itself as the Tigers' season unfolded. At

Fort Hill in 1981, as in the Classic City in 1980, the key to improving from 6–5 to 12–0 had been tenacious and opportunistic defense, a ground-control offense, solid special teams…and, perhaps most important of all, the proper pair of pants.

1982

The Night the Lights Went Out in Georgia

Monday, September 6, 1982, was an historic day for the Clemson-Georgia rivalry, and for college football. The Bulldogs and the Tigers had agreed to move their annual affray to Labor Day night to accommodate a national broadcast in prime time on ABC. Not since 1946 had the Classic City Canines opened their season against the Jungaleers and not since 1903 had the Fort Hill Felines kicked off their campaign against the Dogs.

The last time Clemson and Georgia had squared off either after dark or on a weekday was in 1947, when a Friday night clash between the border rivals was witnessed by 18,000 fans. On this occasion, though, recently-expanded Sanford Stadium would be packed with 82,122 rabid college football enthusiasts there to witness the first season-opening meeting between the two previous national champions in NCAA history. Those who were unable to get tickets could join the largest television audience ever to watch a college football contest on the inaugural weekend of the autumn.

The focus of the sport would be on Athens as No. 7 Georgia, the top team in the land in 1980, welcomed a Clemson club coming off of an undefeated season of its own and ranked No. 9 by the coaches and No. 11 by the sportswriters. The addition of a dozen poles bearing 420 metal-halide bulbs towering 150 feet above the field made possible the first night game between the hedges in more than three decades and highlighted the reality that this encounter between the

Bulldogs and the Tigers was bigger than any of the 50 series meetings that preceded it.

There was just one problem: Herschel Walker wasn't playing.

Walker, who began his junior season as the clear frontrunner for the Heisman Trophy, had broken his right thumb in the first full scrimmage of fall practice. The injury occurred on August 21, just 16 days prior to the titanic showdown in the Classic City. The star tailback underwent surgery the next day to have a pair of pins inserted into his hand and he was expected to miss the first three weeks of the season.

Leading up to the game, the question was asked countless times: "Will Herschel play?" Walker said all along that he wanted to play and that he would play. Vince Dooley consistently offered the opposite answer, emphasizing for the umpteenth time on the eve of the contest, "I don't know how many times I've said it, but I'll say it once again. Herschel isn't going to play. He'll be dressed and he'll sit on the bench, but he won't play."

Dooley's unequivocal statements did little to quell the speculation, however, as a small opening remained which would allow the Georgia head coach to change his mind. Walker was scheduled to be examined again on Monday, and the doctor would deliver his final verdict to Dooley shortly before the 9:00 p.m. kickoff.

With or without Walker, though, both coaches had their hands full. Besides having to alter their regular routines and practice regimens on account of playing on a Monday night, the opposing headmasters had to deal with the issues that accompanied starting the season with a monumental outing on the grandest of stages.

Although the Tigers largely were without injuries, they had to replace 11 starters from their national championship squad, including Jeff Bryant, Jeff Davis, and Perry Tuttle. The Country Gentlemen brought back seven defensive starters (with "bruise brothers" William Devane and William Perry splitting time at middle guard) and their entire offensive backfield returned, as well, but Clemson would field an inexperienced offensive line.

Nevertheless, Danny Ford felt good about his squad, noting, "If they want to be good players and a good team, they can be." Several of the head coach's charges had an extra incentive to play well in Athens on Labor Day night, as the Orange-and-Purple roster contained 26 Peach State natives, 14 of whom (including tailback Cliff Austin and quarterback Homer Jordan) appeared on the depth chart as first- or second-stringers.

A similar desire to impress the folks from back home motivated several Bulldogs, as well. The list of the seven South Carolina natives who suited up for the Red and Black featured a number of notable names, among them a couple of pass-catching ends (Laurens's Norris Brown and Seneca's Clarence Kay) and a pair of tailbacks (Spartanburg's Carnie Norris and Liberty's Tron "Electron" Jackson).

However, the Dogs would have to get it done against the Tigers despite the absence of key figures other than Walker. Early in the week before the game, Brown suffered a stress fracture in his right leg. During practice that Wednesday, end Freddie Gilbert tore his quadriceps muscle to join tackle Jimmy Payne among Georgia's injured defensive line- men. On the offensive side of the ball, right guard Warren Gray aggravated a severely sprained ankle, Norris was held out of contact drills for three days after being banged up in practice, and Scottie Williams was shifted over from third-string tight end to fullback in place of Barry Young.

By the weekend before the game, while other college football teams already were taking the field, both head coaches were starting to show signs of strain. "The waiting is the worst thing," observed Ford. "There's just too much time to wonder if you've done everything...I'm glad we don't have to go through this very often. It's nerve wracking."

Barbara Dooley, who had been asked by the press whether her spouse's claims about Walker were true, sensed that husband Vince was too tense. She could tell that the pressure was starting to get to him, and she knew the Georgia head coach had the added stress of celebrating his 50th birthday on the Saturday before his team faced Clemson with a chance to give him his 141st career victory, which would move Dooley ahead of Wally Butts and make him the winningest coach in Bulldog history. Barbara sent a belly dancer to Saturday's practice to break the tension and lighten the mood.

However overwrought perennial worriers Dooley and Ford might have been, though, the fans were loving every minute of the buildup to the battle. As one booster told *The Atlanta Constitution*, "This isn't like a normal game. This is a happening." Chet Parker, an Auburn fan from Tucker, expressed his agreement with that sentiment by coming to Athens for the atmosphere with no expectation of making it into the stadium.

Although everyone's worst fears about traffic congestion and fan fisticuffs proved un-founded, there was no mistaking the fact that the rivalry had grown more heated during the preceding five years, in which the Dogs los three out of five series meeting with the Tigers. In January 1982, two Clemson University students were arrested for paining orange paws on Sanford Stadium and five University students were arrested for writing "Go Dogs" in shoe polish on Memorial Stadium and the campus statue of Thomas Clemson.

Some visiting boosters took the ribbing they received from their Athenian hosts on Labor Day in stride, noting that trash talk was just a part of the game. However, one Clemson supporter remarked, "We haven't been treated like this in other places."

Former Georgia quarterback Buck Belue summed it up succinctly: "It's no secret Georgia people and Clemson people don't like each other." Over the summer, Herschel Walker had learned that lesson the hard way when he parked his distinctive black Trans Am with a Johnson County license plate outside a shopping center in South Carolina and returned to find the back of his car plastered with Tiger stickers. Walker had to have the bumper replaced.

That growing animosity led the Athens chapter of the Alpha Gamma Rho fraternity to unfurl a banner proclaiming, "Tigers Eat Quiche." Another sign exhibited inside the stadium alluded to the ongoing NCAA investigation of the defending national champions and declared: "What do you call a No. 1 Clemson team? A cheetah."

Tiger fan and Atlanta resident John Fulmer had a retort at the ready. "We know they are worried about us," Fulmer said in response to the printed slogans and verbal abuse. "We earned some respect last year." Cliff Walls, who co-owned an Atlanta Highway bar with former Bulldog offensive lineman Craig Hertwig, grudgingly agreed, observing: "This ain't football. It's war. They declared war on us last year when they beat us."

In the calm before the brewing storm, Dr. Butch Mulherin looked at Walker's hand, advised against allowing the tailback to take the field, but notified Dooley that his Heisman Trophy candidate could play. The Georgia head coach stuck to his plan and started Norris at running back, but Walker never strayed far from Dooley on the sideline, hoping to convince the Bulldog skipper to put him in as a substitute.

After ABC play-by-play announcer Keith Jackson, a native Georgian, was honored by the host school in a pregame ceremony, the anticipated contest at last got underway. It became clear early that both defenses would be dominant and the game remained scoreless until the Bulldogs became the first team to make a mistake.

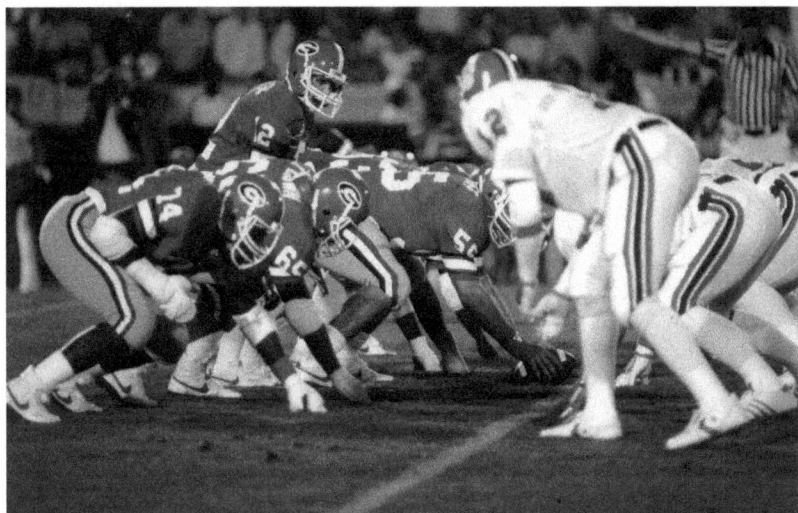

First Year Georgia Quarterback John Lastinger lined up and ready in front of an acclaimed Clemson defense. Photo courtesy of University of Georgia.

Quarterback John Lastinger, starting his first college game as the successor to fellow Valdosta native Buck Belue, directed center Wayne Radloff to hike the ball, but the signal caller bobbled the exchange. The nervous Lastinger fumbled the snap and the loose oblong was smothered by Perry 11 yards in front of the Georgia goal line.

It took the Tigers just three plays to make it into the end zone. Fullback Jeff McCall advanced to the eight yard line on first down, then Cliff Austin went for two more before Homer Jordan received the snap, dropped back as if to pass while the Georgia ends went to the outside, and darted up the middle for a six-yard scoring scamper in a quarterback draw. Place-kicker Bob Paulling's aim was true and the South Carolinians had taken a 7-0 lead with just over seven minutes remaining in the opening period.

The two teams, who would combine for 17 punts over the course of the evening, booted the ball back and forth for the rest of the quarter, but the field position battler gradually was turning the Athenian's favor. Three plays after a 48-yard Jim Broadway punt was downed by snapper Mitch Frix at the Clemson one yard line, the Country Gentlemen faced fourth and one from their own 10.

The snapper to punter Dale "Thunderfoot" Hatcher was high and end Dale Carver, the only Red-and-Black defender assigned to rush, went in untouched. The hometown Dale blocked the visiting Dale's kick and neither Austin nor Hatcher could come down with the football. Georgia right end Stan Dooley, in for the injured Freddie Gilbert, made the grab and fought his way over the goal line. Place-kicker Kevin Butler split the posts to tie the game less than a minute into the second stanza. For the first time since Kent Lawrence's fourth-quarter touchdown run put the Dogs out in front in 1967, Clemson and Georgia were deadlocked at a score other than 0–0.

That point total was unchanged and 10 minutes were left in the half when Herschel Walker came onto the field for the first time. He had talked Vince Dooley into putting him in the lineup, but the junior tailback with the heavily taped hand was employed strictly as a decoy. Walker went left on first down and John Lastinger faked a pitch his way as freshman Tron Jackson skirted the right side on a reverse.

The play went for 40 yards and a touchdown, but Jackson's fellow rookie, center Keith Johnson, was flagged for the illegal use of hands and the resulting holding penalty negated the scoring strike. Walker stayed on the field for the next two snaps without touching the ball on either of them, and he left the gridiron with his offensive teammates as the Dogs faced fourth and 12 from the Clemson 42 yard line.

Ordinarily, Dooley would have sent in Broadway in the clear punting situation, but Butler had told the coach before the game that he felt capable of making a field goal if the offense advanced as far as the Tiger 40. Dooley decided to gamble that the extra six feet wouldn't make that much of a difference. Butler's 59-yard attempt went 57 yards before dropping short of the crossbar.

Each defense continued to get the better of the opposing offense for the balance of the opening 30 minutes. Lastinger completed only four of nine first-half passes for 39 yards against the tight coverage of the Jungaleer secondary and the Bulldogs went to the locker room having gained just three first downs and 97 yards of total offense. Clemson found itself equally stymied by the Red and Black, who allowed Jordan to connect on five of 10 attempts for 31 yards before intermission. The Tigers' halftime tally of 104 yards did not feature even a single offensive possession on which the visitors drove inside the Georgia 40.

One Clemson series ended at that precise point when an aerial thrown by the Orange-and-Purple quarterback was picked off at the home team's 40 yard line by cornerback Tony Flack, the first freshman ever to start a season opener for Vince Dooley. Just 78 seconds remained in the second quarter when the Dogs reclaimed custody of the pigskin. Following a pair of incompletions, Lastinger connected with split end Charles Junior over the middle for a 27-yard pickup and completed another pass to Scottie Williams for nine more. When a pair of Jackson runs over left guard failed to move the chains, Butler was called upon to boot a 39-yarder and the sophomore kicker gave Georgia a 10–7 lead with nine seconds to play until the break.

The Classic City Canines went to the locker room holding a three-point edge, but Lastinger's confidence had been given a boost by the Bulldogs' final drive. Bubba Smith, the former All-Pro defensive end who had embarked on an acting career and was filming in the Peach State, put in an appearance on the Georgia sideline, where he jabbed a finger into the Red-and-Black quarterback's chest and said, "Settle down." Lastinger listened and rebounded from his early jitters.

Walker, who was interviewed by ABC's Jim Lampley at halftime, continued to plead his case with his head coach, offering assurances that the protective cast on his right hand would allow him to play more in the final 30 minutes without undue risk. Dooley finally relented, and, when the Tigers' opening drive of the second half ended in a punt, the question on everyone's mind finally received a definitive answer. Yes, Herschel would play…on e very Georgia offensive series of the second half, in fact.

The Dogs lined up at their own 24 yard line. Lastinger took the snap, took advantage of a Clemson defense whose focus was on Walker, and completed a pass to Kay at the 30 yard line. The tight end scooted to the Orange-and-Purple 23 for a 53-yard gain on his only catch of the contest.

The next snap went to Walker, whose first carry of his junior campaign picked up three yards. The running back threw a block on the ensuing play that allowed Lastinger to find Williams for the 16-yard completion that carried the Red and Black inside the five. Although Walker was thrown for a two-yard loss on the following play, Lastinger made up for it on a quarterback sneak to the one yard line.

Walker went airborne on third and goal, diving over the middle and into the end zone…but the left side of the Georgia line was offsides, so the Classic City Canines were pushed back and forced to settle for a 23-yard field goal to go up 13–7 with 9:20 to play in the third period. Since the series had taken on a new level of competitiveness in 1977, one of the two teams had scored against the other on its opening drive of the second half for six straight seasons.

Because his touchdown was called back on a penalty, Walker completed his college career without having scored against the Tigers. "The

Lastinger in the pocket.

Goal Line Stalker" would break the plane of the goal line at least once in each of the last 11 games of his final season in silver britches, but Clemson would bar him from the end zone in each of his three outings against the Fort Hill Felines. The Country Gentlemen, who similarly held South Carolina's George Rogers scoreless as a collegian, were the only team Herschel Walker faced more than once without scoring a touchdown.

The Bulldog tailback would finish his evening with 11 carries for 20 yards, marking the lowest single-game output of his storied career. Walker broke the 100-yard barrier in each of the Athenians' remaining games (including the bowl) and ended up with a 17-touchdown, 1,752-yard season to capture college football's highest award, but his broken thumb and the Tiger defense held him in check in a game in which Clemson backup fullback Kevin Mack was the leading rusher with 43 yards.

Butler's third-quarter field goal marked the end of the scoring but not the end of the fireworks. Another Georgia march advanced as far as the Tiger 20 before the Country Gentlemen sent Tim Childers on the safety blitz that yielded a sack and a forced 48-yard three-point try. Butler had the distance but the kick went widew to the left.

Clemson took possession following the miss and drove into Bulldog territory on the strength of a 13-yard dash up the middle by Mack. The penetration made it only as far as the Georgia 39 before being halted. Time continued to tick away in the fourth quarter when, on a third down play at the home team's 36 yard line, Jordan lofted a high pass to Austin on the left sideline and saw his errant throw snagged by rover Terry Hoage.

Together with earlier pickoffs by Carver and Flack, the grab marked the Tiger signal caller's third interception of the night. Hoage would finish the season with an NCAA-best 12 interceptions, three more than the national runner-up nine picks notched by his teammate in the Bulldog secondary, safety Jeff Sanchez.

The South Carolinians began their final drive at their own 20 yard line with just under three minutes remaining, still trailing by a scant six points. Clemson marched down the field, picking up a fresh series of downs at the Georgia 41. Jordan's first-down pass was low, short, and incomplete. A sack on second down cost the Jungaleers three yards and the Orange-and-Purple quarterback was pressured into throwing out of bounds on the ensuing snap.

The Fort Hill Felines were down to their final chance. A time out was taken, during which the Bulldog defenders huddled. Senior linebacker Nate Taylor told his teammates, "This is the last play in the world. Let's make it a good one." On fourth down, Jordan was hit from the blind side as he released…and his final pass was intercepted by Taylor to stamp out the final Clemson threat and lock up a 13–7 Georgia victory between the hedges.

As had become the norm, the triumphant team trailed by several statistical measures. The Tigers were out in front of the Bulldogs in first downs (14–10), rushing yardage (129–101), and total offense (249–241). Although each team drew five flags, the Red and Black clearly were more wounded by penalties, which erased a pair of Georgia scores and left the game with only two total touchdowns, both of which resulted from turnovers. The Classic City Canines held the ball for almost 32 minutes of playing time and John Lastinger completed eight of 16 pass attempts for 140 yards.

Homer Jordan put up roughly comparable numbers, going 15 of 28 for 120 yards, but his evening recalled Buck Belue's day in Death Valley the year before. After tossing only nine interceptions in 1981, the Clemson quarterback threw the ball to four different players in red jerseys on Labor Day night. "I really wanted to play well tonight," said Jordan following the loss, "because of that game two years ago. But after the first two inter ceptions I started thinking about that game, and it was tough to keep that off my mind." The senior signal caller once again had failed to live up to his own lofty expectations against the Dogs in his home town of Athens, but his cause had not been aided by a stingy Georgia defense that allowed the Clemsonians to convert just three of their 17 third downs, never permitted an Orange-and-Purple offensive drive to encroach beyond the home team's 30 yard line, and refused to concede as many as 40 yards of real estate to the Country Gentlemen in any single series.

When asked beforehand about the previous season's national championship, Danny Ford had commented, "It has its place in Clemson history, but I'm sure Georgia doesn't care whether we won it or not." The Tiger coach was underselling the Bulldogs' motivation considerably; the Red and Black very much cared that the South Carolinians had reached the mountaintop the year before, and they exacted retribution in 1982 for what had been done to them in 1981.

Georgia had entered Memorial Stadium the previous autumn as the defending national champion and boasting the longest winning streak in Division I-A. The 15 consecutive victories carded by the Dogs

Georgia's Terry Hoage trying to snag an
interception.

had been just two wins shy of matching the school record for the sequential triumphs set in the 1940s, but the Country Gentlemen had spoiled their shot at another title. Now, the shoe was on the other foot: Clemson was the defending national champ with an NCAA-best 13-game winning streak, and the Jungaleers would need just two more victories in a row to match the school mark set in the 1940s. It was the Red and Black's turn to upend their border rival.

The Tiger, somewhat uncharitably, claimed that "the final score wasn't really indicative of the game" and alleged that Ford's squad "never threatened to score after its initial first-quarter 11-yard march." The worries of the sports editor of the Clemson student newspaper were not shared by the school's head coach, though. Ford indicated at his Tuesday press conference that he was encouraged about the season in spite of the loss, which dropped the Tigers to No. 16.

A bye week following the clash in Athens afforded the Fort Hill Felines a dozen days within which to regroup before hosting Boston College. The Eagles no doubt appeared unthreatening at the time the game was arranged—the Jesuit school in Chestnut Hill had not made it into postseason play in four decades and was just four years removed from a winless season—but Clemson caught Boston College on the upswing.

Sophomore quarterback Doug Flutie was in the process of leading the Eagles to a top 10 finish in passing offense, an eight-win regular season, and a Tangerine Bowl berth. In Death Valley, Flutie guided the Bay Staters to a 17–17 tie with the Tigers. The 0–1–1 start caused Clemson to drop from the top 20 altogether, but the Country Gentlemen then proceeded to reel off nine straight victories.

Double-digit wins over Division I-AA Western Carolina and a Kentucky club that would go winless for the fall boosted the Tigers' record before they began conference play and the Fort Hill Felines proceeded to blast their ACC competition. Clemson clobbered George Welsh's first Virginia squad and Duke by a combined 97–14 margin. Cliff Austin established a new school single-game rushing record with 260 yards against the Blue Devils.

After the Tigers registered a 38–29 road win over N.C. State, Bob Paulling kicked three field goals from 40 yards or farther away in the South Carolinians' 16–13 triumph over Sun Bowl-bound North Carolina. At the time of the game, the coaches had the Tar Heels ranked 13th and the Tigers ranked 14th, but the win vaulted Clemson into the UPI top 10.

Another game against a ranked foe followed, as Maryland was pegged as the nation's No. 16 team by the coaches. The Terrapins' last-ditch drive ended when quarterback Boomer Esiason had a pass intercepted by Clemson free safety Billy Davis and the Coun try Gentlemen held on for a 24–22 victory.

The Tigers dealt South Carolina a 24–6 defeat in the ensuing outing, but, for the first time in more than two decades, the Jungaleers did not end their regular-season slate against the Gamecocks. Clemson instead journeyed overseas to take on Wake Forest at the Mirage Bowl in Tokyo on November 27.

The trek to the Far East involved a bit of culture shock for the Tigers, as became apparent when a group of reporters from the Land of the Rising Sun came to interview Danny Ford at the Jervey Athletic Center. The head coach turned to the school's sports information director, Bob Bradley, and asked: "Do I have to speak Japanese?" Bradley replied, "Sometimes I am not sure you can speak English."

Clemson dispatched the Demon Deacons by a 21–17 margin in Tokyo, thereby running the South Carolinians' record to 9–1–1 and capturing their second consecutive ACC championship. The win elevated the Country Gentlemen to a No. 8 ranking in the AP poll and the Cotton Bowl was prepared to extend an invitation to the Orange and Purple. Unfortunately, a trip to the Lone Star State was not in the cards for the Tigers.

James Cofer and Terry Minor, two athletes previously recruited by Clemson, had filed a lawsuit against the University. Although their complaint was dismissed, their story had attracted the attention of the NCAA, which conducted an 18-month investigation into the allegations. On November 22, the day the polls were released that had the Tigers ranked in the top 10 by the coaches and sportswriters alike, the NCAA handed down its punishment for violations dating back to Charley Pell's stewardship of the Fort Hill program.

The stiff sanctions, which Clemson elected not to appeal, consisted of scholarship reductions and a two-year probation during which the Jungaleers could not appear on live television or accept bowl invitations. The TV ban would begin with the 1983 campaign, but Ford decided to keep his team home for the holidays that fall, in an effort to minimize the negative effect on recruiting. The ACC tacked on another year of bowl ineligibility and removed the Tigers from conference championship contention prior to 1985. Clemson protested the league penalties, but these harsh punishments were upheld on appeal.

The only Fort Hill Feline to be present for the Cotton Bowl was free safety Terry Kinard, who was on hand to receive the national defensive player of the year award. Kinard, a unanimous first-team All-American who led the team in both interceptions and tackles, became the 10th overall selection in the 1983 NFL draft. Although nine of his Tiger teammates were selected in that same draft, Clemson's 21-1-1 two-year run had come to a bitter end.

In Athens, the Dogs had little time to revel in the victory that made them the only team to beat the Country Gentlemen in a span of two seasons. Five days after their Monday night conquest of the defending national champions, the Red and Black were scheduled to host Brigham Young in a contest between the sixth-ranked team in the AP poll and the 19th-ranked team in the UPI poll.

BYU came into Sanford Stadium sporting a six-game winning streak and a string of three straight seasons of double-digit victories. The Cougars' high-powered offense was led by quarterback Steve Young, but the Georgians succeeded in holding the visitors from the WAC to one offensive touchdown. Kevin Butler's 44-yard field goal with 71 seconds remaining lifted the Red and Black to a 17–14 win over LaVell Edwards's Holiday Bowl-bound outfit.

After emerging from Columbia with a 34–18 triumph over the Gamecocks, the Bulldogs reeled off four straight SEC victories over Mississippi State, Ole Miss, Hall of Fame Bowl-bound Vanderbilt, and Kentucky by a cumulative score of 116–59 to boost the Classic City Canines' ranking to No. 3 in both polls. Against the Rebels, Butler drove home a 59-yard field goal to set a new school record.

A 34–3 win over Memphis boosted Georgia to second in the coaches' poll just in time for the Red and Black to meet a top 20 Florida club in Jacksonville. Stan Dooley recovered three fumbles by Gator quarterback Wayne Peace in a regionally-televised rout before the largest crowd ever to see a game in the Sunshine State. The Bulldogs trounced Florida by a 44–0 score on the same day that top-ranked Pitt fell to Notre Dame and Georgia took over the No. 1 ranking in the November 8 poll.

The Dogs remained atop the polls with a 19–14 win over an Auburn outfit that would finish the fall with nine wins following a Tangerine Bowl victory. The triumph on the Plains clinched a third consecutive conference crown for the Red and Black, prompting play-by- play announcer Larry Munson to declare: "Oh, look at the sugar falling from the sky!"

A 20-point win over Georgia Tech concluded the Bulldogs' second 11–0 regular season in three years and set up a national championship bout between No. 1 Georgia and No. 2 Penn State in the Superdome on New Year's Day. Despite the two teams' respective rankings, the Nittany Lions were a four-point favorite in New Orleans and the Pennsylvanians proved the oddsmakers correct.

Joe Paterno's squad leapt out to a 20–3 lead before the Classic City Canines began a furious comeback. John Lastinger completed four of five passes on a 34-second drive in the final minute of the first half to narrow the gap to 10 points and Georgia pulled to within four inside the four-minute mark of the final period. Penn State picked up two first downs on its final possession to run out the clock and claim the national championship with a 27–23 victory.

Like Clemson, Georgia ended the 1982 campaign on a down note, but the Bulldogs' 11–1 finish earned them a No. 4 final ranking while the Tigers checked in at No. 8 in the AP poll. The last shock of a surprising season came when Herschel Walker decided to fore go his senior season and play football professionally for the USFL's New Jersey Generals.

The 1982 Heisman Trophy winner left school following a three-year college career in which he set 41 University of Georgia, 16 Southeastern Conference, and 11 NCAA records. Not counting bowl games, Walker rushed for 5,259 yards and scored 52 touchdowns. The three-time consensus All-American's No. 34 jersey was retired in 1985. Herschel's days wearing the red and black produced three conference crowns, a national championship, and a 33–3 record for the Bulldogs. His only regular-season loss was to the Clemson Tigers.

1983

Fit to be Tied

On opposite sides of the Savannah River, Vince Dooley and Danny Ford looked ahead to the coming season and saw similar causes for concern. Each coach had two quarterbacks, several tailbacks, and multiple question marks.

The Bulldogs would start four seniors on the offensive line, with the lone underclassman, sophomore center Keith Johnson, boasting significant playing experience, but Georgia was still trying to settle on a runing back to fill the void left by the early departure of Herschel Walker.

As Dooley wrestled with that crucial decision, he continued to move senior Barry Young back and forth between fullback (where he had been the backup for the last two years) and tailback (where he offered the maturity lacked by the likes of freshman David McCluskey or sophomore Keith Montgomery). Senior John Lastinger and sophomore Todd Williams likewise were vying for playing time under center, while eight new faces were to be found among the 11 starting defenders after safety Jeff Sanchez sustained the broken arm that would take him out of the lineup for the entire autumn.

The Tigers shared all these problems and more. Center Cary Massaro passed up his final year of eligibility shortly before the start of the season and Chuckie Richardson, Clemson's only player with game experience at linebacker, spent much of fall practice struggling with injuries. Ford's biggest concern, though, was at the tailback spot, where the depth chart was without a speedster who had spent more than one year with the program. The Jungaleers' dual field generals were option quarterback Mike Eppley and passer Anthony Parete.

With so much uncertainty surrounding the two clubs, both coaches had to have been pleasantly surprised with the way the fall began. On September 3, Memorial Stadium opened the new upper deck over the north stands to bump the arena's capacity over 80,000 in time for a 44–10 throttling of Western Carolina. Sophomore tailback Terrence Flagler got loose for 139 yards against the Division I-AA Catamounts, earning a starting nod for the following week's road encounter with Boston College.

On the same Saturday that the Tigers took care of business against WCU, a Georgia squad ranked 13th in the coaches' poll hosted UCLA for a rain-drenched night game against a Pac-10 outfit led by quarterback Rick Neuheisel and slotted as the UPI No. 12 team. Herschel Walker was in Sanford Stadium as a spectator for the nationally-televised tussle with the Bruins, in which the Dogs secured a 19–8 victory when Red-and-Black senior safety Charlie Dean returned an interception 69 yards for a touchdown in the final 30 seconds. Georgia had led the nation in interceptions in 1982 and, in the opening outing of 1983, the Athenians picked off four of the Californians' passes. In their first game since the loss of Walker, the Classic City Canines racked up 228 yards on the ground against a UCLA club bound for its second straight Rose Bowl win.

The Bulldog's regular-season winning streak now stretched to 20 games, with their last loss on a date other than New Year's Day having come on their previous trip to Death Valley. As the Athenians prepared to journey to Lake Hartwell, they did so with the full awareness that, in the last five series meetings between Clemson and Georgia, the home team had prevailed in each instance. The September 17 showdown between the Country Gentlemen and the Dogs would take place on the sixth anniversary of the Tigers' 1977 upset of the Red and Black in Sanford Stadium.

Following the first Saturday of the season, however, Georgia enjoyed a September 10 open date, while Clemson had a game to play in Chestnut Hill. In the Bay State clash with Doug Flutie's Eagles, the South Carolinians appeared cursed from the start. Flagler, who had aggravated a preseason knee injury, had to be scrubbed from the lineup at the last minute and replaced on the first team by Stacey Driver. After taking a 16–3 lead, the Tigers proceeded to surrender four second-half touchdowns in a 31–16 setback at Alumni Stadium in which Liberty Bowl-bound Boston College garnered 281 rushing yards on 57 carries.

The loss in Massachusetts placed added emphasis on the Georgia game for a young Clemson club that would start six freshmen against the Dogs. Tiger defensive tackle Ray Brown, a Rome, Ga., native facing his home state team for the final time in his collegiate career, declined to dance around the importance of the outing: "It could be the difference between a winning season and a losing season." The visiting Athenians were wary, as well. Bulldog cornerback Darryl Jones pointed out beforehand that, "when you go into Death Valley you find the noisiest fans in the world and you find a pretty good football team."

The Tiger's Scott Freeman spelled out the familiar script for cage matches between the border rivals when predicting that "there will be no passing in Saturday's game, just hardnosed running and tough-minded defense. As usually happens in a Clemson-Georgia game, a break at just the right time will probably decide the winner." Tom Mc-Collister of *The Atlanta Journal-Constitution* concurred, noting, "There will be little razzle-dazzle, but a great deal of jarring of bones."

For his part, Brown understood all the reasons why it mattered which team emerged victorious from expanded Memorial Stadium: "I don't hate Georgia; it's still my home... But it's such a rivalry, bigger now than even South Carolina. It's more political, because it's for national recognition." The Bulldogs came into the game ranked seventh in the coaches' poll and 11th in the AP top 20.

Both head coaches shared their players' sentiments concerning the significance of the showdown. Vince Dooley declared that the rivalry dividing the nearby schools was "a series as heated as we have, a game as intense as we play." "If we're not ready to play this week," said Danny Ford, "I'll take every one of our players to the infirmary to check out their heads."

The untelevised contest got underway at 1:00 in the afternoon, following a pregame ceremony honoring Terry Kinard as the Clemson athlete of the year. The largest crowd ever to see a football game in the Palmetto State—more than 81,000 fans—was present to learn which team would outduel the other, and, although everyone on hand would be at least somewhat disappointed in the outcome, the assembled members of the Bulldog and Tiger faithful at least learned who would be running the ball for the respective combatants.

Dooley had decided late in the week to make Young his first-string tailback rather than throw youthful speedsters McCluskey and Montgomery into the starting role in such a hostile environment. Ford had his decision made for him when what was thought at first to be a bruised knee forced Flagler to undergo arthroscopic surgery to repair cartilage damage on Friday afternoon. Freshman Kenny Flowers would spell Flagler, making his first start in place of the player who had been the Country Gentlemen's leading rusher through the season's first two games.

The scoreless opening quarter largely favored the visitors, in spite of the fact that Red-and-Black flanker Kevin Harris separated his shoulder on the third play of the game. Even though an early Georgia drive ended in an interception by Clemson free safety Billy Davis, the Dogs crossed midfield on each of their first five possessions.

The Tigers' first series advanced as far as the Classic City Canines' 35 yard line, but, when Jungaleer place-kicker Bob Paulling lined up for a 52-yard field goal try, Bulldog rover Terry Hoage skirted the edge of the Orange-and-Purple line to halt the pigskin in its flight. It was the first time in his career at any level that Paulling had a field goal attempt blocked.

Late in the first period, Georgia began a 13-play drive covering 64 yards and culminating in the first points of the contest. The Bulldogs were facing third and 12 on their own side of the field when Lastinger connected with receiver Jimmy Hockaday for a 15- yard pickup to midfield. The senior signal caller followed that up with a 14-yard comple tion to flanker Herman Archie.

After McCluskey gained two yards on fourth and one, Lastinger fumbled the ball forward, only to have tailback Melvin Simmons fall on the loose oval for a nine-yard pickup to the Clemson 16. The march was capped off by a 26-yard Kevin Butler field goal 55 seconds into the second stanza.

The Bulldogs built on their 3–0 lead within the next three minutes once freshman flanker Ray Williams turned the ball over on a pass reception followed by a fumble. The Tigers' loss was Georgia's gain, as Bulldog defender Mike Jones pounced on the free football at the home team's 28 yard line. A sack of Todd Williams by middle guard William Perry forced another Butler three-pointer to put the Red and Black up by six with 11:15 to play in the first half.

The balance of the second quarter belonged to the Tigers, though. The South Carolinians moved 49 yards in eight snaps on the strength of a 14-yard run by fullback Kevin Mack sandwiched between a 13-yard reception by split end Shelton Boyer and an 11-yard Eppley scamper to carry the Country Gentlemen inside the Bulldog 25. Paulling's 37-yard field goal with 3:30 showing on the clock cut the Georgia lead in half.

The rest of the Red and Black's advantage was erased in short order. Clemson kicked off and the Dogs set up shop at their own 20 yard line. Perry, anticipating the Athenians' snap count, blew past Johnson and into the visitors' backfield. The 320-pound nose guard encountered McCluskey behind the line of scrimmage, clothes lined the Bulldog ballcarrier with a bruising forearm tackle, and caught the Georgia running back's airborne fumble at the 16 yard line.

The resulting drive lasted all of one play, as Flowers went off left tackle on a diversion play and went into the end zone untouched. "I think any tailback could have scored with that hole," said Flowers, who ended the afternoon with 58 yards on a dozen carries. For the third straight season, a Perry fumble recovery inside the Georgia 35 yard line had produced a swift scoring strike by the Jungaleers.

Paulling's extra point made the score 10–6 in favor of the Tigers. Just 10 seconds of game time had elapsed since Clemson's previous score. The Fort Hill Felines continued to hold that four-point lead at the break, in spite of the fact that the Bulldogs had held the ball for more than 20 of the first 30 minutes of play.

As he had done against UCLA two weeks earlier, Dooley rotated his signal callers in Death Valley. Lastinger, who had spent part of the summer with his leg in a cast after offseason knee surgery, started the game and played during the odd-numbered quarters, whereas Williams directed the drives during the second and fourth frames.

As the afternoon wore along, it increasingly appeared that Dooley would have to count on one of his two quarterbacks to give the team an offensive spark, for the Bulldogs' ordinarily reliable special teams did not perform consistently on the banks of Lake Hartwell. Punter Chip Andrews shanked a pair of punts, while place-kicker Kevin Butler would miss a 50-yard field goal attempt prior to a wild final five minutes of play.

Clemson's second-quarter dominance carried over into the third stanza, in which the Tigers moved 45 yards downfield in eight plays. The Country Gentlemen's starting fullback demon strated why he deserved the nickname "Mack Truck" when he went off right tackle on third and 14 for a 33-yard run to the Georgia 25. Mack tallied 91 yards on 15 carries to lead all rushers.

Paulling booted a 38-yarder to stake the Jungaleers to a seven-point lead just over four minutes into the penultimate period, and, as had been the case for both teams in the first half, a score by one squad was followed swiftly by more points for that same club. The Tigers kicked off to Simmons, whose earlier recovery of Lastinger's fumble had allowed Georgia's initial scoring drive to continue. The senior tailback was being called upon to return a kick for the first time in his collegiate career.

The kicked pigskin slipped through Simmons's grasp and the Bulldog deep man was unable to track it down. "I just didn't look the ball in all the way," he later explained, "and once it went through my arms I couldn't find it. It was right under my foot." While Simmons was unable to locate the loose oblong, it was visible to on rushing cornerbacks (and native Georgians) Tyrone Davis and Perry Williams, the latter of whom took possession of the football at the Red and Black's seven yard line.

The Tigers initially advanced as far as the Georgia four yet lost yardage on a brief series in which Eppley squandered a pair of time outs before Paulling drove home a 40-yard field goal. Just 39 seconds after the Clemson kicker's previous three-pointer, the home team had extended its lead to 16–6.

The margin threatened to grow even larger later in the third period when Paulling was sent in to attempt his fifth field goal of the day. Hoage

**In his first collegiate start, freshman tailback Kenny Flowers rushed
for 58 yards against Georgia.**

once again swept around the short corner of the Orange-and-Purple line and secured his second blocked kick from the foot of the Tiger senior.

The tide shortly thereafter began to turn in favor of the Dogs when a forced fumble from Flowers just inside Georgia territory was snatched up by freshman defensive end Calvin Ruff. From their own 46 yard line, the Classic City Canines commenced the only sustained touchdown drive by either team in their last two clashes.

The march was not without its fits and starts, however. Todd Williams was sacked for a loss of five and a pair of early holding penalties threatened to set back the Red and Black, but the Tigers declined the second flag on a play that produced a four-yard gain to set up third and 21 for the Dogs.

Prior to that point, the Athenians' sophomore signal caller had completed one pass for 12 yards, so it appeared that the South Carolinians had made a shrewd choice by taking the down rather than the yardage. What the home team did not know was that Williams would connect on 10 of his 17 aerial attempts for 157 yards and a touchdown in the fourth quarter, starting with the 19-yard pass to Archie that carried Georgia to the Clemson 46 yard line.

McCluskey's five-yard jaunt on fourth and two allowed the Bulldogs to retain possession of the football. The visitors maintained their momentum by varying the snap count that Perry previously had discerned, enticing the Tiger middle guard to jump offsides. When the Red and Black faced third and three at the Jungaleer 20, Williams ran for four yards. When Georgia faced another third and three at the Clemson nine yard line, the Bulldog quarterback once more scampered for four yards.

On the 14th play of the 54-yard drive, Williams completed an eight-yard pass to tight end Clarence Kay for the Classic City Canines' first offensive touchdown against the Tigers since 1980. Butler drilled the point after and the Country Gentlemen's lead was cut to 16–13 with slightly more than nine minutes remaining in the contest.

Although the Georgia head coach sent in his place-kicker with little hesitation, Dooley drew some criticism for that decision. *The Greenville Piedmont's* Scott Regan questioned why the Dogs had not elected to go for two and set up a possible game-winning field goal. The Red-and-Black skipper defended the call by noting that too much time was left on the clock to risk a low-percentage play that could have killed the Bulldogs' newfound momentum.

While Dooley did not say so, he might well have held in the back of his mind the memory of the decision he had made on the Sanford Stadium sideline six years earlier to the day, when he directed his team to go for the win rather than the tie. Prior to that afternoon, he had posted a 10–1 record against the Tigers; from that date to this, Dooley's Dogs had gone 3–3 in contests with Clemson. The Red and Black had not lost on three straight trips to Fort Hill since the first three series meetings to take place in the Palmetto State and Dooley was not anxious to have that particular piece of history repeat itself.

The score remained unchanged as the clock ticked below five minutes, but the Bulldogs were driving. Georgia clawed its way inside the Tigers' 35 yard line, only to have freshman linebacker Henry Walls register the sack of Todd Williams that compelled the visitors to settle for a 56-yard three-point try. Butler, who had missed a 50-yarder already, saw his latest field goal attempt go wide left. The scoreboard showed 4:25 to go.

Fewer than three minutes remained when the Dogs got the ball back at their own 20. The Classic City Canines were carried out to the Georgia 44 by consecutive completions from Williams to Archie, who would catch seven passes for 85 yards that afternoon. The sophomore quarterback then found end Jamie Wisham for 39 yards.

The three pass plays had earned the Bulldogs a first down at the Country Gentlemen's 17 yard line, but, when Barry Young was flagged for holding on the next play, the Athenians' march came to a halt. Georgia made it as far as the 14 yard line before Dooley turned to Butler on fourth and seven. The junior kicker atoned for his earlier misses by making the 31-yard field goal that knotted the score at 16 points per side with 38 seconds to play.

Both teams took shots at splitting the uprights from the vicinity of midfield in the time that remained. With the ball resting on their own 49 yard line, the Tigers relied upon the foot of Donald Igwebuike, who tried a 68-yard field goal that would have surpassed by three feet the existing NCAA record. Igwebuike's kick, which was attempted with a scant seven seconds showing on the scoreboard, fell well short. It was the South Carolinians' third failure in six three-point attempts against Georgia.

The Bulldogs took over one yard inside Tiger territory with time left for one more play. The Jungaleers' missed field goal was followed by a Red-and-Black attempt on the very next snap, and, with one second to go, Kevin Butler took a stab at a 66-yard kick into the wind. Butler, too, came up short on the final play of the game. It was the Athenians' third failure in six three-point attempts against Clemson.

The 16–16 final score produced the first series tie in two decades and left no one satisfied. Ray Brown tried to put the best possible face on the outcome, pointing out, "We have their respect and they have ours, for whatever little that's worth." Brown's teammate, Tiger nose guard William Devane, declared that the result left him feeling "empty" and William Perry agreed that it was "just like you never played." Clemson defensive end Jeff Wells put it best when he said: "It feels like a fight where you extend your right and he extends his right and you each get it right in the face."

Neither head coach was pleased, although both were proud of the way their players performed in the intense, hard-hitting contest. While admitting that the game "was disappointing," Vince Dooley tried to take a philosophical approach. The Bulldog skipper commented, "We won the fourth quarter and, because of that, at least we didn't lose the game."

Danny Ford, who had made good on his pregame promise that his squad would not come out attired in orange pants, described the inconclusive ordeal as "60 minutes of football which seemed like five hours." The Clemson headmaster also recognized that the game might have gone on even longer had his quarterback not burned two time outs in a single possession on which his team lost ground.

The Red and Black's Edward Thomas actually saw some positives in the draw, though. The assistant sports editor of the University of Georgia student newspaper believed the tie had a beneficial cooling effect on what threatened to become an overheated rivalry. As Thomas pointed out, the absence of a winner and a loser contributed to more cordial relations between Bulldog and Tiger partisans, who spoke to one another on the way out of Memorial Stadium with a level of neighborliness sorely lacking in recent clashes between the nearby foes.

The game was deadlocked on the scoreboard, but not on the stat sheet. There, the Dogs held the upper hand in first downs (21–14), passing yardage (216–63), and total offense (346–240). The Red and Black attempted twice as many passes (28) as their hosts (14), and the Athenians had custody of the football for almost 37 minutes of clock time.

However, the Tiger defense took charge of the line of scrimmage and limited Georgia to 130 yards on the ground. No Bulldog player tallied more than 34 rushing yards—a figure that provided the visitors with a cruel reminder that the tailback who had worn that number no longer was in the lineup—and the Red and Black had just two runs from scrimmage of greater than 10 yards. Clemson also was the victim of fewer "takeovers," as each team lost a pair of fumbles yet the Country Gentlemen did not throw an interception.

The one redeeming feature of the day from the Bulldogs' perspective was that none of their major rivals fared any better. The same Saturday that saw Clemson and Georgia deadlocked after 60 minutes also featured fourth-ranked Auburn losing to third-ranked Texas, 15th-ranked Florida struggling to beat Indiana State by four points, and, perhaps best of all, Dick Sheridan's Furman team defeating Georgia Tech at Grant Field.

The Yellow Jackets were the next opponent on the slate for a Clemson club that stood at 1–1–1 for the second year in a row despite being outscored 31–0 in the fourth quarters of its last two outings. After almost two decades as an athletic independent, the Ramblin' Wreck was rolling into Death Valley for its first conference game as a full-fledged member of the ACC.

The Country Gentlemen delivered a 41–14 throttling to the Engineers to begin a third straight undefeated run through league play. The Tigers reeled off victories against Virginia, Duke, N.C. State, Wake Forest, and Peach Bowl-bound North Carolina by an average margin of 29–18. The triumph over a Tar Heel unit then ranked in the top 10 in both polls lifted Clemson into the AP top 20.

This set up a showdown with Maryland, the No. 11 team in the estimation of the sportswriters, which would allow the Orange and Purple to earn on the field the ACC championship they were ineligible to claim in the record book. The Terrapins and the Tigers tangled on "Spirit Blitz Weekend" at Fort Hill, when 3,000 Clemson students arrived at 7:00a.m. to help inflate the 363,729 balloons which were released as the team ran down the hill.

The inspired South Carolinians built up a 42–7 lead on Maryland as Mike Eppley threw three touchdown passes. Kevin Mack, playing in his final home game, accounted for 186 of Clemson's 350 rushing yards and he scored for the final time while wearing one shoe; the Tiger fullback had lost the other half of his footgear on a 56-yard touchdown run. Bobby Ross's Terrapins, who would end the autumn in the Citrus Bowl, fell to the Jungaleers by a 52–27 score.

Clemson climbed to No. 13 in time to take on South Carolina in Columbia. The Tigers' 22–13 win over the Gamecocks gave the Country Gentlemen their eighth straight victory to cap off a 9–1–1 campaign complete with a 7–0 conference ledger. Even though probation prevented the Fort Hill Felines from accepting a bowl bid or receiving a ranking in the coaches' poll, the Orange and Purple finished as the AP No. 11 team.

The tie with the Tigers dropped the Dogs out of the top 10 and caused Vince Dooley to reassess his quarterback quandary. Because Georgia had been shut out in Death Valley during the first and third quarters—the ones in which John Lastinger was directing the offense—Todd Williams was given the starting nod for the following Saturday's date with the Gamecocks between the hedges.

While Georgia emerged victorious from the South Carolina game by an 18-point margin, Williams was injured in the outing, necessitating that Lastinger take over again in time for the Bulldogs to begin SEC play. The Red and Black ripped through Mississippi State, Independence Bowl-bound Ole Miss, Vanderbilt, and Hall of Fame Bowl-bound Kentucky in succession, outscoring those four opponents by a combined 123–52 score.

After carding a 17-point win over Temple, the Bulldogs traveled to Jacksonville for their second series meeting with the Gators when both teams were ranked in the top 10. Trailing 9–3 in the third quarter with the ball resting at their own one yard line, the Classic City Canines went on a 16-play, 99-yard march to claim a 10–9 triumph over a Florida outfit that would spend the holidays in the Gateway City for the Gator Bowl.

No. 4 Georgia then returned home to host No. 3 Auburn in a battle for SEC su- premacy. Bo Jackson led the Plainsmen to victory between the hedges to earn a Sugar Bowl bid. The Tigers went on to post an 11–1 record and capture a No. 3 final ranking. The Bulldogs rebounded to outlast Georgia Tech in Atlanta and were off to the Cotton Bowl to face undefeated and second-ranked Texas.

A Red-and-Black loss to the Longhorns in the Orange Bowl 35 years before had deprived the Dogs of a shot at the 1948 national championship and Georgia looked to return the favor in Dallas. Texas held a 9–3 lead late in the fourth quarter when a fumbled punt by the Lone Star State squad gave the Classic City Canines custody of the football deep in Longhorn territory.

On third down, Lastinger went 17 yards on an option run to score the touchdown that gave Georgia a 10–9 victory. That night, No. 1 Nebraska fell to No. 5 Miami in the Orange Bowl by a 31–30 margin to give the Hurricanes the national championship that Texas would have won in the absence of the Georgia quarterback's heroics. The Bulldogs completed the season with a 10–1–1 ledger and a No. 4 final ranking in both polls.

As the 1983 campaign came to a close, Clemson was able to boast of a 30–2–2 record over the past three seasons, giving the Tigers the country's best resume over that period. At the same time, Georgia could claim a 43–4–1 record over the past four seasons, giving the Bulldogs the nation's best resume over that period. The tie between the two programs that could argue plausibly that they were the best in the NCAA had done nothing to settle the differences between them, which set the stage for a showdown between the border rivals the following fall that might well have been the most epic of them all.

1984

The Butler Did It

Georgia quarterback Todd Williams trotted out onto the field for the Bulldogs' final drive. The ball was resting at the Classic City Canines' 20 yard line and the Red and Black were staring down the barrel of a second straight tie in their series with the Clemson Tigers after the visiting Jungaleers had booted a 48-yard field goal to snarl the score with 2:10 showing on the clock.

In many ways, a draw would have been a blessing for the Athenians, who had arrived at Sanford Stadium as a three-point underdog to the second-ranked Fort Hill Felines. Williams had experienced an outing as awful as that endured by Buck Belue in Death Valley three years previously, as the Georgia signal caller tossed five interceptions in the course of the afternoon. The Dogs had trailed the favored Tigers by two touchdowns at intermission.

The Red and Black were in it now, though, and they were in it to win it. Williams dumped the ball off twice to start the home team's last possession, but the Bulldogs had advanced only as far as their own 31 yard line when the Georgians executed a delay draw play as the clock ticked below 80 remaining seconds.

The quarterback faked the handoff to the fullback, who plunged through the line and blocked the middle linebacker. The center took on the opposing left tackle and the tailback—in this case, Tron Jackson—cut off the center's block and drove through the hole. "It was a 23 draw and the hole was there," the running back remarked afterwards. "It was a big hole. You could have drove a transport truck through it."

The play was good for a 24-yard gain to the Clemson 45 yard line. The next two plays picked up only a yard and Williams, much to Vince Dooley's chagrin, took the Bulldogs' last time out to avoid a delay of game penalty on third down. An incomplete pass thrown high and out of bounds made it fourth and nine with 17 seconds to go.

Place-kicker Kevin Butler took center stage. The senior specialist had been concerned that the game might come down to a late field goal, so he had been working on splitting the uprights from far away. On the Wednesday before the game, Butler had made four 62-yard attempts in a row in practice, but that preparation had not prevented him from missing a chip shot in the second quarter on Saturday.

Butler had arrived in Athens as a bit of a reclamation project. After being heavily recruited, the kicker saw all but one of his scholarship offers disappear when he was injured as a high school senior.

Dooley still wanted him to come to Georgia, though, and Butler rewarded the coach's confidence in him by scoring more points with his toe than any player in SEC history *en route* to becoming the first kicker inducted into the College Football Hall of Fame. He would replicate that success at the next level by becoming the Chicago Bears'

Bulldog tailback Tron Jackson's 24-yard run on a draw play set up placekicker kevin Butler's game-winning field goal.

all-time highest-scoring specialist during an eight-year career with the professional franchise.

Butler had been at his best in the border rivalry with the Tigers. As a freshman, he had scored all of Georgia's points against Clemson in 1981 before going on to account for seven of the Bulldogs' 13 points in 1982 and 10 of the Red and Black's 16 points in 1983.

He already had 11 points to his credit against the Orange and Purple on the sunny September afternoon later described by *Atlanta Journal-Constitution* columnist and rabid Bulldog partisan Lewis Grizzard as "a wonderful day on the Georgia campus. We are talking blue, cloudless sky, a gentle breeze and a temperature suggesting summer's end and autumn's approach."

However, even though Butler would go five for six on field goal attempts from farther than 50 yards away in 1984, there was the nagging fact that, for all his heroics against the Country Gentlemen, the upperclassman had not been entirely lucky on long three-point tries when facing the Jungaleers. In the previous two years, Butler had missed five field goal attempts of 48, 50, 56, 59, and 66 yards versus Clemson.

In the booth high above, Georgia play-by-play announcer Larry Munson set the stage for the listening audience that was unable to watch the game on television due to the lingering sanctions against the Tigers. "So we'll try to kick one 100,000 miles," grumbled Munson in his trademark dour gravelly delivery. "We're holding it on our own 49 and a half, gonna try to kick it 60 yards plus a foot and a half."

The place-kicker's foot hit the pigskin. "Butler kicked a long one, a long one," Munson called out, his voice rising with the arcing oval. The ball was airborne for six seconds. "Oh, my God!" shouted Munson, "Oh, my God!" Butler had known the moment it left his toe what the outcome would be, but the 82,122 fans, as well as the other players and the coaches, had to wait as the football seemed to float forever in the direction of the self-same goalposts in the west end zone where he had missed a short kick two quarters before.

Anyone who had listened to the poor-mouthing coming out of Athens during the week before the game would have been shocked that Georgia had even the opportunity to attempt a would-be game-winning field goal. Bulldog running backs coach Mike Cavan, who had tamed the Tigers as a player in 1968 and scouted Clemson for 12 years as an assistant coach at his *alma mater*, described Danny Ford's bunch as the most talent-laden at the skill positions of any Orange-and-Purple club he had ever seen. Both Cavan and Dooley compared the offensively explosive 1984 Jungaleers favorably to their 1978 and 1981 counterparts.

The Peach State news media generally agreed. Although *Atlanta Constitution* sports editor Jesse Outlar predicted a three-point Georgia win, his colleague Tony Barnhart pronounced that "Clemson may bring its best team ever to Athens Saturday" and the *Journal- Constitution* conceded that "it's hard to figure why they come in favored by just a field goal." Five out of seven *Red and Black* prognosticators forecast a Tiger triumph, and one of the other two pundits predicted another tie. Even the homers didn't like the home team's chances.

More than merely Vince Dooley's customary pessimism fueled that widespread opinion. The Country Gentlemen began the autumn ranked fourth in the Associated Press poll. While No. 1 Auburn and No. 3 Pittsburgh fell on the opening weekend, Clemson clubbed Appalachian State in a 40–7 smackdown to improve to No. 3. New No. 1 Miami also tumbled as the nation's top-ranked outfit, but the Tigers rolled to a 55–0 win over a Virginia team that would end the season with a Peach Bowl victory and a top 20 ranking. The manhandling gave Clemson its largest margin ever over a bowl-bound opponent.

The Fort Hill Felines crept up to the No. 2 spot and Tiger quarterback Mike Eppley, who had completed 21 of 31 aerials for 307 yards and four touchdowns in the team's first two games, claimed the NCAA lead in pass efficiency. The Jungaleers ranked sixth nation ally in scoring and received 15 first-place votes from the sportswriters. In addition, Clemson boasted an offensive line topheavy with seniors and fielded three tailbacks who each had rushed for 100 yards on the young season: Stacey Driver, Terrence Flagler, and Steve Griffin. Driver averaged six yards per carry; Flagler picked up almost eight yards per rush.

The Tigers were no slouches on the other side of the ball, either. The Clemson D was ranked 15th in the land in total defense. The line was anchored by brothers William and Michael Perry, the former of whom entered the tilt in Sanford Stadium within striking distance of the school sack record. The Perry brothers and their teammates had surrendered just 329 *combined* yards in their first two games.

An open date followed the South Carolinians' shellacking of the Cavaliers, enabling the Tigers to return to their lair, stare across the state line towards the Classic City, and await their September 22 showdown with the Dogs. For their part, the Red and Black had entered the fall as a marginal top 20 outfit and impressed few viewers with a seven-point home victory over Southern Miss after trailing the Golden Eagles at the break.

All the Bulldogs seemed to have going for them was a bye week of their own prior to the Clemson tilt and a 15–1 all-time record against the Tigers between the hedges. Split end Herman Archie was the lone offensive starter from the 1983 campaign who was back at his familiar position, and the only other returnee from the previous year's first team was Keith Johnson. The junior lineman, whose coaches wanted to move him from center to tackle, had not seen the field since the Cotton Bowl due to persistent back problems which were expected to limit his playing time against the Orange and Purple.

Senior safety Jeff Sanchez likewise had missed most of the week's practices leading up to the Clemson game with a sore back, while an injury sustained by Todd Williams would require the Georgia quarterback to wear a pad on his elbow. To these troubles were added an inexperienced offensive line and the loss of six defensive starters from a 1983 outfit that had outscored its opponents 99–34 in the fourth quarter.

Nevertheless, familiarity had bred contempt and emotional intensity was likely to prove to be the great equalizer in the latest series clash between the gridiron titans. *The Tiger's* Foster Senn identified the reason a close game was likely: "The annual contest has turned into a war of hate between the two teams...Clemson and Georgia are two fierce rivals that always go at it hard, and Saturday's game will feature two excellent teams, despite what Danny and Vince say.

The *Journal-Constitution's* Barnhart concurred, but with a caveat. The college football writer described each side as viewing the other as "a team that it positively, genuinely and unequivocally dislikes with a passion reserved for none other...There are older, more established rivalries, but none has grown to such an intensity in such a short time." Even so, though, Barnhart recognized the reality: "Given Clemson's defensive strength, Butler could be Georgia's most potent offensive weapon."

The contest got underway at 1:30 in the afternoon and it did not take long for the assemblage to see why the visitors were ranked second and the hosts were ranked 20th. The Tigers kicked off and the Bulldogs lost eight yards on their first possession before punting.

The South Carolinians took custody of the pigskin and moved 58 yards in seven snaps. Driver guided the Tigers downfield with two runs totaling 29 yards before Eppley completed a 16-yard strike to tight end K.D. Dunn over the middle. The senior receiver covered the final seven yards separating him from the end zone with Sanchez clinging to him in a futile effort to bring him down.

Place-kicker Donald Igwebuike's point after try was successful to give Clemson a seven-point lead with more than 10 and a half minutes left to play in the opening period. The scoring drive had been sparked by the combined efforts of a pair of native Georgians, as Driver hailed from Griffin and Dunn was a product of Decatur.

The Bulldogs went back on offense with no more success than they had enjoyed before. Williams launched a pass which was intended for Archie but instead found its way into the hands of free safety Ronald Watson from Jefferson, Ga. A 14-yard interception return by the senior defensive back gave Clemson the ball in Red-and-Black territory, but a clipping penalty followed by an Eppley interception rendered the Georgia quarterback's miscue harmless.

Williams was not similarly fortunate later in the quarter, though, when he underthrew tailback Lars Tate and saw his pass picked off by linebacker Chuckie Richardson. The Dogs' first four drives ended in a pair of punts and a couple of interceptions. The Tigers, in the meantime, were adding to their advantage. Eppley found Dunn again for 26 yards to carry the Country Gentlemen inside the Athenians' 10 yard line, setting up a 22-yard Igwebuike effort that extended the Clemson lead to 10–0 inside the six-minute mark in the first quarter.

The Georgia quarterback's struggles continued in the second stanza, when a long pass from Williams to Archie was snagged by cornerback Reggie Pleasant at the visitors' 20 yard line. Butler, however, proved to be as much a mainstay of the Bulldogs' offensive arsenal as Barnhart had anticipated.

A little more than two minutes into the second quarter, a 72-yard march by the Classic City Canines (on which two of the 13 plays saw third downs converted into first downs) was capped off by a 34-yard Butler field goal. Later in the period, the Dogs drove inside the Clemson 10 and the senior kicker's 26-yard attempt went wide left, but, once the two teams had traded turnovers, Tate scampered 11 yards to put Butler in a position to boot a 51-yarder and cut the Tigers' lead to 10–6 with 4:45 left until halftime.

The Fort Hill Felines responded by traversing 70 yards of real estate in five snaps, with more than half that distance covered in a single 38-yard jaunt by Flagler. Three plays later, Eppley hooked up with the sophomore tailback on a 27-yard touchdown pass that sailed over rover John Little's extended fingers and into Flagler's waiting arms. It was

Eppley's longest completion of the day. Igwebuike's aim was true and Clemson was up by a 17–6 margin inside of two and a half minutes.

The South Carolinians were not finished, though. When the Classic City Canines reclaimed custody of the oblong, a pass in the flat to tailback Andre "Pulpwood" Smith was picked off by diving cornerback Tyrone Davis to return possession to the visitors. It was Williams's fourth interception of the first half by a fourth different Clemson defender. The Bulldog signal caller, just three of whose first 11 passes had been caught by players wearing the proper color jersey, had more interceptions than completions at that juncture.

Although the Tigers advanced just four yards in three plays, it was enough to enable Igwebuike to divide the uprights on the 43-yard field goal that staked the Country Gentlemen to a 20–6 lead. The final 54 seconds elapsed and Clemson went to the locker room leading by two touchdowns. Grizzard would later report that the man sitting in front of him remarked, "I just hope we don't get embarrassed."

Vince Dooley had opined before the game that the Dogs would need the contest to be another low-scoring affair for his club to have a chance. Georgia defensive coordinator Bill Lewis was equally clear on what it would take for the Bulldogs to win: "The key to our football team and this game is that we somehow, by hook or by crook, have to get the game into the fourth quarter and still have an opportunity to win." By that measure, matters were not looking well for the home team.

The Red and Black kicked off at the outset of the second half but the Bulldogs caught a break on the fifth play of the third quarter. Just before intermission, Davis had set up a Clemson score with an interception at the Georgia 30 yard line; shortly following the break, Eppley fumbled a handoff and defensive end Carlyle Hewatt pounced on the loose pigskin 30 yards in front of the Tigers' goal line. The Dogs closed that distance in seven snaps.

A two-yard dive by Tate on fourth and one gave the Classic City Canines a fresh set of downs at the Clemson 19. Three plays later, on third and 10, Williams saw Davis in single coverage on Archie and changed the play at the line. The receiver ran an up pattern, the quarterback lofted a long high pass, and Archie came down with the ball in the right corner of the end zone. It was Williams's longest completion of the day. Butler's kick reduced the deficit to 20–13 not quite five minutes into the penultimate period.

The Georgia scoring strike had begun at the Clemson 30 yard line, but the Bulldogs' next series ended at that same spot, where strong safety Kenny Danforth became the fifth Tiger defenseman to intercept a pass from Williams. Fortunately for the home team, both signal callers were equally careless with the football.

Eppley led the Tigers to a first down at the Georgia 38, but, on a third-down sweep, the Clemson quarterback failed to see that the trailing back had been taken to the ground. While going down, Eppley pitched the oval to a teammate who was no longer there and cornerback Kevin Harris, who had forced a fumble and picked off a pass in the opener against Southern Miss after being moved over from the offense, scooped up the spheroid for the Dogs.

A 66-yard scoring drive began with an 11-yard completion from Williams to Smith, but the bulk of the work on the nine-play march was done on the ground by Jackson and Tate. After Williams found Archie at the Clemson 40 for a 17-yard pickup on third and 13, Jackson got his first carry of the season. The Liberty, S.C., native had served a one-game suspension to start the fall and he saw the field for the first time late in the third quarter.

When he got the ball, Jackson skirted right end for 11 yards to carry the Athenians within three feet of the goal line. The final yard was bridged by freshman tailback Cleve land Gary, who dived into the end zone for the touchdown. Butler connected on his second extra point try of the ballgame, and, with 73 seconds to go in the third period, the scoreboard showed the contest was knotted at 20 points per side.

Grizzard described the moment by stating that "my mouth was dry, and my hands were shaking, and this Clemson fan who had been running his mouth the whole ballgame suddenly shut his fat face." The fourth quarter began with the score still tied and it remained that way for most of the next 10 minutes, thanks chiefly to Georgia cornerback Tony Flack, who intercepted Eppley passes—one at the Bulldogs' 47 yard line, the other at the Red and Black's six-yard stripe—on consecutive possessions by the Country Gentlemen.

The Tigers' inability to hang onto the ball persisted as the contest's closing canto continued. A 31-yard scamper by Eppley once more carried Clemson into Georgia territory, but the ball was stripped from the Orange-and-Purple signal caller's grasp at the end of his long run. Linebacker Calvin Ruff came up with the pigskin for the Bulldogs to notch the twelfth turnover of a clash in which strong emotions produced multiple defensive takeaways off of quarterback miscues.

Mike Eppley accounted for all seven Clemson turnovers, throwing a trio of picks and losing four fumbles. Although the Dogs never failed

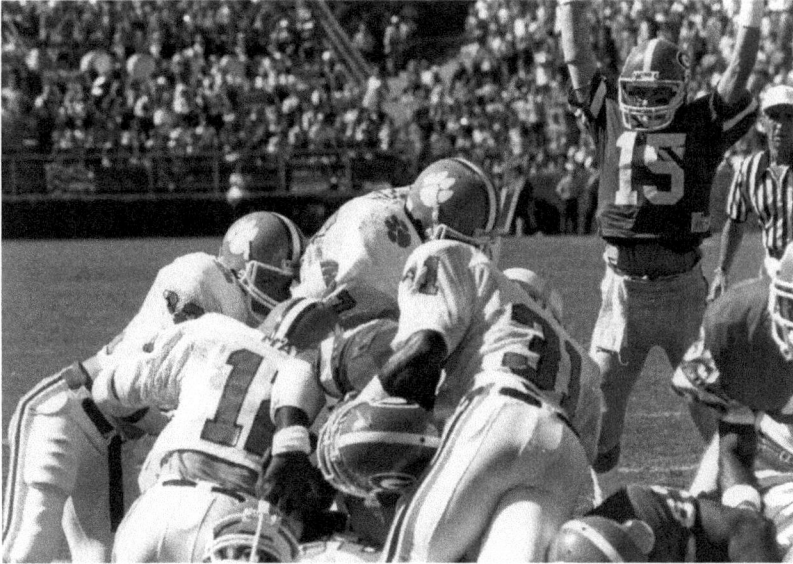

Georgia quaterback Todd Williams signaled the touchdown after freshman tailback Cleveland Gary scored from the one yard line to tie the game.

to retrieve the ball after they had put it on the ground, Todd Williams tossed five interceptions, three of which came on passes intended for Herman Archie. The Georgia end had just two receptions for 36 yards and he dropped a long pass before making his third-quarter touchdown grab.

It was Williams, however, who did the better job of bouncing back from his mistakes. Eppley came into the game with a 16–1–1 record as a starter, but he played like a rookie at times. The Bulldogs blitzed less and disguised their coverages more in the second half, leading the Tiger QB to check off at the line often. Together with the crowd noise which affected Clemson's ability to audible, these tactics created the confusion that produced a pair of interceptions. Following two of Williams's turnovers, Eppley gave the ball right back, but the Georgia signal caller erased four first-half interceptions by leading four second-half scoring drives. Meanwhile, five of the Jungaleers' seven giveaways came after intermission.

Once Ruff recovered Eppley's latest fumble at the home team's 45 yard line, the Dogs gained yardage using the ground game in an eight-play drive that featured four of the 17 carries with which Gary became the Classic City Canines' leading rusher on the day. The march stalled when the Athenians were forced to fall on a bobbled handoff, but Butler was successful on a 43-yard three-pointer. With just over six minutes to play, Georgia had taken its first lead with a 23-20 edge.

The Tigers answered with a 12-play drive that garnered 48 yards and threatened to earn even more. On third and 10, Eppley threw a perfect pass to Dunn, who would finish the afternoon with four catches for 68 yards and a touchdown. The Clemson tight end should have had a fifth reception for a first down, but he dropped the pass and forced the South Carolinians to settle for a game-tying 48-yard Igwebuike field goal. Eppley's day was done after 11 completions on 28 attempts for 161 yards, two touchdowns, and three interceptions.

Georgia responded by marching 36 yards in eight plays to put Butler in a position to win the game with a 60-yard three-point try. The senior kicker had the wind at his back, but the breeze died down as he lined up for the attempt. Butler was the first to know whether he had made good on his shot at redemption, and he telegraphed the result for the rest of the crowd before the football even reached the crossbar when he leapt up, ran toward the east end zone, and sank to his knees near the 20 yard line.

Just before 4:30 in the afternoon, in the bright sunshine that shone down on Sanford Stadium from above, a football that had taken flight with 17 seconds showing on the clock finally passed between the goalposts with 11 seconds remaining to give the Red and Black a 26–23 lead. The long field goal broke the school record previously set by Butler and tied the all-time SEC mark, yet it split the uprights with room to spare, clearing the crossbar by at least five yards; the kick might well have been good from 70 yards away.

Butler, who was still trembling in the locker room afterwards, was mobbed by his teammates as cheers and applause rained down from the stands. "The stadium," proclaimed an emotional Larry Munson from the press box, "is worse than bonkers. 11 seconds. I can't believe what he did!"

Neither could anyone else. Vince Dooley admitted that he "thought the percentages were against him" and Danny Ford said he believed "he would miss it." Todd Williams allowed as how he "was praying the whole time. I knew it was gonna save my neck if he made it." The only person who was not surprised was Kevin Butler himself, who told the press: "I knew it was good when I kicked it. It was the best feeling I've ever had."

Kevin Butler kicked 77 field goals in his college career, but none of them was bigger than his record-setting 60-yarder against the Tigers in 1984.

It did not take long for the realization to sink in that everyone on hand had witnessed an historic moment, however. Ford opined, "That ball must be flat now. He kicked the fool out of it." Dooley, not ordinarily given to effusive praise, repeatedly threw around the word "miracle" and tried to put the moment in its proper context: "I think that it will be in the Butts-Mehre Heritage Hall, where people can walk in, and pick up that phone and push the button and see Kevin Butler kick that record-breaking field goal to win the ballgame. That's going to be a very exciting play, just as Buck's pass to Lindsay, and…this has got to be one of the greatest in Georgia history."

Butler knew what the kick meant to him personally. "It was like electricity was going all through my body," he remarked. "There has never been anything like it in the world. I'm going to remember this day for the rest of my life." The epic nature of the event, though, was best captured by Lewis Grizzard, who penned an open letter to the son he hoped one day to have. Wrote the newspaper reporter in perhaps his most memorable and moving column:

"I hugged perfect strangers and kissed a fat lady on the mouth. Grown men wept. Lightning flashed. Thunder rolled. Stars fell, and joy swept through, fetched by a hurricane of unleashed emotions.... Saturday in Athens was a religious experience. I give this to you, son. Read it and re-read it, and keep it next to your heart. And when people want to know how you wound up with the name 'Kevin' let them read it, and then they will know."

For the moment, though, 11 seconds still remained and Butler had one more kick to make. The celebration following the field goal had drawn a 15-yard penalty, which was assessed on the ensuing kickoff. Butler sent the ball hurtling downfield and Ray Williams took it at the 20 yard line, advancing as far as the Clemson 30 before tossing a lateral across the field to fellow wide receiver Terrance Roulhac.

The Tiger sophomore saw 70 yards of open field before him and took off down the sideline for the end zone. He had passed midfield when he found the border walled off by Bulldog defenders, so Roulhac darted out of bounds around the Georgia 40 yard line. The return man was hit after passing outside the white lines, so a flag was thrown, and the officials convened to discuss the situation.

If Roulhac had gotten off the field before time expired, a personal foul penalty would be assessed and Clemson would have a chance to tie the game with a long field goal. If no time remained on the clock at the end of the play, the hit occurred after the game was over and, therefore, was not an infraction. Representatives of both teams gathered in front of the visitors' bench while the officials huddled, and referee Robert Aillet eventually emerged to declare that time had expired, no foul had occurred, and the game had ended. An amazing 26–23 Bulldog victory had entered the record books and been etched into history.

Dooley went to shake Ford's hand, but the Clemson coach's attention was elsewhere. He was looking for an official to explain what had happened on the final play, and he was unable to find one. The traditional handshake never happened, but Ford later came to the Georgia locker room to apologize to Dooley for whatever words had been exchanged on the field.

The Tiger skipper subsequently acknowledged that the officials' decision "wasn't what lost the game for us," as the team that had led 20-6 at the break had been outscored 20-3 in the second half. After speaking with former ACC supervisor of officials Norvelle Neve, Ford said on the Sunday following the controversial contest, "I found out that the ruling was correct – that is, if there was no time left on the clock."

The statistical battle was in most respects as close as the score indicated. Georgia led by one in first downs (18-17) and Clemson led by two in rushing yards (195-193). Both teams punted four times apiece. While the Jungaleers nearly doubled up the Dogs through the air (161-89), David Jones of *The Greenville News* reported that "Georgia was outrushed and outpassed Saturday afternoon, but the Bulldogs were not outplayed." The home team held the ball for almost 32 minutes.

Opportunistic defenses competing intensely in a hard-hitting battle had produced a dozen takeovers but had proven unable to prevent the opposing offenses from combining for 49 points, the most tallied by the two squads against one another in a decade. The 23 ticks placed on the scoreboard by the Tigers were the most they had scored against Georgia since 1974 and the Country Gentlemen had never before notched more than 18 points in a loss to the Red and Black.

Kevin Butler completed his career against Clemson with 34 total points to his name, or almost 59 per cent of the Bulldogs' four-year tally versus the Fort Hill Felines. Against the Tigers, Butler had kicked one field goal as a freshman, two field goals as a sophomore, three field goals as a junior, and four field goals as a senior. His point total against the Orange and Purple increased annually throughout his collegiate career.

The result gave Georgia its 45th victory in a span of 50 games while dealing Clemson just its third loss in the Jungaleers' last 38 outings. Two of those three setbacks came against the Dogs during an intense period in which the border rivalry pitted perennial national powers. The titanic 1984 struggle between the old foes marked the end of an era, though. It would be another three years before Clemson and Georgia again met in a game in which both were ranked.

One week after Butler's historic game-winner, the Bulldogs dropped a seven-point decision in a night game in Columbia against a South Carolina squad that would earn a Gator Bowl berth and a No. 11 final AP ranking with a 10-win campaign that included a season-ending victory over Clemson. That same Saturday, the Tigers traveled to Atlanta and also fell by a touchdown to a Georgia Tech squad that would cap off the autumn with a triumph over the Red and Black between the hedges. September 29, 1984, would mark the first day on which Clemson and Georgia both lost football games since September 15, 1979.

The Country Gentlemen's disappointment at the loss on the football field in the Classic City was deepened by the news that Clemson's first All-American, O.K. Pressley, had passed away on September 22, the same day of the epochal clash in Sanford Stadium. Pressley, who had played on the 1927 Tiger team that faced the Bulldogs, had been inducted into the Clemson Hall of Fame the year before his death.

Both teams followed up their memorable game with otherwise largely forgettable seasons. After consecutive setbacks in the Peach State knocked the Jungaleers from the top 20, the Fort Hill Felines got back on track with five straight victories over North Carolina, Duke, N.C. State, Wake Forest, and Independence Bowl-bound Virginia Tech. The latter battle showcased two of the nation's top defensive linemen in the Tigers' William Perry and the Hokies' Bruce Smith.

After that, the bottom fell out for the Country Gentlemen, who were beginning to feel the effects of the scholarship limitations imposed as a part of the harsh NCAA sanctions levied against them. With a first-place finish in the ACC at stake, the Tigers took a trip to Baltimore, where they were whipped 41–23 by a Maryland squad then in the midst of a seven-game winning streak. The Terrapins completed a 9–3 season with a Sun Bowl win to wrap up a No. 11 final ranking in the coaches' poll.

Clemson fell to the Gamecocks in Death Valley to finish with a 7–4 record, and the penalties imposed by the conference prohibited the Orange and Purple from accepting a bowl bid. For just the second time in an eight-year stretch, the Tigers had won fewer than eight games, stranding Danny Ford's team well short of the lofty heights to which the club had aspired at the outset of the autumn.

Despite the Bulldogs' loss to South Carolina, it appeared at first that the victory over Clemson would springboard another successful campaign for Georgia. On the Tuesday following the triumph against the Tigers, the *Red and Black* opinion page took a break from publishing political editorials to declare, "We can't wait for the rest of the season."

A five-game winning skein over Alabama, Ole Miss, Vanderbilt, Hall of Fame Bowl- bound Kentucky, and Memphis allowed the Dogs to climb as high as No. 8 on the strength of their 7–1 ledger. That was the last hurrah for the Classic City Canines, who fell to AP No. 10 Florida, AP No. 18 Auburn, and Georgia Tech in succession.

The Gators finished 9–1–1 and ranked third by the sportswriters after being put on probation (and stripped of both their bowl eligibility and the first SEC championship in school history) for the NCAA violations that got Charley Pell fired three games into the fall. The

Plainsmen finished 9–4, won the Liberty Bowl, and were the country's consensus No. 14 team. The Yellow Jackets finished 6–4–1 for their first autumn with fewer than five losses in nearly a decade. The trio of rivals beat the Bulldogs by a combined margin of 83–30. Georgia had not lost to all three season-ending foes since 1977.

The Red and Black received a bid to the Citrus Bowl on December 22, marking their earliest post season engagement since the 1974 Tangerine Bowl. Georgia held a 17–9 lead on Florida State with four minutes remaining in the game, but the Seminoles returned a blocked punt for a touchdown and tied the game with a two-point conversion. A 70-yard Kevin Butler field goal attempt fell a foot short of the crossbar and the game ended in a draw, sending the Bulldogs into the offseason sporting a 7–4–1 ledger and without a top 20 final ranking for the first time in five years.

Clemson and Georgia had risen in unison at the dawn of the decade and had begun sliding back to the pack together, as each ended the 1984 regular season with four losses and seven wins. That the twin juggernauts emerging from such a small geographic radius had been utter equals was attested to by the facts that, over six series meetings starting in 1979, the Bulldogs held a narrow lead in won-lost record (3–2–1), the Tigers held a narrow lead in points scored (87–85), and neither team won on the other's home field.

Although the ferocity of the battles and the closeness of the scores would persist, the ancient and increasingly bitter rivals would no longer continue to clash at so lofty a level. That chapter in series history was now closed, but, thanks to Kevin Butler, the greatest period of competition between the Classic City Canines and the Fort Hill Felines certainly had ended with a bang.

1985

Go You Red Britches, Action Jackson, and Little Makes a Big Difference

Vince Dooley's Dogs limped into their 1985 showdown with the Tigers mired in a slump and having something to prove. Eight games into their 1984 slate, the Red and Black had boasted a 7–1 record and had won 51 of their previous 57 outings, but a late-season collapse saw Georgia go 0–3–1 down the stretch.

The Classic City Canines' winless streak continued into the autumn of 1985, when Alabama quarterback Mike Shula led the visiting Crimson Tide on a game-winning drive in a nationally-televised contest between the hedges on Labor Day night. A marked lack of healthy quarterbacks hampered the Bulldogs, as injuries to David Dukes (torn rotator cuff), James Jackson (sprained ankle), and Todd Williams (strained knee ligaments) forced redshirt freshman Wayne Johnson into action under center against the Red Elephants.

Johnson connected with split end Jimmy Hockaday to cut into Bama's 13–3 lead, but, after defensive end Calvin Ruff covered up a blocked punt in the end zone to give Georgia a 16–13 advantage, Shula guided the Tide on a four-play touchdown drive covering 71 yards in the final 50 seconds to give the visitors the victory. Alabama went on to notch nine wins (including a triumph in the Aloha Bowl) and end the year ranked in the top 15.

The Bulldogs welcomed Baylor between the hedges on September 14 under circumstances similar to those in which Dooley's club entered their outing against Clemson in 1970. A decade and a half earlier,

Georgia's home victory over Hootie Ingram's Tigers had stopped an 0–5–1 skid, and now a win over the Bears ended an 0–4–1 slump.

Baylor, which had finished under .500 in three of the previous four seasons, gave the Classic City Canines a scare in Sanford Stadium. Two long reverses by Georgia flanker Frederick Ferdale Lane, one for 35 yards and the other for 33 yards and a touchdown, enabled the Dogs to escape with a 17–14 win over the Bears. The Southwest Conference squad would leap out to a 7–1 start, end up at 9–3 after a Liberty Bowl win over LSU, and be ranked 15th in the final coaches' poll.

As the Red and Black prepared to head up I-85 to Lake Hartwell, though, everyone among the Bulldog faithful was acutely conscious of the malaise that gripped the program in Athens. After tallying one big win after another throughout the early 1980s, the Dogs now found themselves without a signature victory in almost a year. Since Kevin Butler's famous field goal had shocked the second-ranked Tigers, Georgia had gone 0–2–1 against ranked teams.

Now Butler was gone; the Red-and-Black place-kicker had been drafted in the fourth round by the Chicago Bears. Punter Chip Andrews likewise had been lost to graduation, and, although the Bulldogs returned 14 starters from the preceding campaign, fullback Andre Smith was an academic casualty who would not take the field in 1985.

Furthermore, Dooley's charges had not claimed victory over Clemson in Death Val- ley in nearly a decade, since Ray Goff and Matt Robinson guided the Bulldogs to a win in the Palmetto State in 1976. In fact, Georgia had gone 2–3–1 in its last half-dozen games outside of Athens. Dooley, however, had a trick up his sleeve which was designed to revive that old Red-and-Black magic.

The Country Gentlemen who awaited the Dogs at Fort Hill seemed to have slipped a bit themselves. Danny Ford's Tigers had lost no more than one game in any of the three seasons from 1981 to 1983, posting a 19–0 ledger in conference play in the process, but Clemson had dropped four of its last nine decisions in 1984, beginning with the South Carolinians' defeat between the hedges.

Thanks to the lingering effects of NCAA and ACC sanctions, the 1985 Tigers had twice as many freshmen on their roster as they had seniors. There were limits to what those 24 rookies could learn from those dozen upperclassmen in their final year of eligibility, as only five Clemson seniors had started a college game. Among the departed stars from the previous year's squad was middle guard William

Perry, who had been selected in the first round of the NFL draft by the selfsame Chicago Bears who later chose Kevin Butler, as well.

In spite of the adversity they faced, the Country Gentlemen kicked off the campaign in more favorable fashion than did the Dogs, opening the autumn with a 20–17 victory in Blacksburg over a Virginia Tech squad bound for its sixth straight winning season. Clemson lost five fumbles against the Hokies, but cornerback Perry Williams set a record for the Orange and Purple by deflecting five passes versus VPI.

Sophomore quarterback Randy Anderson, making his first start for the Tigers, set school records for attempts and completions by a signal caller in his initial first-team ap pearance. In a 17-point fourth-quarter outburst in the Old Dominion, Anderson evaded a sack to connect with wide receiver Ray Williams on a 46-yard touchdown toss and also completed a 41-yard pass to tailback Stacey Driver on the visitors' closing drive.

Ford sent a walk-on place-kicker onto the field to attempt the would-be game-winning field goal. Before coming to Fort Hill, the Jacksonville, Fla., sophomore had not set foot on a gridiron since his pee-wee league days as a youngster in the Sunshine State. "I came to Clemson for its engineering program," the specialist later explained. "I did not play high school football, I played high school soccer. When I did not get a soccer scholar ship offer at a major school, I opted for the school with the best engineering program, and that was Clemson." The underclassman's name was David Treadwell, and his 36-yard field goal on the last play of the game lifted the Tigers to victory over Virginia Tech.

Clemson and Georgia, each of which had finished a season ranked No. 1 in the previous five years, both ended the 1984 campaign unranked and neither was tabbed as a top 20 team heading into their showdown in South Carolina on September 21. It was the first time neither the Bulldogs nor the Tigers were ranked on the day of the game since 1979, but the sportswriters' low estimation of the combatants did nothing to disabuse either team of the intention to make their 1985 clash the ninth consecutive classic in series history.

The oddsmakers evidently considered the two teams to be more or less evenly matched, as the home team took the field as a three-point favorite, which was about the edge that was to be expected for a squad enjoying the advantage of playing on its own field. To counteract that benefit to Clemson, Dooley turned to his equipment manager, Howard Beavers.

Knowing that the Tigers typically came out clad in orange pants for big games, Beavers spoke to Dooley before the season and suggested breaking out the red pants the Bulldogs had taken to wearing on the road during the 1970s. The Dogs had last been seen sporting the red uniform pants with the wide white stripe up the side in the 1980 season opener against Tennessee in Knoxville, just before the permanent return of the traditional silver britches.

Georgia wore what The Tiger's Kevin Bobo called "their bright red pants" against Clemson. Dooley, expressing a skepticism reminiscent of Frank Howard's following the Jungaleers' 1967 win over N.C. State while wearing orange shoes, claimed to doubt that the scarlet britches would make much of a difference. "Quite frankly," he said, "I am not big on trousers or jerseys or that type of thing, but rather, I am concerned with what is inside." Nevertheless, when the game was won, the Bulldog coach acknowledged, "I think that what was inside those pants today certainly got the job done." Dan Magill would later call Dooley's bluff, declaring of the victory: "I am positive that he really thought the red britches were a vital factor."

The Bulldogs were not alone in making symbolic gestures that Saturday afternoon. Just prior to the 3:40 p.m. kickoff, the Clemson cheerleaders bore out to midfield an orange box shaped like a casket and labeled "Probation." As a cannon went off, the Country Gentlemen's costumed tiger mascot emerged from the coffin to mark the end of the Jungaleers' time in the wilderness.

After a two-year absence, the TV cameras had returned to Death Valley for the first nationally-televised game ever broadcast from Memorial Stadium, and the 81,500 fans assembled in the stands constituted the second-largest crowd in the arena's proud history. The energy evident by the shores of Lake Hartwell was put on full display by Adubarie Otorubio, the three-time All-American soccer star who sailed the opening kickoff between the goalposts for a touchback.

On their second possession of the outing, the Bulldogs took a little over four minutes to put up the initial points by either team. A 15-yard scamper by freshman fullback Keith Henderson, followed by a five-yard facemask penalty tacked on at the end of the run, carried the Athenians to the home team's 33 yard line and the drive culminated in a 26-yard field goal off of the toe of freshman place-kicker Steve Crumley. Georgia had taken a 3–0 lead with six minutes to play in the opening frame.

The Red and Black kicked off to Terrance Roulhac, who had returned a kick amid such controversy a year earlier. The Tiger wide receiver brought the oval out to the 35 yard line to set up a seven-play march spanning 65 yards in three minutes. Anderson, after recovering a Clemson fumble at the host squad's 45 yard line, took advantage of the Classic City Canines' young secondary.

The Bulldogs were still smarting from the loss of All-American safety Jeff Sanchez, who had led the team in interceptions in his senior year the previous season. Anderson spotted Jim Riggs streaking downfield and took advantage of the breakdown in Georgia's inexperienced defensive backfield by completing a 43-yard strike to the junior tight end. Riggs went into the end zone untouched for his first career touchdown reception. With three minutes remaining in the first quarter, the Tigers had gone out in front by a 7–3 margin.

That score remained unchanged at intermission, though not for lack of effort on the part of the combatants. Senior flanker Herman Archie dropped a surefire touchdown pass in the end zone on the Bulldogs' first possession of the second quarter, and Clemson linebacker Henry Walls picked off a pass in Georgia territory to set up a 56-yard field goal attempt by Otorubio with 30 seconds left in the first half. The three-point try went wide to the left to keep the Country Gentlemen's advantage at four points heading into the locker room.

The Bulldogs' only points had come on a nine-play, 61-yard drive ending in a field goal on the visitors' second series of the contest. After halting the Georgians on fourth down at the Clemson 30 yard line, the Fort Hill Felines went 57 yards in 10 plays on their second possession of the third quarter. A 21-yard completion from Randy Anderson to Ray Williams led to a 30-yard David Treadwell field goal to extend the Jungaleer lead to seven points inside the seven-minute mark in the penultimate period.

The fireworks got underway in the fourth quarter and the initial spark came from Dooley's decision to change quarterbacks. Wayne Johnson had served as the Dogs' signal caller throughout the Baylor game the week before and the rookie field general started the Clemson game. With Johnson under center, the Tigers expected the Dogs to go to the air, so Dooley elected to mix things up by sending sophomore James Jackson into the game.

The quarterback from Camilla played the entire second half, but he did not truly light a fire under the Georgia offense until early in the final stanza. Noting that Clemson's de fensive ends, apparently still anticipating the pass after Johnson's previous presence in the contest, were playing soft, Jackson elected to take advantage of his superior speed against an Orange-and-Purple defensive front featuring a trio of freshmen. The Georgia quarterback went around left end for 17 yards and followed that up one play later with an 11-yard touchdown run on an option keeper around right end. The score came at the end of a series traversing 67 yards and knotting the score with just over 13 minutes remaining in the game.

Georgia kicked off, Clemson commenced its initial possession of the fourth quarter, and the Tigers wasted no time in reclaiming the lead. Anderson led the home team down the field in less than two minutes, completing a 40-yard strike to Roulhac to set up the 40-yard field goal by Treadwell that put the Jungaleers back in front by a 13–10 margin with 11:35 showing on the scoreboard.

The Dogs answered on their next drive. The South Carolinians' ensuing kickoff gave the Classic City Canines custody of the pigskin at the visitors' 20 yard line and the Red and Black moved out across midfield. Jackson's option runs to the right set the stage for the third-down reverse which Fred Lane took around left end for a 36-yard gain to the Clem son 12 yard stripe, where Tiger cornerback Delton Hall made a touchdown-saving tackle.

Tailback Tron Jackson went off tackle on the next snap for a six-yard pickup to halve the distance to the goal line. Henderson skirted the right side of the line on the ensuing play and appeared bound for the go-ahead touchdown when the freshman fullback fumbled on the three yard line. The loose oblong represented potential disaster for the visiting Athenians. *The Greenville News's* Ron Green had pointed out on the day before the game that, in the previous eight series meetings between Clemson and Georgia, the team that led in total offense had won just once, but the team with fewer turnovers had not lost in eight tries.

That trend ended in Death Valley that day, as the Bulldogs gave the ball away three times on an interception and a couple of lost fumbles while the Tigers tossed a pair of picks yet never failed to cover up the pigskin when they put it on the ground. The free football squirted into the end zone in the midst of a mass of colliding bodies, yet only a few of them even saw the oblong was up for grabs.

Clemson free safety A.J. Johnson was one of the players who spotted the spheroid and Tiger defensive tackle Steve Berlin was another. "I saw the ball loose in the end zone," Berlin explained afterward, "but, by the time I could get to it, Georgia had two guys on it." The first of those was Bulldog center Pete Anderson, who would earn All-American honors that season and be declared the player of the game by CBS for his efforts in Death Valley that day.

The Red-and-Black center dived over tight end Troy Sadowski, who was still blocking for Henderson, to retrieve the football for the first touchdown of his college career. After the game, Anderson joked, "I'd love to play tailback next week." Although such a position switch was not to be for the Georgia offensive lineman, his heads-up play gave the Athenians the lead with a little under eight and a half minutes to go. In their 2001 athletics history Clemson: Where the Tigers Play, Sam Blackman and his co-authors noted of Pete Anderson's fumble recovery: "No opposing offensive lineman has scored a touchdown in a game since."

Although one Anderson—Georgia's Pete—had staked his squad to a 17–13 advantage, another Anderson—Clemson's Randy—set about erasing the deficit at his earliest opportunity. The Tiger signal caller went back to Riggs, who had opened the scoring for the Country Gentlemen in the first half. The home team's tight end picked up 17 yards on the resulting reception, so the Clemson quarterback again intended to hook up with Riggs on the ensuing snap.

Georgia center Pete Anderson was named player of the game after recovering a fumble in the end zone for a touchdown in Death Valley.

This time, though, the Orange-and-Purple signal caller would see his efforts thwarted by junior rover John Little. The Bulldogs' All-American defensive back, who had surrendered a touchdown pass to the Tigers in Athens the year before, stepped in front of Anderson's throw and plucked the pigskin out of the air. Riggs, the intended receiver, explained following the game: "I don't think Randy ever saw him. I never saw him. I stuck my hands out there and he stuck his out there. It was a perfect interception."

Little made the grab at the Clemson 45 yard line and advanced the oval six yards on the return. The Georgia rover had snagged the first of the two interceptions that would provoke Vince Dooley to observe afterwards, "I just can't say enough about the performance of John Little today. He gave an All-American effort." Noting that the Bulldog defensive back also tallied 25 return yards on special teams, the Georgia coach continued, "Two big interceptions, returned punts, he did it all."

After Little's pick, the Dogs succeeded in running over the three minutes off of the game clock before Crumley's 31-yard field goal extended the Georgia lead to 20-13 inside the final five minutes of the contest. The Tigers got the ball back, but, when Randy Anderson threw three incomplete passes in succession, the Red and Black resumed possession at their own 39 yard line with just over four minutes remaining in the game.

The Bulldogs attempted to run out the clock, but, in an era of thrilling finishes in the series, a Clemson-Georgia game simply could not end without additional drama. Accord ingly, the contest's leading rusher, tailback Lars Tate, marred a 16-carry, 96-yard day by coughing up the football at the opponent's 38 yard line, near the point at which the Classic City Canines had begun their previous scoring drive. Tiger strong safety Kenny Danforth recovered the fumble, reviving the home team's hopes as the Country Gentlemen regained custody of the pigskin in good field position with 102 seconds showing on the scoreboard.

Terrence Flagler and Terrance Roulhac each hauled in an 11-yard pass from Randy Anderson to take the Tigers to the Georgia 36 yard line. Although Clemson still had time to score, the orange-clad quarterback went for it all on the next play. Anderson, who had hooked up with eight different receivers under the relentless pressure of the fierce Bulldog pass rush, was flushed from the pocket before firing the ball at wide receiver Shelton Boyer for the would-be tying touchdown with just under a minute remaining.

It was then that John Little made the play that led *Red and Black* sports editor Ivan Aronin to surmise that the Georgia rover was "playing with the ghost of Terry Hoage." Little leapt over both Boyer and Bulldog teammates Gary Moss and Miles Smith to snatch his second interception of the afternoon, pulling in a game-saving pick in the end zone with 57 seconds left to preserve the Athenians' seven-point win.

Danny Ford's postgame assessment of the outing was brief and to the point: "It was a typical Georgia game." That wasn't entirely so, though; not only had the team that won the turnover battle lost the game, but the very same Tigers who had tallied 17 fourth-quarter points to beat Virginia Tech the week before had surrendered 17 fourth-quarter points to the Red and Black. The Bulldogs had scored more than 17 *total* points against the Jungaleers just twice in the previous eight series meetings. To top it all off, the visiting team had won the Clemson-Georgia game for the first time since 1977. Perhaps there was something to the red britches, after all.

Over the course of the afternoon, the Red and Black had amassed 360 rushing yards, very nearly equaling their output from the season's first two games combined. In the third autumn following Herschel Walker's departure from the Classic City, the carries contin ued to be distributed among a variety of backs, with Tron Jackson, David Mc-Cluskey, and Lars Tate getting their share of the touches and a pair of 6'2", 210-pound freshmen, Keith Henderson and Tim Worley, starting to show signs of future success. In all, seven Bulldog backs made contributions.

The game's most positive development for the Athenians, however, was the emergence of James Jackson. The sophomore signal caller showed little early proficiency as a passer, completing just three of his 11 aerial attempts for a mere 34 yards, but Jackson provided a spark to the offense by leading the Bulldogs' unstoppable option attack expertly.

Jackson's numbers alone did not tell the full story. While lining up under center, he kept the ball a dozen times for nearly 70 yards, but, under his guidance, the visiting team held the ball for nearly 35 minutes. Georgia picked up the requisite yardage on 15 of 23 third down tries over the course of the contest. In the final stanza, the Dogs went six for seven on third down and held the ball for more than 11 minutes. It was no wonder that Ara Parseghian, who served as part of the CBS broadcasting team present in Death Valley that day, said of Jackson, "Vince Dooley has found his quarterback."

The setback dropped Clemson to 1–1 and marked only the third time under Danny Ford that the Orange and Purple had lost a game in which they led after three quarters. The Tigers opened ACC play the following Saturday with another loss in Death Valley to a Peach State opponent, as the Hall of Fame Bowl-bound Yellow Jackets handed the Country Gentlemen a 14–3 setback. A third straight defeat came against Kentucky in Lexington. The Fort Hill Felines had lost three in a row for the first time in 10 years.

Four games into the fall, the Tigers sported an NCAA-worst minus-11 turnover ratio. At his weekly press conference, Ford explained the problem with his team. "We're just not clicking," he told reporters. "'Clickness' is the word I'm looking for. Is that a word? Well, if it's not, it is now." After Frank Howard delivered a pep talk to the players the following Thursday, the South Carolinians righted the ship and went on a four-game winning streak against league foes Virginia, Duke, N.C. State, and Wake Forest.

Despite that midseason hot streak, Clemson came up short in three of the team's last four games. The Tar Heels claimed their first win in Death Valley since 1971 when North Carolina scored the go-ahead touchdown with 10 seconds showing on the game clock. One week later, Maryland defeated the Country Gentlemen by kicking a game-winning field goal with three seconds left after tying the contest on a controversial play.

The Cherry Bowl-bound Terrapins pulled even with the Jungaleers when quarterback Stan Gelbaugh completed a pass to tight end Ferrell Edmunds in the end zone. There were two problems with the scoring strike, though: Gelbaugh had not received the snap from center until after the expiration of the 25-second play clock, and Edmunds had lost possession of the pigskin after briefly having his hands on the airborne football. Ford was furi ous that Maryland erroneously was awarded a touchdown on the play, and he expressed his outrage with such intensity that the Clemson coach was barred from the sideline for the following year's showdown with the Terps in College Park.

The Orange and Purple beat the Gamecocks in Columbia as a result of the 136-yard rushing effort that took tailback Kenny Flowers over 1,000 yards for the season. The win over South Carolina earned Clemson an Independence Bowl berth opposite a Minnesota squad whose second-year head coach, Lou Holtz, had just been hired away by Notre Dame. John Gutekunst had taken over the Golden Gophers and would become the second college football head coach to begin his career in a bowl game. Danny Ford had been the first.

In just their second meeting with a Big Ten team, the Country Gentlemen turned the ball over on each of their first three possessions, but, because Flowers had his seventh 100- yard outing of the season, Clemson led by a field goal at the start of the fourth quarter. For the fifth time in their last 13 games, however, the Tigers proved unable to hang onto a lead in the final period.

A one-yard touchdown run by the Golden Gophers' Valdez Baylor in the final five minutes sent the Tigers to defeat by the same 20–13 margin by which they had lost to the Dogs. Although Clemson managed only a 6–6 record to register their first non-winning season since 1976, the Orange and Purple were competitive, losing four games by seven or fewer points. Nevertheless, the Fort Hill Felines failed to defeat any bowl-bound opponents and none of the Country Gentlemen's six victims finished with a record better than 6–5.

For the Classic City Canines, the big win in Clemson initially appeared to serve as a springboard for another successful season of the sort to which the Bulldog faithful had become accustomed during the early 1980s. Georgia rebounded from the season-opening loss to Alabama and ran its record to 7-1-1, inexplicably tying Vanderbilt in Nashville to snap an 11-game series winning streak over the Commodores but beating South Carolina, Ole Miss, Kentucky, Tulane (which then was in its first year under head coach Mack Brown), and Florida by at least two touchdowns apiece.

The victory in Jacksonville was particularly significant, as it marked the Bulldogs' first win ever over a No. 1-ranked team. The probation-hampered Gators, who were ineligible to attend a bowl game, had carried a 7-0-1 ledger with them to the St. John's River after ascending to the top spot in the AP poll the week before. Florida was brought back down to earth by the Bulldogs, who dealt the Saurians a 24–3 setback to improve the Red and Black's poll position. Once-beaten Georgia was awarded the No. 12 ranking in both major polls.

As had been the case the year before, though, the Dogs could not sustain their success through the last leg of the campaign. The Classic City Canines fell by two touchdowns against Cotton Bowl-bound Auburn between the hedges, marking Georgia's third straight loss to the Plainsmen and sending Vince Dooley's record against his alma mater south of .500, as the longtime Red and Black head coach now stood at 10-11-1 against the Tigers from the Loveliest Village.

The Bulldogs still were ranked 20th in both polls, but their subsequent narrow loss to a Georgia Tech team that would end the season with a 9–2–1 record dropped the Classic City Canines to a disappointing bowl berth for the second straight year. This time, the Red and Black would take on UPI No. 20 Arizona in the Sun Bowl. History repeated itself once again in El Paso, where the game ended in a tie, just as the previous year's Citrus Bowl engagement had.

At 7–3–2 and trailing a three-game winless streak, Georgia once again finished the season outside the top 20. Nevertheless, the future appeared bright for the Bulldogs, who could look forward to beginning the 1986 campaign with James Jackson under center and Keith Henderson and Tim Worley lining up in the backfield. What no one on either side of the state line yet knew, though, was that the next two showdowns between the Red and Black and the Orange and Purple would be settled by Clemson's walk-on kicker, David Treadwell.

1986

A Great Opportunity

Fifty-eight minutes and forty-nine seconds had elapsed in a game that appeared destined to end in a second tie in a span of just four series meetings. The 56 points tallied so far had already made this the highest-scoring Clemson-Georgia game in history, eclipsing the 55 ticks put on the scoreboard in the 1920 contest, but the Tigers were determined to tack on a few additional points.

"I can, I will, I want to and I see a great opportunity." That slogan had become the mantra of the Fort Hill Felines, who had come into Sanford Stadium remembering the 17 fourth-quarter points they had surrendered to Georgia the year before. Clemson also arrived in Athens stinging from a season-opening 20–14 setback sustained at the hands of Virginia Tech, a team that had not previously beaten the Country Gentlemen since 1954.

Bill Dooley's Gobblers had been outgained by their hosts and the Tigers had stopped VPI 10 times in 14 third-down tries. However, the Orange and Purple had lost two of their four first-half fumbles to the Hokies and Clemson's inexperienced secondary had conceded 242 yards through the air. Bill Spiers, who had answered Tiger coach Danny Ford's news- paper advertisement seeking a new punter, had a kick blocked for the decisive touchdown.

Thus, it was an 0–1 Clemson club that found itself tied at 28 with the 14th-ranked Red and Black between the hedges, 64 yards away from the Bulldogs' end zone and 71 seconds away from the final buzzer.

Ford, naturally, elected to run the ball.

The oval went to Terrence Flagler on first down. The Tiger tailback, in for the injured Kenny Flowers, would finish the day as the South Carolinians' leading receiver (with three catches for 58 yards) and their leading rusher (with 10 carries for 90 yards). The extra carries he received against the Dogs allowed him to pass the 1,000-yard mark for his career in the backfield.

On the first play of the contest's final drive, Flagler added to his rushing tally by taking the ball from the Clemson 36 to the Georgia 49 on a sprint draw down the left sideline. 59 seconds showed on the scoreboard.

Sophomore quarterback Rodney Williams kept the ball on an option play on the ensuing snap, picking up 15 yards on the left side. The ball rested at the 34 yard line with 53 seconds left.

On the visiting sideline, Ford was getting an earful from former Auburn offensive coordinator Jack Crowe, who had come to Lake Hartwell to work with the Clemson QBs. The assistant wanted to throw the ball, but the head coach was worried about being taken out of field goal range if his signal caller dropped back to pass and was tackled behind the line of scrimmage.

It was not entirely clear, though, whether the Country Gentlemen were within field goal range in the first place. Early in the fourth quarter, place-kicker David Treadwell had missed what would have been a tiebreaking field goal from 39 yards away. Ford, in fact, was thinking of letting his other specialist, Rusty Seyle, try the three-point shot this time.

Clemson ran the ball into the line twice, picking up the final five yards of a game- deciding 35-yard drive in which not a single pass had been attempted. Ford called a time out as the clock crept closer to zero.

Gathering the team around him, the Tiger head coach reminded his players of their motto: "I can, I will, I want to and I see a great opportunity." Treadwell and his teammates trotted out onto the field. Ford had asked the junior kicker whether he was up to the task of booting a 46-yarder and Treadwell assured him that he was, so in he went.

Before the ball could be snapped and set down on the tee, however, Georgia coach Vince Dooley called a time out of his own in an effort to "ice" the kicker. The Jungaleers milled about in the huddle during the delay.

Tight end Jim Riggs, who had caught Clemson's only touchdown pass against the Athenians the year before, looked at the Orange-and-Purple place-kicker and spoke. Although Riggs would start 11 of the

Tigers' 12 games that autumn, he had been replaced on the first team this day by Jerome Williams, who had lined up at tight end on the South Carolinians' first offensive snap against the Red and Black because he was the better blocker of the two.

Riggs was in the game now, though, and he had a question for Treadwell: "Do you want us to get away from you?" The Clemson kicker did not speak a word in reply; he only nodded. The other 10 Tigers on the field moved away from Treadwell, leaving him alone to look toward the uprights he was about to attempt to split. He picked out the "28" on the scoreboard—the place- kicker would not recall afterwards whether it was the Clemson "28" or the Georgia "28"—and determined to make that his target. *I can, I will, I want to and I see a great opportunity.*

Four seconds remained in the game.

Regardless of whether Treadwell's aim was true, the kick would settle what had been a very even game. Each team had earned exactly 20 first downs and each had been penalized precisely 30 yards. Both teams fumbled the ball thrice, losing possession all three times. Had the Tigers held the football for 33 fewer seconds over the course of the 60-minute con test, the time of possession would have been altogether even. Clemson had turned the ball over more often, throwing two interceptions to the Bulldogs' one, but the visitors held the edge in total yardage (428–383). The Classic City Canines led in passing yards (211–149) while the Fort Hill Felines had the advantage in yards gained on the ground (289–182).

Such a close contest had been foreseen by the coaches and players on both sides of the state line. Georgia running backs coach Ray Goff anticipated a physical game, remarking beforehand that Clemson would "line up and knock you in the mouth." Bulldog linebacker John Brantley was looking forward to a brutal battle: "This is one to see who the men are. It is the kind of game where women and children need to be sitting in the top level because bones are going to be cracking. It's going to be really intense."

Across the border, senior flanker Terrance Roulhac expressed a common lament among the Tiger faithful ("Somehow Georgia always beats us") and his sentiment was echoed by Danny Ford, who observed, "They're taught they can whip us in the fourth quarter."

Knowing the South Carolinians would give Georgia a great game, Vince Dooley said "Clemson will come with orange in their eyes," while Tiger secondary coach Bill Oliver believed "Georgia's going to do whatever it takes to win." Red-and-Black rover John Little, one of the heroes of the previous season's showdown, presciently predicted, "It always seems to come down to the last play in the game. If one key mistake is made by a team, it usually happens in the fourth quarter."

Both teams came into the game in dire need of good news after unusually stressful offseasons. A June 20 incident involving Flowers, free safety A.J. Johnson, and former Clemson players Craig Crawford and Duke Holloman had drawn University reprimands for "a mistake in judgment" and made for a tense summer by the shores of Lake Hartwell.

Worse still, the star tailback and his teammates potentially faced charges of criminal sexual assault, kidnapping, and larceny in connection with the highly-publicized off-campus events involving a fellow player's mother. On September 2, after hearing testimony and deliberating for more than seven hours, a Pickens County, S.C., grand jury refused to indict any of the football players.

The Bulldogs' troubles also had involved the court system but they had not ended nearly so happily. Jan Kemp, a University of Georgia professor who had been fired in 1985, sued her former employer over her termination. Kemp claimed that her criticism of the treatment given to athletes had been the basis for her dismissal and the trial of her case produced a verdict of $2.8 million in the former professor's favor.

Even though the judge's award later was reduced to $1.08 million, the lawsuit and its outcome had been an enormous public relations disaster for the University. Consequently, the effects of the trial were swift and significant. Three top figures in the University administration resigned or were reassigned, including longtime president Fred Davison. The University Council formed a 12-member Ad Hoc Committee on Academic Policies, which issued a report making 37 separate recommendations, including a proposal to require all athletes to meet standard admission requirements.

After such unpleasant offseasons, both teams were ready to get back to the gridiron. The Tigers, however, lost their opener against Virginia Tech, in a game in which the Orange and Purple held the ball for six minutes longer than the Hokies, and the Bulldogs struggled against an overmatched Duke team...although the fans in Athens may not have minded, in light of what they saw on the Classic City Canines' first play from scrimmage.

Georgia quarterback James Jackson had continued to mature as a signal caller and Dooley had decided to open up the offense, publicly promising before the season began that the Dogs would be throwing out of the shotgun on the first snap of the fall. Sure enough, the Red and Black lined up in the shotgun on the inaugural play of the season for the first time in Dooley's 23-year tenure and Jackson completed a nine-yard pass to tailback Tim Worley.

Back to the shotgun went "Air Dooley," and, this time, the Georgia QB handed off to fullback Keith Henderson for an eight-yard gain. After that opening series, the Bulldogs would not line up in the shotgun again for the remainder of the game. "You didn't think we were going wild, did you?" Dooley gently chided the media during postgame questioning.

On paper, the Bulldogs' 31–7 opening win over the Blue Devils appeared encouraging. Jackson's passing performance (16 of 22 for 193 yards and a touchdown) paced a balanced attack that saw the Red and Black racking up 202 yards through the air (the most for a Georgia team since the 1983 Clemson game) and 284 more on the ground. To top it all off, Vince Dooley tied his mentor, former Auburn coach Shug Jordan, with his 176th career victory.

However, the Dogs' weaknesses were exposed by Duke, much as the Country Gentlemen's had been by VPI. Only a fumble recovery on the goal line had kept the Classic City Canines from trailing at the break and, for all the passing yards tallied on the day, the wide receivers were not getting involved, as half of Jackson's completions were to running backs. Worst of all, the Georgians put the ball on the ground five times, losing all five fumbles, and the culprits included talented backs Henderson, Worley, and Randy Jackson.

The Clemsonians, though, had troubles, as well, even after the grand jury rendered the decision that (in the word of A.J. Johnson's attorney) "vindicated" the players under suspicion. Although his legal worries were behind him, Kenny Flowers faced an uphill climb to live up to the preseason Heisman Trophy hype Clemson was trying to generate for him. An ankle injury and a knee bruise hampered his ability to practice as much as the distraction of the potential charges he had faced.

In addition to fielding a new secondary, the Tigers likewise were young up front on offense. An injury to Eric Nix necessitated that underclassman Jeff Bak start at center for the Jungaleers, which meant that the Clemson O-line would feature four sophomores and a junior. Although the middle of the Country Gentlemen's forward wall (Bak, right guard John Phillips, and leftguard Pat Williams) featured a trio of 12-game starters that fall, fellow sophs Fall Deluliis and Jeff Nunamcher would split time at right tackle during the 1986 cam-

Tiger tailback Terrence Flagler contributed team-leading tallies in rushing (90 yards) and receiving (58 yards) to Clemson's triumph between the hedges.

paign, doubtless to the dismay of the person charged with the task of emblazoning equipment with the players' names.

Due perhaps to the inexperience of the Tigers' young offensive line so early in the season, the Dogs managed to halt Clemson's progress on the visitors' first series. Such success seldom recurred for the Red and Black in their regionally televised September 20 showdown with the Orange and Purple, which kicked off between the hedges at 3:30 in the afternoon on the second Saturday of the season for both teams.

The initial returns may have been promising for the Bulldogs defensively but those positive results did not translate at first to the offensive side of the ball. When the Georgia D recovered a Tiger fumble at the Clemson 26 yard line in the first quarter, the early scoring opportunity was squandered by the Classic City Canines, who ran three players, incurred a penalty, and sent in place-kicker Steve Crumley for a 50-yard field goal attempt, which he missed.

Fortunately for the Red and Black, the South Carolinians were not through being careless with the football. Clemson punt returner James Lott absorbed a hit from Keith Henderson which jarred loose the pigskin and rover Mike Brown fell on the loose oval at the visitors' 29 yard line. An 18-yard pass from James Jackson to split end Cassius Osborn on first down sparked a five-play, two-minute drive that ended in tailback Lars Tate's one- yard fourth-down dive over the left guard and into the end zone. Crumley's kick was good and Georgia led 7–0 with a little under nine minutes remaining in the opening period.

The Tigers answered on their next possession. Taking the ball at their own 28 yard line, just three feet from the point at which Lott had surrendered the oblong on the visitors' previ ous series, Clemson put together a seven-play, two-and-a-half-minute drive highlighted by a pitch to Flowers on a draw play. The Orange-and-Purple tailback scampered 57 yards down the left side before being stopped just four yards from paydirt. Flowers subsequently scored, go ing into the end zone from two yards out on a toss sweep. Treadwell's extra point tied the game.

Because Flowers had twisted an ankle during his long run, Flagler was sent in at tailback after the Tigers' first scoring series. Before the Fort Hill Felines regained custody of the pigskin, though, the Dogs had something to say on their ensuing possession. After evening the score, Clemson kicked off and Worley took the ball out to the Georgia 39 on the return. The Red and Black took just under three minutes to go out in front once more.

Responding to the Jungaleers' seven-play scoring drive with a seven-play scoring drive of their own, the Bulldogs proceeded to cover the 61 yards separating them from the goal. On third down, Henderson got behind outside linebacker James Earle in the middle of the field and Jackson hit him in stride for a 32-yard touchdown pass. Georgia's 14-7 lead lasted roughly six minutes before a strange sequence of offsetting turnovers set up another Clemson score early in the second quarter.

Near the home team's goal line, Tiger quarterback Rodney Williams underthrew Clemson wide receiver Ray Williams and the pass was picked off by Bulldog cornerback Gary Moss. The intended target of the visiting QB's errant aerial refused to give up on the play, however, as Ray Williams tracked down Moss, tackled him, stripped the ball, and recovered the forced fumble. The play gave the Country Gentlemen the ball at the Georgia 11 for a net gain of 16 yards for Clemson on the exchange of giveaways.

The Tigers ran three plays in the next 42 seconds, culminating in the nine-yard touchdown pass to Flagler that left the contest snarled at 14. Clemson kicked off and Georgia went on another march, moving 64 yards in a little over four minutes. A tipped pass was hauled in by tight end Troy Sadowski at the 20 yard line to set up a 15-yard touchdown run by Jackson on an option keeper. The Bulldog quarterback's 43 yards over the course of the game made him the home team's leading rusher, as Henderson and Worley finished the day having tallied 40 rushing yards apiece.

The Red and Black's touchdown lead held up for the next five minutes and 33 seconds, for the Jungaleers took the Georgia kickoff and went 74 yards with the ball in 11 snaps. One series after the Dogs made a meaningful gain off of a tipped ball, John Brantley deflected a Clemson pass yet Ray Williams brought it in anyway for his only catch of the afternoon.

The Tiger wide receiver picked up 20 yards on the play to carry the Country Gentlemen to the 21 yard line. The possession ended in a one-yard touchdown run by fullback Tracy Johnson to tie the game anew with 3:12 left until halftime. The score remained 21–21 at the break. After intermission, the South Carolinians were set up with outstanding field position when Lars Tate fumbled at the Bulldogs' 35 yard line. Clemson linebacker Norman Haynes, an Ath ens native and the Jungaleers' leading tackler for the day, recovered the football for the visitors.

The Tigers ran the ball seven straight times before punching it in on a quarterback sneak from the one to stake the Fort Hill Felines to their first lead of the day. In addition to going nine of 18 for 149 yards through the air, Rodney Williams gained 52 rushing yards on 10 carries that afternoon. Treadwell converted on the point after try to give the Country Gentlemen a 28–21 edge.

Just five plays later, the Athenians again surrendered possession of the pigskin to their guests. James Jackson's pass was intended for Tim Worley but it found its way instead into the waiting arms of Clemson's Dorian Mariable, who took the ball down to the Georgia 27. The South Carolinians appeared to be on the verge of extending their lead when Rodney Williams again underthrew a receiver and an aerial meant for Terrance Roulhac was intercepted by Bulldog safety Steve Harmon five yards short of the end zone.

The Red and Black had been granted a reprieve and they made the most of it. With 95 yards of real estate before them, the Classic City Canines moved the ball out to the 22 yard line on their next three snaps. Jackson spotted the Clemson free safety playing up close, so the Georgia quarterback looked to go deep on the ensuing play.

Flanker Fred Lane took off downfield and got behind cornerback Perry Williams. Off a play fake, Jackson hooked up with Lane for a 78-yard strike. The touchdown brought the combatants once more into perfect alignment on the scoreboard and marked the longest TD pitch and catch by a Bulldog tandem since Buck Belue's famous pass to Lindsay Scott in Jacksonville six years before. The play marked Jackson's second touchdown pass of an afternoon on which he went 12 of 27 for 211 yards through the air.

There were just under two minutes remaining in the third quarter, but the fireworks subsided for a short while thereafter. The balance of the third period and the bulk of the final stanza were scoreless, although Clemson missed a chance to reclaim the lead when Treadwell pushed his 39-yard field goal attempt with 10:19 left in the contest and the kick sailed over the right upright to preserve the deadlock.

As the clock ticked under five minutes in the fourth quarter, the Bulldog offense resumed its steady march. In spite of having scored four touchdowns that afternoon, the Red and Black had found themselves stymied for much of the day by the Tiger D. In addition to tackling well, the Tigers had tried with substantial success to confuse Georgia by using different looks, including a "stack" formation with the linebackers aligned directly behind the defensive linemen.

Nevertheless, after a lengthy dry spell, the Dogs moved the ball from their own 23 yard line to their opponents' 15. A potentially game-winning score seemed virtually assured when disaster struck. Facing a Clemson blitz, Jackson kept the ball and tried quickly to turn the corner around right end.

Without being touched, the Georgia quarterback fumbled.

Afterwards, all Jackson could offer by way of explanation was a simple statement of undeniable fact: "The ball just came out." A.J. Johnson pounced on the oval at the Clemson nine yard line to give the Tigers new life.

The visitors weren't out of the woods yet, though. The Jungaleers had halted the Classic City Canines' drive for the would-be go-ahead score, yet 4:39 remained and the Country Gentlemen were scrimmaging in the shadow of their own goalposts. The week before, the Fort Hill Felines had fallen to Virginia Tech on a blocked punt deep in their goalposts. In a contest that already had featured nine turnovers, the South Carolinians could not afford to serve up the game's tenth giveaway.

The Bulldogs swiftly put the Tigers in a second-and-18 situation. Georgia defensive coordinator Bill Lewis had his defensive backs playing a "deep third," with each defender covering one-third of the gridiron deep downfield. Flagler, who had put the ball on the ground at the VPI eight yard line one week earlier, ran a wheel route, running toward the sideline as if about to receive a pass in the flat before turning upfield and making a diving catch on the left sideline at the 25 yard marker.

Two plays later, a 21-yard run by Flagler took the Orange and Purple to midfield. Because they punted from that point rather than from their own end zone, the Tigers were able to pen the Dogs deep and Georgia was unable to do much with its final possession. The Red and Black gained six yards on three plays before booting the ball back to their guests, whose final chance got underway from their own 36 yard line with 1:11 remaining to play.

There began the drive that went as far as the Bulldog 29 before the game was turned over to David Treadwell to decide. Dooley called his last desperate time out and a pair of Clemson seniors, Brian Raber and Terrance Roulhac, knelt alongside teammate Keith Jennings on the sideline. The three Tiger players grasped one another's hands, bowed their heads, and prayed while every other man, woman, and child in Sanford Stadium looked to David Treadwell as he finally lined up for the fateful field goal try. *I can, I will, I want to and I see a great opportunity.*

The Clemson place-kicker put his foot into the ball as the last seconds ticked away to nothing. The kick was up and holder Todd Schonhar was the first to know the result. He realized right away that the field goal was good, so, much as Kevin Butler had done on that same field two years before, the holder jumped up and yelled, "We won! We won!" The rest of those assembled in Athens waited for the officials to confirm Schonhar's verdict, and, when they did, Treadwell was mobbed at midfield by his teammates.

The 31–28 final margin gave the Clemson Tigers their second win ever between the hedges and dealt the Georgia Bulldogs the second loss in their history in a game in which the Red and Black scored at least 28 points. Previously, only Texas in the Orange Bowl on New Year's Day 1949 had given up 28 points to the Dogs yet gone on to win the game.

At the conclusion of the contest, the all-time Clemson-Georgia scoreboard read 985 for the Red and Black and 585 for the Orange and Purple. Through 55 rivalry showdowns, the Bulldogs led the historic series scoring by exactly 400 points. The continuing closeness of the annual affrays was underscored by the fact that, eight years earlier, the Athenians had held an overall 398-point edge over the Tigers after 47 clashes.

The Columbia Record's Doug Nye minced no words in summing up the South Carolinians' dramatic victory in Sanford Stadium. "It was the biggest victory for Clemson," Nye stated, "since the Tigers defeated Nebraska in the Orange Bowl five years previously to win the national title."

On the opposite side of the field, the devastating nature of the loss was attested to by Vince Dooley after the game. When asked if he was pleased with his team's passing effort, the longtime Georgia coach replied, "You're pleased when you win. We had 211 yards. But it doesn't make any difference if it's 411 if you don't win."

Nevertheless, the Bulldogs bounced back from the defeat to beat the Gamecocks by five in Columbia and the Rebels by four in Athens in order to improve their record to 3–1. A nine-point loss in Baton Rouge to an LSU squad that would end the season in the Sugar Bowl was followed by a three-game winning streak during which the Red and Black bested Vanderbilt, Kentucky, and Richmond by a cumulative tally of 97–38.

Clemson placekicker David Treadwell drilled a 46-yard field goal in the closing seconds to beat Georgia in Sanford Stadium.

Another loss followed in Jacksonville to Florida, but the Dogs managed to dodge an 0-3 ledger against teams named Tigers by beating Citrus Bowl-bound Auburn on the Plains in the infamous "between the hoses" game, in which Georgia fans who stormed the field after the visitors' 20–16 victory were sprayed down with water. A 31–24 win over Georgia Tech in Sanford Stadium snapped a two-game losing streak to the Yellow Jackets and the Classic City Canines' 8–3 record earned them a bid to the Hall of Fame Bowl to face Boston College.

The Bulldogs drew first blood in Tampa, taking a 7–0 first-quarter lead on a James Jackson touchdown run, but the Eagles reeled off 20 straight points to take a 13-point halftime lead. The Red and Black came roaring back after intermission, when a 28-yard field goal, a five-yard TD run by Jackson, and an 81-yard interception return by Gary Moss staked Georgia to a 24–20 lead with just under 12 minutes remaining.

Boston College had time for one final drive, however, and it appeared at first that the Dogs had held on fourth down at their own 27 yard line, but a pass interference penalty revived the Eagles' hopes and they scored the game-winning touchdown with 32 seconds showing on the clock. The loss dropped the Athenians to 8–4 and left Georgia unranked in either the final coaches' poll or the final sportswriters' poll for the third straight season.

Clemson, by contrast, rode the wave of its big win between the hedges to another successful season. The victory over Georgia began a five-game winning streak for the Tigers, who defeated Georgia Tech, The Citadel, Virginia, and Duke in succession by a combined tally of 117–23.

The win over the Yellow Jackets in Atlanta was sparked by Terrance Roulhac's return of the opening kickoff, which he took four yards deep in his own end zone and brought out as far as the Ramblin' Wreck's 19 yard line. Following the 24-point triumph at Grant Field, the Tiger faithful chanted, "We own Georgia! We own Georgia!"

The Jungaleers' win over The Citadel earned the Orange and Purple an AP ranking and Kenny Flowers proved against the Blue Devils that he had recovered from his ankle injury in Athens by breaking Buddy Gore's school record for career rushing yards.

No. 16 Clemson suffered a 27–3 road loss in the rain to a No. 20 N.C. State club that was bound for a Peach Bowl berth under first-year head coach Dick Sheridan. Terrence Flagler rebounded by having a field day against Wake Forest, catching two touchdown passes and adding a pair of TD runs in the Country Gentlemen's 28–20 victory over the Demon

Deacons. Flagler, who was bound for All-American honors that autumn, not only turned one of his carries into a career-long 88-yard jaunt, but also set an individual school record with 274 all-purpose running yards.

The Tigers wore orange pants for their 38–10 win over North Carolina in Death Valley to set up a showdown with the Terrapins in Baltimore. Both Clemson coach Danny Ford and Maryland coach Bobby Ross guided their teams from the press box due to ACC-imposed suspensions; Ford had joked with Frank Howard during the week before the game that perhaps the Baron of Barlow Bend ought to stroll the sideline for the Fort Hill Felines. David Treadwell's 20-yard field goal with two seconds showing on the clock earned an ACC championship-clinching tie for the Orange and Purple.

A second straight deadlock followed when the Fort Hill Felines tied the Palmetto State Poultry 21–21 in the season-ending rivalry game between Clemson and South Carolina. The 7-2-2 Tigers headed to Jacksonville for a December 27 date with No. 17 Stanford in the Gator Bowl. The Country Gentlemen were forced to punt on their first postseason possession, but the Jungaleers proceeded to score on their next five drives.

In the second quarter, Clemson recovered a fumbled Cardinal kickoff return deep in Stanford territory and Ray Williams scored his first touchdown of the season on a 14-yard reverse. A 46-yard David Treadwell field goal and the performance of Gator Bowl MVP Rodney Williams through the air (8 of 11 in the first half) and by way of the option gave the Tigers a 27–0 lead at intermission.

The Cardinal came to life in the second half, however. Stanford's All-American tailback Brad Muster ran for one touchdown and caught a pair of TD passes after the break to bring the Pac-10 squad within six points of the South Carolinians. Although Clemson was compelled to punt with 1:43 remaining in the fourth period, a stout Tiger D held on fourth down to preserve a 27–21 victory.

By virtue of having claimed their first bowl win since the conclusion of their 1981 national championship season, the Orange and Purple ended the year with a No. 17 ranking in the final AP poll to mark the South Carolinians' first top 20 finish since 1983. The postseason victory and the conference title capped off a successful campaign by the shores of Lake Hartwell, confirming for Clemson what the Tigers had known when they claimed just their second win in Athens since 1914. They could, they did, they wanted to…and they made the most of what they correctly saw was a great opportunity.

1987

Treadwell, Take Two

It had not been a pretty day and it had not been a pretty game, but the 18th-ranked Bulldogs at least appeared to be on the verge of an outcome they would find pleasing. On a rainy afternoon by Lake Hartwell, Georgia led No. 8 Clemson 20–16 with roughly six and a half minutes remaining in the game. The Tigers were out of time outs and were about to have to punt the ball back to the visitors, who expected to run some time off of the clock and head down I-85 towards Athens carrying a victory in their hip pocket.

After the game, Danny Ford assured the news media that "you all saw a good football game. I know I saw a good football game, not error free but they never are error free." The Clemson coach was being generous; both teams had been complicit in a contest fraught with miscues, and Ford's Georgia counterpart, Vince Dooley, was acutely aware of how poorly his club had performed in the kicking game.

Ray Sherman, the Bulldog assistant charged with overseeing kickoff returns, had opined in the days leading up to the showdown in Memorial Stadium, "We've got to be great on special teams." It would have been hard to argue that the Classic City Canines were even good in that department. The day had showcased a long run by Georgia punt returner Nate Lewis, but that lone bright spot had been overshadowed by a missed field goal, a pair of Joey Hester punts that each went fewer than 30 yards, a fumble on a bobbled fair catch, a failure to have enough members of the punt team on the field (which cost the visitors a time out), and a botched fake field goal.

The abundance of errors in the kicking game convinced Dooley, who had expressed some uncertainty in the preceding week whether he would rely on Steve Crumley or freshman John Kasay for field goal attempts, to send in a new safety man for Rusty Seyle's forthcoming punt. Lewis stayed on the sidelines and Mike Bowen took his place as the Red and Black's punt returner.

Bowen was a walk-on who had transferred to Georgia from SMU after the Mustangs' football program was given the "death penalty" by the NCAA. His mission was simple: rather than risk a turnover by attempting to field a slippery ball in the soggy conditions, Bowen was to keep the Country Gentlemen from downing the oblong too close to the goal line. In this endeavor, as in most other aspects of special teams play that day, the Bulldogs were wholly unsuccessful.

Punting from the 44 yard line, Seyle put his foot into the ball. Bowen let the oval bounce at the nine, expecting the pigskin to bound into the end zone for a touchback. The Georgia deep man's expectation fell an inch shy of becoming reality, as Chinedu Ohan batted the ball backwards to keep it in the field of play, allowing outside line-backer John Johnson to tiptoe along the goal line and down the ball at the one. Johnson, a freshman from LaGrange, Ga., had verbally committed to the Dogs during the recruitment process before ultimately electing to don the orange and purple. Along with Savannah native Rusty Seyle, John Johnson was among the 24 Tigers from the Peach State.

The Red-and-Black offense lined up in its own end zone with 6:23 show ing on the clock. On the Bulldogs' first play from scrimmage, signal caller James Jackson ran it up the middle on a quarterback sneak. 300-pound starting middle guard Tony Stephens plugged the hole and halted Jackson's progress. The Georgia QB barely made it past the goal line; Stephens said afterwards, "I thought I had him."

Stephens lined up in the center of the Tigers' big defensive line. The Coun try Gentlemen's three-man front was three-deep at every position and was the largest concern of a Bulldog offensive line averaging 264 pounds per man. At 6'1" and 280 pounds, right tackle Michael Dean Perry was the *smallest* member of the Fort Hill Felines' first-string D-line. The weighty trio carried such heft that, when a student was given the duty of driving Perry, Stephens, and 295-pound start-ing left tackle Raymond Chavous from the athletic dorm to the sta-

Defensive linemen Raymond Chavous (79), Tony Stephens (65), and Michael Dean Perry (91) made up a formidable front for the Tigers.

dium, he was unable to exceed a speed of five miles per hour because his Toyota was sitting too close to the ground.

Perry came into the Georgia game needing just three sacks to take the all-time school record from his big brother, William. Together, the triumvirate and their understudies had limited Clemson's first two opponents, Western Carolina and Virginia Tech, to three rushing first downs, 11 first downs overall, and 33 rushing yards on 61 attempts, for an average of just over a foot and a half per carry in a pair of games which, like the Tigers' contest against the Bulldogs, were marred by rain.

Of course, those figures had come against the Division I-AA Catamounts and a Hok ie squad bound for a 2–9 finish under first-year head coach and VPI alum Frank Beamer. Clemson defensive coordinator Tom Harper was well aware of the challenge the Dogs would pose to his unit's statistical dominance. "I've got a horse," Harper explained, "and he's been impressive in a couple of races. But now I'm getting ready to put him in a big stakes race. This week, we'll find out if he's a thoroughbred."

The initial indicators had not been promising for the Jungaleers. Georgia had rolled to 118 rushing yards and 13 first downs by halftime, but the Tigers had tightened up defensively in the final two periods. After intermission, the Bulldogs were limited to 39 yards gained on the ground and the visitors moved the chains just twice. "Nobody gets that many first downs on us," explained outside linebacker James Earle, who added: "In the second half, we stood our ground."

Not for the first time that afternoon, the Orange and Purple anticipated what the Dogs were about to do. On second down from the one yard line, Jackson took the snap and rolled to his left, going to the outside on a sweep. Right corner James Lott "knew they were going to run outside, because that's what they do best." The Tigers had a full blitz on, rotating their defensive ends to the outside, sending the inside linebackers up the middle, and bringing the outside linebackers off the corners.

Jackson's teammates in the offensive backfield were charged with the duty of running interference for him, but the flood of oncoming orange overpowered the visitors. Lott shed a block with a spin move and got the Georgia quarterback by the ankles, holding him up long enough for strong safety Gene Beasley and weak-side linebacker Vince Taylor to converge on Jackson and make the tackle two yards deep in the end zone. The official signaled safety and the Bulldogs' four-point lead was halved.

"I had nowhere to go," explained Jackson afterwards. "I tried to string it out as far as I could and hope to find a seam so I could cut upfield. All I wanted to do was get it out of the end zone. Yeah, I thought we might surprise them with it, but they fought off the blocks. I don't know what else I could have done."

Dooley immediately accepted full responsibility for the play call, which he described using the words "dumb," "poor," and "stupid." Recognizing that he "should have run right at them, taken our chances and punted it out of there and let them try to score," the Georgia coach acknowledged: "I don't know that I've ever felt as bad personally about losing a football game for a team that played as hard as we did. But it was all my fault."

Dooley likely was being too hard on himself. The 24-year veteran of the Red-and-Black sideline understood that there sometimes were advantages to giving up a safety late in a game, which he had considered doing under similar circumstances against Clemson in 1980.

Then, as now, Dooley opted against such a strategy, recognizing that the difference between 20–16 and 20–18 was the difference between being beaten by a touchdown and beating beaten by a field goal.

Among the odd quirks of the Clemson-Georgia rivalry was the bizarre fact that debatable calls on two-point plays had plagued Dooley three times in 11 series meetings, perhaps costing the Classic City Canines the victory or the tie against the Fort Hill Felines in 1977, 1983, and 1987. The decision to go for two against Charley Pell's first Tiger team even after a penalty led to a 7–6 Jungaleer win; the election not to go for two and risk a momentum- killing miss four years before had produced a 16–16 tie with the Country Gentlemen; and, now, the choice to run to the outside had given the Orange and Purple a safety.

Dooley's recurring regrets about two-point mishaps were not the only aspect of the contest to have followed a familiar script. The Bulldogs' nationally-televised September 19 scuffle with the South Carolinians in Death Valley conjured up memories of their tussle between the hedges one year earlier.

Then, as now, Georgia likely had needed only to keep the ball moving to notch a victory when James Jackson carried the oval to the outside in the face of a Tiger blitz and met with drive-ending disaster. In 1986, it had been the Athenian signal caller's abrupt fumble; in 1987, it was the safety that forced the Red and Black to boot the ball back to the Clemsonians, who, also in a repeat of the previous year's performance, would mount a final drive as the clock ticked down towards zero, once again using only running plays to set up a potential last-second game-winning David Treadwell field goal.

Tailbacks Terry Allen and Wesley McFadden traded carries during the nine-play drive that followed the Classic City Canines' free kick from the 20 yard line. Allen would run the ball 16 times for 97 yards by the end of the afternoon, whereas McFadden would tally 52 yards on a dozen rushes. The Tigers began their final possession at their own 42 with 5:38 to go and they moved a little more than half the length of the field on the ground. The South Carolinians' march appeared to stall at the Georgia 30, where the home team faced third and seven.

For his part, Treadwell was not worried, for he saw another parallel: one year earlier, he had kicked the decisive three-pointer from essentially the same spot, which he judged "a good omen." Allen, however, took the next carry for a first down inside the 15 yard line, setting up a 21-yard chip shot for the Clemson place-kicker. Treadwell, a senior, had gone his entire collegiate career without ever having missed a field goal in the final eight minutes of a game, so there was no doubt that he could make this one.

He had to get onto the field first, though. Clemson's clock management had been as error-prone as Georgia's special teams. The Tiger sideline had mishandled several situations regarding play calling and personnel substitutions, necessitating that the Orange and Purple squander their time outs one by one.

An injury to Jerome Williams had caused a shortage of tight ends for the Country Gentle men, who shuffled the players around in ways that proved wasteful. According to Clemson offensive coordinator Jack Crowe, Ford had wanted to pass on a play in which the South Carolinians had a tackle lined up at tight end, requiring the coaches to stop the clock. It was one of five times the Tigers called a time out to avoid a delay of game penalty that afternoon.

Such sideline miscommunications at one point caused Clemson to call time outs on two consecutive plays. When the Fort Hill Felines mistakenly lined up in a power formation after an illegal motion penalty on first down had pushed them back, Ford called the entire offense to the sideline during the ensuing time out. The clock stoppage saw the head coach delivering a tongue-lashing in which he asked his players forthrightly whether they wanted to win.

As a result, the home team was without any remaining time outs three minutes into the final period. The clock kept running as the Clemson offense rushed off of the field and the Tiger field goal unit came on in its place. Treadwell had last looked at the scoreboard while 50 seconds yet remained and Ford self-admittedly "was about to panic" when he saw his players huddling up as the precious seconds passed.

Fewer than 10 of those seconds remained, in fact. "I could just see us standing there as time expired," said the Clemson coach during postgame questioning, calling to mind the 1963 tie between the two old foes in which the Dogs ran out of time before running a play after recovering a fumble on the game's final snap.

The ball was hiked and set down. Treadwell approached. The steady progression on the scoreboard showed five seconds left and they continued slipping away.

Everyone had known going into the game how momentous the showdown was likely to be. Both teams were ranked in the top 20. Eight of the previous 10 series meetings had been settled by a touchdown or less and neither team had beaten the other by more than 12 points since the Bicentennial. Due to the expansion of Georgia's SEC schedule, there would be a three-year hiatus before the border rivals renewed hostilities again in 1990. For those reasons alone, the contest carried consequences.

The Tigers had an extra incentive to emphasize the outcome, though. Clemson brought back 17 starters and was widely considered a contender to capture the Country Gentlemen's second national championship in a seven-season span. Before the game, both *The Atlanta Journal-Constitution*'s Tony Barnhart and *The Greenville News*'s Dan Foster penned columns arguing that the outing, while big for both teams, was bigger for the home team.

The rationale was simple: Clemson had eight games remaining after the Orange and Purple played the Red and Black, of which six would be hosted at Frank Howard Field and none was likely to be against a top 20 team. The Bulldogs could expect to be challenged by two more sets of Tigers in No. 3 Auburn and No. 4 Louisiana State, but, if they could get by Georgia, the Fort Hill Felines could face smooth sailing all the way to the No. 1 ranking.

Foster pointed out that the Orange Bowl intended to have scouts at Saturday's Clemson-Georgia game and that the second-toughest test on the Jungaleers' slate was expected to be their season-ender against the in-state rival Gamecocks on November 21. As Foster noted, "Clemson's last trip to the Orange Bowl, and its last three to the Gator Bowl, were guaranteed before the team ever got on its buses to play South Carolina, just as Carolina's 1984 trip to the Gator Bowl was locked before it played Clemson."

Therefore, the *Greenville News* columnist concluded, "The Clemson-USC game will not be a bowl factor – for either – if everything else goes well." Foster added that "no team in the top 10 is as heavily favored to win its last eight games as the Tigers are" and Barnhart concurred that "Georgia represents the major stumbling block between Clemson, an undefeated regular season and a chance at its second national championship this decade."

Knowing the stakes were so large, the combatants chose costumes appropriate to such high drama. The Clemsonites not only had broken out their trademark lucky orange pants, they had even donned a special new style of the familiar uniform britches, which Ford had unveiled to the team by wearing them underneath his warm-up pants, removing his outer garment to reveal the new attire underneath, and announcing: "We're wearing these." The satiny orange pants worn for the Georgia game were made of a shiny material,

David Treadwell (18) joined teammates Duane Walker (47) and Robbie Chapman (62) for the opening coin toss, but it was what Treadwell did at the end of the game that mattered most for the Tigers.

featured a small tiger paw near the top, and had black and white piping down the side.

The Dogs responded in kind. The Athenians were well aware of the significance of the previous year's game between the hedges, which was commemorated, along with the Country Gentlemen's other road wins over ranked teams, in the "Graveyard" at the practice field entrance behind the Jervey Athletic Center. Clemson's 1986 victory in the Classic City joined such previous noteworthy away games as the Tigers' 1977 triumph in Sanford Stadium in becoming the Orange and Purple's tenth conquest of a top 20 team in the opponent's home stadium.

Georgia looked to avenge the prior season's affront to Bulldog dignity, although Vince Dooley took his time in settling upon the proper method by which to attempt to counteract the Country Gentlemen's home field advantage. On Friday night, the Red-and-Black head coach dispatched his equipment manager, Howard Beavers, back across the state line to Clarke County to retrieve the red britches the Dogs had worn on their last trip to Lake Hartwell two years before.

The participants now being garbed appropriately for the latest installment of their 90-year-old rivalry, all that remained was for the scarlet-panted Georgians and the saffron- slacked South Carolinians to get down to the serious business of playing a football game. Echoing the sentiment he had expressed so colorfully the year before, senior linebacker John Brantley succinctly summed up the recent history of the series: "It's going to be a street fight. It's going to be one of those blood-and-guts kind of games where the women and children should sit in the upper deck." History, apparently, was not all that saw fit to repeat itself regarding this memorable game.

The contest was televised by CBS Sports...for the most part, that is. A flexible wave- length wire caught fire in the third quarter, short-circuiting the video transmitter and interrupting the broadcast for seven minutes. Former Clemson standout Banks McFadden was honored at midfield prior to kickoff when the legendary Tiger great's basketball and football numbers were retired.

When the game at last got underway, Georgia took the opening kickoff and moved methodically down the field, covering 56 yards in a dozen plays. After senior signal caller James Jackson hooked up with classmate Lars Tate on a 17-yard screen pass to the Clemson eight yard line, Steve Crumley connected on a 21-yard field goal to give the visitors an early three-point advantage. The drive had eaten up the first 6:16 of the opening period.

The rest of the initial quarter passed without either team tacking additional points onto the scoreboard until the first of the Bulldog special teams miscues aided the Tigers in tying the game. Joey Hester's first punt was short, traveling only 29 yards to set up Clemson with good field position.

In response to the Red and Black's opening 56-yard, 12-play drive, the Orange and Purple proceeded to go 60 yards in 12 snaps, keeping the chains moving with a 20-yard completion from Rodney Williams to Gary Cooper. The possession produced a 30-yard David Treadwell field goal to knot the score with a little over two minutes left in the first frame.

It had appeared during the autumn's first two outings that special teams were among the Bulldogs' strengths. After facing Virginia and Oregon State to open the campaign, the

Classic City Canines ranked in the top five nationally in kick returns. The visitors hoped to be able to break one for long yardage in the kicking game against the Tigers, who had surrendered a 92-yard touchdown on a kickoff return to Virginia Tech one week earlier.

Initial indications had been promising for the Dogs, who would return Clemson's first five kickoffs for a cumulative 135 yards over the course of the afternoon. The Georgians were looking for a momentum-swinging runback, though, and, early in the second quarter, Nate Lewis produced what the Athenians sought.

Upon receiving a Clemson punt at his own 24, Lewis saw the wedge before him and followed his blockers. Mike Guthrie and Richard Tardits provided effective interference for the return man, who streaked down the right sideline, put a move on Seyle to freeze the punter, and scooted the remaining 25 yards into the end zone for Lewis's first career punt return for a touchdown. Crumley converted, and, with 14:31 left until halftime, the Bulldogs led 10–3.

The visitors' lead did not last long, for the Georgia celebration which followed Lewis's electrifying dash incurred a 15-yard penalty to enable the Tigers to begin the ensuing possession at their own 41. The Jungaleers needed just four plays and fewer than two minutes to cover the 59 yards separating them from their intended destination.

The Country Gentlemen picked up a combined four yards on the first two snaps of the series before Williams's third-down pass to flanker Keith Jennings netted 17 yards and put the home team at the Red and Black's 38. From there, it was all Tracy Johnson, as the Clemson fullback scampered the rest of the way to the end zone for the highlight of his 11-carry, 72-yard day. Treadwell tied the game with his extra point with 12:36 showing on the clock.

Having already gotten their only quality special teams play of the day out of their collective system, the Dogs proceeded to waste a chance to break the deadlock. Dooley had been asked about the choice between his two place-kickers before the contest and the coach had answered, "Normally, I would go with Crumley, but if it was a long way I'd consider Kasay."

Perhaps Dooley should have heeded his own wisdom, but, in any event, the Red and Black made it as far as the Tiger 24 later in the period, only to have Crumley miss the 41- yard field goal attempt that would have put the Classic City Canines back out in front. The junior specialist later explained, "There was perfect execution. It just faded out."

Georgia's next possession ended in an even more ignominious special teams gaffe. From the Bulldog 23 yard line, Hester went back to punt. He mishandled the wet ball, which went through his hands. After Hester finally got control of the slippery pigskin, he shanked an 11-yard punt. The Red-and-Black D managed to hold the Orange and

Purple zero to seven yards on the next three plays, but Treadwell's ensuing three-point try was good from 44 yards, securing a 13–10 edge
for the home team with just over two and a half minutes left until the
break.

Clemson kicked off and, starting from their own 36, the Bulldogs
took nine plays to travel 53 yards. Jackson's pass to split end John
Thomas picked up 20 yards to the Tiger 17 and the Athenians thereafter found themselves 11 yards from paydirt with 20 seconds remaining. Although Georgia had one first-half time out left, Dooley did not
stop the clock to allow his team the chance to run one more play. Instead, he sent Crumley onto the field to attempt a 28-yard field goal.

Dooley's decision would not be the Georgia coach's last question-
able call concerning the use of time outs that day, but the kicker's wobbling three-point try managed to make it through to put 13 ticks per
side up on the scoreboard eight seconds before intermission. The score
stayed snarled at the break.

The Dogs were given another opportunity to retake the lead early
in the second half when Clemson fumbled and the Georgians recovered. The possession culminated with the Red and Black lining up for
what would have been a 46-yard effort to divide the uprights, but the
Bulldogs proceeded to botch a bold gambit.

Crumley waited in the backfield as though getting ready to boot a
three-pointer. Lewis was stationed on the right wing with the wide side
of the field to the left. Holder David Dukes went into the appropriate
stance to place the ball for a left-footed kicker. There was, however, a
problem.

Crumley was a right-footed kicker.

The fake field goal formation was designed to allow Lewis to go
into motion, receive the handoff from Dukes, and take the ball around
left end for the first down. Although the positioning of the holder fa-
cilitated the handoff, it also ran the risk of tipping off the opposition, as
an alert defender might notice the fact that Dukes was aligned improp-
erly for an actual field goal attempt. "We're supposed to run the play so
quickly that the defense shouldn't have time to react," Dukes described.

Perhaps the Clemson defense shouldn't have had time to react, but
react they did, aided by the raucous Memorial Stadium crowd. Because
the play was dependent upon precise timing, Lewis was under orders
to go into motion at the sound of Dukes's voice. Since the fans in the
stands were so loud, however, Lewis could not hear the holder, so he
began moving when the ball was snapped instead.

The Tigers sniffed out the fake, the play took too long to develop, and the ballcarrier was dropped for an eight-yard loss. Just as they would later realize Jackson was going to run to the outside on the play that produced the fourth-quarter safety, the Jungaleer defense had picked up on Dukes's unusual location to shut down the attempted trickery.

Indeed, the wily Clemson D appeared to be inside the Bulldogs' helmets throughout the second half. Michael Perry revealed afterwards that the Country Gentlemen had spotted another Georgia tendency. Whenever the Dogs lined up with split backs, the play was either going to be a pass or a draw.

Armed with that information, the Fort Hill Felines were able to blunt the Red-and-Black attack after the break. Lars Tate, who had rushed for 350 yards in Georgia's first two games, ran the ball 19 times for 84 yards in Death Valley. Despite Rodney Williams's poor passing performance (6 of 16 for 76 yards, no touchdowns, and an interception), the Tigers ended the day in front of the visitors in first downs (19–15), rushing yards (261–157), total yards (337–268), offensive plays (72–62), and time of possession (35:40–24:20).

Georgia's kicking game woes continued after the fake field goal attempt was smothered. The Dogs had to burn a time out when they found themselves preparing to receive a punt with only 10 members of the return team on the field because Nate Lewis was speaking with Ray Sherman on the sideline. The Bulldog deep man's greatest mistake, though, came at the end of the Tiger drive immediately after he had been thrown for a loss on the fourth-down fake.

Clemson's ensuing possession ended in a 37-yard punt by Seyle, who had overcome his troubles from the first two weeks of the autumn to average 41.8 yards per punt against the Dogs. Lewis signaled for a fair catch, but he took his eye off of the incoming football. The punt returner bobbled the oblong, which bounded off of his shoulder pad and fell to the ground. Snapper David Spry recovered the fumble for the South Carolinians at the Georgia five yard line.

The Country Gentlemen did not take maximum advantage of the chance they had been afforded. The Tigers were flagged for illegal motion on first down and Rodney Williams later rolled out and stumbled for a six-yard loss. All told, the three plays just after the turnover *cost* Clemson eight yards, so the home team had to settle for a 29-yard Treadwell field goal, but the Fort Hill Felines led 16–13 with fewer than six minutes still to go in the third quarter.

The Tigers were in a position to extend their lead early in the final period. On their next drive after going up by three points, the Jungaleers went on the march from the Clemson 20 to the Georgia 26 despite the persistence of sideline issues that exhausted the last of the home team's supply of time outs. Treadwell was called upon to try a 43-yarder, but the holder got the ball down slowly and the Dogs were able to get a hand on the oblong as it sailed aloft. The miss represented the only one of the Clemson kicker's five tries that day not to yield points.

Georgia took over on downs still trailing by three and with 74 yards of real estate stretching out between the line of scrimmage and the plane of the goal line. James Jackson, who would finish the afternoon having hooked up on nine of his 19 aerial attempts for 111 yards, guided a drive on which he completed a 16-yard pass to tight end Troy Sadowski before going 36 yards through the air on third and 10 to Kirk Warner.

Warner leapt up and hauled in the pass at the Clemson 22. Lars Tate carried the ball to the eight yard line and the next handoff went to freshman Rodney Hampton, who started to the left and found himself face to face with five Tiger defenders. After briefly halting in the vicinity of the five yard line, Hampton continued to his left, turned the corner, and scored the first rushing touchdown allowed by the Orange-and-Purple D in the 1987 season.

Georgia had staked its claim to a 20–16 lead that recalled the final score from the Bulldogs' tussle with the Tigers in the Red and Black's national championship campaign seven years before. One second less than nine minutes remained in the game.

There followed the Rusty Seyle punt that was downed at the one, the James Lott tackle in the end zone for the resulting safety, and the Tiger march down the field as the seconds bled away into the ether. The Classic City Canines had closed out the first half by mounting a 53-yard, nine-play drive ending in a tying field goal with eight seconds left; the Fort Hill Felines were now closing out the second half by mounting a 53-yard, nine- play drive which the home crowd hoped would end in a winning field goal…although, if it did, it would do so with far fewer ticks remaining on the clock.

Curiously, the Bulldogs had chosen to hold onto their last two second-half time outs while the Country Gentlemen ran off more than five and a half minutes of game time. Georgia did not use them to stop the clock during Clemson's final drive and buy the Red and Black more time with which to work, in the hope of getting a kickoff return to set up a long field goal try for the victory. Dooley admitted afterwards that this, too, had been an error on a day chock full of them.

The seconds slid off the scoreboard as Treadwell put his toe into the pigskin. This time, the drama was minimal; in his college career, the Jungaleer place-kicker would win five games within the final two minutes of play, and this was one of them. Treadwell made the kick with ease and Clemson led 21–20 with two seconds left in the game.

With these precious seconds the Dogs were unable to do anything, so that score stood as the final margin. The hometown fans stormed the field to celebrate the Tigers' first back-to-back wins over the Red and Black in consecutive seasons since 1905 and 1906. Follow ing the mistake-laden game in the rain, Danny Ford summed up his reaction to the victory for the press: "Maybe we didn't win this one the right way. But right now, who cares?" Then, remembering the three-year break in the series that was about to begin, the Clemson coach added, "But to tell you the truth, I don't think I can take too many more of these."

The Tigers carried their 3–0 record and top 10 ranking into conference play the following Saturday, when the Country Gentlemen hosted a Georgia Tech outfit in its first year under the direction of new head coach Bobby Ross. After having gone 999 kickoff and punt returns without scoring a touchdown, the Jungaleers ended a 17-year gap between TD returns with a 95-yard kickoff return for a touchdown by Joe Henderson and a 78-yard punt return for a touchdown by Donnell Woolford in a 33–12 victory over the Yellow Jackets. Henderson's scoring scamper produced the South Carolinians' first kickoff return TD since Hal Davis's runback against Georgia in 1962.

The Orange and Purple opened October with successive victories over Virginia and Duke to run their unbeaten streak to 11 straight games since their last loss at N.C. State the year before. After a lackluster win over the Blue Devils, Clemson hosted the Wolfpack at Frank Howard Field on October 24 as the No. 7 team in the nation.

The Tigers were shocked to find themselves down 30–0 at halftime, but Rodney Williams nearly brought the Orange and Purple back with a career-best 271-yard passing performance in which he set an NCAA record with 46 second-half attempts. The rally featured a trio of fourth-quarter touchdowns yet finished just shy of success as Clemson fell to unranked North Carolina State by a 30–28 margin. The Fort Hill Felines tumbled to 14th in the AP poll and Dick Sheridan's Pack club went on to lose three of its last four outings to finish 4–7.

Ford's Country Gentlemen rebounded from the disheartening loss by reeling off three straight victories. Against Bill Dooley-coached Wake Forest, the Tigers trotted out the orange pants once more and also allowed Rodney Williams to be spelled in the first half by backup quarterback Chris Morocco. The Clemson signal caller's father, Anthony "Zippy" Morocco, had been a three-year letterman for the Red and Black in the late 1940s and early 1950s.

With wins over North Carolina and Maryland, the Tigers worked their way back up to eighth in the polls heading into their date with No. 12 South Carolina in Columbia. Ford had carded his 75th career victory against the Terrapins, but the Gamecocks prevailed in the season-ender at Williams-Brice Stadium by a 20–7 score. Clemson dropped to 9–2 in the outing in which Michael Perry broke his older brother's conference record in tackles for loss.

The Tigers' 6–1 ACC mark still was good enough to capture an outright conference championship for the Orange and Purple, who were bound for their first New Year's Day bowl game since the 1981 season. In the Citrus Bowl on January 1, Clemson would face Joe Paterno's 20th-ranked defending national champion Penn State Nittany Lions.

The Jungaleers acquitted themselves capably in Orlando. Rodney Williams earned bowl MVP honors for the second straight season with a 214-yard passing performance in which he was aided by Keith Jennings's seven receptions for 110 yards. The addition of Terry Allen's 105 rushing yards meant that Clemson had a 200-yard passer, a 100-yard receiver, and a 100-yard rusher in a single outing for the first time since 1969. The result was the worst postseason defeat ever suffered by a Penn State squad in a 35–10 thumping.

If the Dogs found the setback in Death Valley deflating, they did not show it in wins over South Carolina and Ole Miss in the next two weeks. After a narrow defeat (26–23) suffered at the hands of a seventh-ranked LSU team that would end the season with a 10–1–1 record and a Gator Bowl victory, the Red and Black reeled off wins over Vanderbilt in Nashville, Kentucky in Athens, and Florida in Jacksonville (in a game in which freshman John Kasay kicked his first career field goal).

Georgia's troubles with Tiger teams persisted at home against No. 12 Auburn on November 14, when the Plainsmen paid a visit to Sanford Stadium and administered a 27–11 spanking to the Bulldogs. The Classic City Canines' oldest rivals from the Loveliest Village went on to earn a 9–1–2 record, an SEC title, and a No. 7 final ranking following a Sugar Bowl tie with Syracuse.

The Dogs closed out the campaign with a 30–16 victory over Georgia Tech in a game played on a rainy night in Atlanta. The 8–3 mark attained by the Athenians earned them a Liberty Bowl berth on December 29, the latest date the Red and Black had been in ac tion since the end of the 1983 campaign. Although Arkansas held a 17–7 lead after three quarters in Memphis, Georgia battled back to tie the game on a James Jackson touchdown run and John Kasay's 39-yard field goal with no time left on the clock gave the Bulldogs a 20–17 win over the Southwest Conference foe that had bested them in two previous postseason meetings.

The year's final Associated Press poll recognized Clemson (10–2) as the nation's No. 12 team and ranked Georgia (9–3) 13th. Between them, the Bulldogs and the Tigers had lost five games, and four of those setbacks had come at the hands of teams that finished in the AP top 15. At the end of the season immediately preceding the temporary cessation of their longstanding rivalry, the Fort Hill Felines and the Classic City Canines were separated by one poll position in January, which seemed somehow appropriate for two tough teams who had been separated by one point when they met on the field in September.

1990

No Vince Dooley, No Danny Ford, and No Contest

Something was...different. Memorial Stadium was still Death Valley. Both teams' uniforms essentially were unchanged. The contest still loomed large as an important date on each school's schedule. Nevertheless, the dawning of a new decade had brought to the Clemson-Georgia series an unmistakable air of change.

For one thing, there was the fact that the Red and Black were a shadow of their former selves. Despite having won eight or more games in seven of the previous 10 campaigns, the Dogs had stumbled out of the gate after star tailback Rodney Hampton left school early for the NFL and four defensive starters were ruled academically ineligible on the eve of the season.

Granted, the Athenians were 3–1, but they had come up short against Louisiana State in Baton Rouge and sneaked by Southern Miss, winless Alabama, and East Carolina between the hedges in a trio of nailbiters decided by one, one, and four points, respectively. A winning record could not mask the truth that only inches separated Georgia from an 0–4 start against the weakest part of the Classic City Canines' schedule.

Still, that wasn't the biggest difference.

Perhaps the oddity was to be found in the broadcast booth, where ESPN's Dave O'Brien was calling the game in place of gravelly-voiced Bulldog radio announcer Larry Munson, who was recovering from back surgery. From the time the beloved Munson had become the

Classic City Canines' play-by-play man in 1966 to the time he opted out of traveling to the Red and Black's first away game of the season against Alabama in 2007 (one week before the legendary broadcaster's 85th birthday), the 1990 clash with Clemson was the only Georgia game Munson missed in 42 years.

That wasn't it, either, though.

An even more unusual aspect of the 1990 clash between the Bulldogs and the Tigers was the reality that it represented a resumption of the rivalry following a two-year interruption. The SEC had expanded its conference schedule from six games to seven in 1988, necessitating that the Red and Black begin taking turns between home-and-away exchanges of games against Georgia's longstanding Palmetto State rivals, Clemson and South Carolina.

The Gamecocks had been up first, hosting the Dogs in Columbia in 1988 and traveling to Athens in 1989, and now the Country Gentlemen reclaimed their spot on the Athenians' slate. The two-year break during which Clemson and Georgia did not meet on the gridiron marked the first instance of the Bulldogs and the Tigers failing to play one another in consecutive seasons since 1960 and 1961.

Nevertheless, even that wasn't the most important change.

No, the most noteworthy alteration was that, for the first time in more than a quar ter-century, a Clemson-Georgia game was being played with someone other than Vince Dooley standing on the Bulldog sideline and, for the first time in a dozen years, a Clemson-Georgia game was taking place with the Orange and Purple being coached by anyone besides Danny Ford.

For many fans on both sides of the Savannah River, separating the rivalry from the two coaches who had elevated it to national prominence was impossible. To any Georgian or South Carolinian who had come of age as a football fan after the glory days of Wally Butts and Frank Howard, Vince Dooley and Danny Ford defined their respective programs, and the nine-year war waged between them was an epic struggle fought at the highest level.

Although he left under happier circumstances than his counterpart at Lake Hartwell, Dooley had been the first to go. In December 1988, following the attainment of his 200th career victory in the regular-season finale of his silver anniversary season between the hedges, the legendary Georgia coach announced that the Bulldogs' upcoming bowl game would be his last on the sidelines for the Red and Black. Following a thrilling Gator Bowl victory over Michigan State, Dooley took over as the school's full-time athletic director and left the coaching duties to someone else.

Settling upon that someone else proved to be somewhat difficult, though. Dooley had taken over a Georgia program that had posted eight losing seasons in the 11 years just prior to his arrival in Athens and restored it to the place of national prominence it occupied under Wally Butts in the 1940s. By the time he rode off into the sunset sporting the 201–77–10 ledger that made him the winningest coach in school history, Dooley had guided the Dogs to 20 bowl games (including nine straight in the 1980s), six SEC championships, and the 1980 national title. Nine of his last 14 teams had finished with at least nine wins and Dooley had gone 17–7–1 against Florida, 19–6 against Georgia Tech, and 15–6–1 against Clemson. The latter ledger made him the winningest coach for either school in the history of the border rivalry.

Despite the accomplishments of the program Dooley would hand off to his successor, however, the Red and Black had a real problem finding a coach willing to take the job. Depending upon whom one asked, Georgia Southern head coach and former Georgia defensive coordinator Erk Russell was offered the job and turned it down. North Carolina State head coach Dick Sheridan was next in line, and he reportedly was Classic City-bound when he had a change of heart and elected to remain in Raleigh. Arkansas head coach Ken Hatfield's name later came up but was shot down when the Hogs' skipper told reporters "they never offered it to me. All they did was talk to me."

Ultimately, and surprisingly, the job went to James Rayford Goff. The former Bulldog quarterback, who was the permanent captain of Dooley's third SEC championship squad and the 1976 conference player of the year, had spent the preceding eight years on the Georgia staff, heading up the Red and Black's recruiting efforts while coaching, in turn, the Athenians' tight ends, offensive linemen, and running backs.

Goff was still six months and eight days shy of his 34th birthday when he was named his alma mater's head football coach on January 2, 1989, but the Moultrie native was a Georgia man through and through, so hopes were high even if Dooley's successor was an unproven commodity.

The Bulldog faithful could take comfort in the fact that prior head coaching experience had never been a prerequisite for success in Athens. Since the hiring of former North Carolina A&M head honcho Bull Whitney in 1906, the Red and Black had been led to great success by Alex Cunningham, Herman Stegeman, George Woodruff, Harry Meh-

As a senior quarterback in 1976, Ray Goff had been part of a 41-0 Georgia victory in Death Valley, but, when he returned to Clemson as a head coach 14 years later, he found himself on the other side of a lopsided score.

re, Wally Butts, and Vince Dooley, each of whom came to the Georgia job with a lifetime ledger of 0-0.

What gave Peach State partisans pause, though, was the fact that the four previous University of Georgia alumni to have coached the Red and Black (Charles Herty, Marvin Dickinson, George Woodruff, and Johnny Griffith) between them had compiled a 45–42–5 record as the head man at their *alma mater*. Of the four Georgia graduates who had helmed the program prior to Ray Goff, only Woodruff had finished above .500 for his career.

Ford's departure from the Death Valley sideline was more acrimoni ous, although the hiring of his successor went more smoothly. At the end of an 11-year tenure as the head coach at Fort Hill that had begun when he was 30 years old, the man who had guided the Tigers to the 1981 national championship was pressured to resign by the Clemson administration.

Recruiting violations had landed the Orange and Purple on NCAA probation following the 1982 campaign, a sanction that deprived consecutive 9–1–1 Tiger teams of the opportunity to compete in bowl games that year and in 1983. On January 5, 1990, less than a week after the Country Gentlemen capped off a 10-win campaign with a Gator Bowl victory, the NCAA outlined 14 rules violations purported to have been committed by the Clemson football program between 1984 and 1988. The 15-page report accused six coaches of recruiting violations and alleged payments to players.

Ford was unequivocal in maintaining his innocence. "I deny any wrongdoing on my part," he wrote, "and I am confident that an impartial review of the facts will so prove." However, the school administration feared additional sanctions and believed the potential punishment might be lessened if Ford was no longer employed at Clemson. After a $1 mil lion settlement (which included the University's pledge to pay the balance of the mortgage on Ford's farm) was negotiated, the embattled coach formally resigned on January 18.

Ford left behind a record of achievement at Fort Hill that included six first-place finishes in the ACC, eight seasons of eight wins or better, and the Tigers' first national championship in any sport. His last four Clemson teams had gone 38–8–2 and won four straight bowl games. In addition to posting winning marks of 7–3–1 against in-state rival South Carolina and 6–5 against pesky Textile Bowl foe N.C. State, Ford had compiled a 4–4–1 record against Georgia that made him the first Tiger head coach since Bob Williams to have beaten the Red and Black more than once during his Clemson career.

Three days after Ford officially stepped down, Ken Hatfield was named as his succes sor. Although it would be difficult to replace Ford, who left with a 96–29–4 ledger, the new head of the Tiger football program brought a 55–17–1 record with him from his days with the Razorbacks. Although Hatfield's winning percentage in Fayetteville (.753) had not quite been the equal of Ford's in the Palmetto State (.760), the newcomer didn't trail the former coach by much.

An Arkansas alum, Hatfield had guided his *alma mater* to six straight postseason appearances between 1984 and 1989, taking the Hogs to a pair of Liberty Bowls, an Orange Bowl, and a couple of Cotton Bowls. All of these were losses for the Hogs, however, which drew a stark contrast between the new Clemson coach and his predecessor. Ford had gone 6–2 in bowl games. Still, that was the postseason; what mattered first and foremost was how the new guy fared against the Country Gentlemen's regular slate.

In May, the Fort Hill football program received a light punishment for impermissible extra benefits that did not include scholarship restrictions or bans on bowl bids or television appearances. As the former head coach had promised would be the case, the NCAA cleared Ford of any direct wrongdoing. With the specter of possible sanctions having been lifted, the Ken Hatfield era got off to a solid start the following September when a Tiger team that returned eight defensive first-teamers commenced the campaign in dominant fashion.

Rover Arlington Nunn returned an interception for a touchdown and flanker Doug Thomas returned a kickoff for another score *en route* to a 59–0 waxing of Long Beach State in the 10th-ranked Orange and Purple's opening outing. Following a 20–7 loss in Charlottesville to a Virginia team that would start the season with seven straight wins and be ranked No. 1 in the nation for three weeks during October, the Orange and Purple defeated Independence Bowl-bound Maryland in Baltimore thanks to another kickoff return for a touchdown by Thomas.

Wins over Appalachian State and Duke by a combined 74–7 margin followed to boost the Tigers to 4–1 and No. 13 in the coaches' poll as they prepared to host the Bull dogs on October 6. "Prepared" was the key word, as Hatfield's Country Gentlemen were ready to welcome the visiting squad, of whom Goff would observe afterwards, "I don't think we were ready today. I don't think we are as bad as we looked."

Even so, the Red and Black looked pretty bad.

A befuddled Georgia offensive line struggled mightily to block the Clemson blitz, resulting in losses of eight yards on the Bulldogs' first play from scrimmage and four more on their third snap. Those two plays—on which linebacker John Johnson stopped flanker Kevin Maxwell on an ill-fated reverse and defensive tackle Vance Hammond registered a sack—set the tone for the entire afternoon just moments after the 1:00 kickoff before 84,000 fans.

Because neither Peach State quarterback had time to throw, both Preston Jones (2 for 12) and Greg Talley (5 for 11) produced tepid stat lines and collectively passed for just 50 yards, 14 of which came on the Andre Hastings reception that gave the visitors their longest gain from scrimmage of the day. Hastings also tacked on 76 yards on three kickoff returns. The Athenians drew six penalty flags in the first quarter of Danny Ford's first game in Memorial Stadium as a spectator.

A seven-play Georgia drive in the first quarter netting 25 yards before ending in a Scot Armstrong punt went down in the record book as the Classic City Canines' longest drive in Death Valley. Defensively, the Dogs held their own in the early going, limiting the Tiger offense to a 47-yard field goal attempt at the end of a drive covering only seven yards. Chris Gardocki drove home the try for the first points of the contest three and a half minutes into the opening period. Gardocki, a four-time All-ACC specialist who finished the autumn ranked fourth in the nation both in placekicking and in punting, would go on to tie a school record with four field goals in a single outing.

The first compelling indicator that the Orange and Purple truly were ready to romp came on their second possession, when fewer than five minutes had elapsed in the first frame. On a first-down option play, the Bulldog defensive back whose responsibility was the pitch man instead took the quarterback, enabling Clemson's freshman tail-back, Ronald Williams, to take the pitch, head down the sideline, cut back at the 15 yard line, and go untouched for 51 yards to score the touchdown that made it 10–0 for the home team. Williams would go on to gain 128 yards on the ground, nearly surpassing all on his own the total offensive output the Red and Black would generate as a unit (131 yards, the worst for a Georgia squad since 1984).

Also for the first time since 1984, the Bulldogs had a punt blocked. In the second quarter, Armstrong went back to boot the ball away after the Athenians failed to convert—Georgia was one of 13 on third down—and Tiger linebacker Doug Brewster burst through, once again without a Bulldog laying a hand on him, and covered up the punt. The South Carolinians recovered the ball on the visitors' 28 yard line and Gardocki extended the Country Gentlemen's lead to 13–0 with a 25-yard field goal.

Jones, an Anderson native who considered his trip to Clemson as a visiting quarterback to be a homecoming of sorts, later remarked, "We felt good at halftime. Clemson was up 13–0, but we had given them a lot of their points with a blocked punt, and they had had only one big play on offense. But we were stopping them on defense."

Jones's assessment was not invalid, as the Classic City Canines held nearly a one-minute first-half lead in time of possession and had gained more first downs in the first two quarters (5) than the Fort Hill Felines could claim (3). That state of affairs would not last long, as Georgia tallied only three first downs and 39 yards after halftime.

The second half got underway with a Tiger drive that bled nearly six minutes off of the game clock. Just over nine minutes remained in the third quarter when Gardocki drilled his third field goal from 30 yards away to build up a 16–0 advantage. Georgia's 92 yards of total offense before intermission were not accidental, as Clemson demonstrated on the Bulldogs' next possession. The Tigers allowed the Red and Black to gain only eight yards and the visitors once again were compelled to punt.

Although the Orange and Purple racked up an impressive 224 rushing yards in the second half, the home team committed a miscue late in the third quarter. A fumble by Clemson quarterback DeChane Cameron was pounced upon by Georgia's freshman defensive tackle, Willie Jennings, at the Tiger 27 yard line, and, although the Dogs proceeded to lose four yards on three plays in the ensuing possession, John Kasay connected on a 48-yard field goal with 14 seconds remaining in the period to prevent the shutout.

The Country Gentlemen responded with a 13-play drive taking more than six minutes, during which Clemson converted on second

In addition to handling the punting duties for the Tigers, specialist Chris Gardocki also kicked a record-tying four field goals against the Bulldogs.

and 20 when fullback Tony Kennedy scampered up the middle for a 23-yard gain. Gardocki's three-pointer from 25 yards away capped off the 72-yard march, opened up a 19–3 lead, and made him the first Fort Hill Feline since David Treadwell in the 1987 showdown between the two squads to boot four field goals in a single game. That achievement must have been a satisfying one for Gardocki, a Peach State native who had attended the same high school that produced Kevin Butler.

In the first half, an interception by Orange-and-Purple corner-back Dexter Davis had halted one of two Georgia drives across mid-field (each of which ended at the Tiger 47 yard line); free safety Norris Brown added a second-half pick of his own to begin a seven-play, 45-yard march culminating in a five-yard run by Williams for his second touchdown of the day.

The freshman tailback's score made it 25–3 with under three minutes remaining in the game, but a successful two-point conversion try put the home team ahead by 24. Although there was some grousing about Hatfield's decision among the Bulldog faithful, Goff took a different view, noting: "I was more concerned about the 34 than the two."

In any event, the Red and Black had no one to blame for the Tigers' touchdown drive but themselves. Georgia's freshman defensive line-man, Tracy Huzzie, incurred a personal foul penalty by taking the ball from the Clemson running back after the end of the play and spiking it to give the Country Gentlemen a first down six yards from the end zone. It was one of mul tiple mistakes by the Classic City Canines, who drew three flags on special teams for failing to allow the Tiger returner adequate room within which to field a trio of the Bulldogs' 11 punts.

Georgia linebacker Mo Lewis, who made a dozen tackles (including a quarterback sack) during an otherwise dismal day for the visitors, later commented on the fact that "we started giving them penalties and doing stupid things. I'm disappointed about that." Lewis and his team-mates on the defensive side of the ball were on the field for nearly 21 minutes in the second half as Clemson ground out 341 rushing yards (the most gained against a Bulldog squad since 1984) on 76 offensive snaps, 66 of which were running plays.

A trio of freshman tailbacks took the field for the Tigers and one of them, Rodney Blunt, finished off the scoring with a 26-yard touch-down scamper with just under a minute and a half remaining. For his part in the blowout, Orange-and-Purple offensive lineman Stacy Long earned ACC player of the week honors for the first of two times during his senior season with six knockdown blocks against Georgia.

The Athenians, meanwhile, held the ball for just 53 plays as the Clemson defense harried the visiting signal callers, recording three sacks and six tackles for loss while breaking up five passes and intercepting two more. The Dogs attempted to run the ball on first down 12 times in the first half, only to face second and long on nine occasions. Matters were not helped by the fact that emerging star Garrison Hearst was given only three second-half carries, two of which came on the final two plays of the game.

After Georgia suffered its worst loss since falling to Kentucky in 1977, Bulldog linebacker Torrey Evans summed it up succinctly: "It was an old-fashioned butt whipping." Writing for *The Atlanta Journal-Constitution*, Scott Reid put it more lyrically: "When was the last time somebody rolled through Georgia as easily as Clemson did in its 34–3 victory on Saturday? Florida in 1984? Virginia in 1979? Sherman in 1864?" Dan Foster of The Greenville News did not delve quite as far back into the past when declaring the result "a victory that transcended 85 years of Clemson history."

However one chose to put it, though, the Death Valley manhandling was decisive to the point of being historic. Georgia picked up only eight first downs, two of which came by penalty and none of which came through the air, while Clemson moved the sticks a whopping 22 times. While the result was unsurprising, given the strengths and weaknesses of the two combatants, the outcome represented a stark departure from recent trends in the series.

In Ray Goff's senior season as a Bulldog, the Classic City Canines had invaded Memorial Stadium and run away with a 41–0 victory to give Georgia its 28th victory over the Orange and Purple in its last 35 tries. During that 70-season span (1907–1976), the Red and Black had enjoyed a trio of two-game winning streaks and longer series victory skeins of three games (1911–1913), eight games (1964–1973), and 10 games (1920–1954).

After taking seven straight meetings between 1900 and 1906, the Country Gentlemen had beaten the Bulldogs in 1909, 1914, 1955, and 1974 and tied the Athenians in 1910, 1919, and 1963. Otherwise, the rivalry had been tinted red rather than orange for seven decades. Since the Orange and Purple's 7–6 victory between the hedges in 1977, though, the series had been remarkably even. In the 11 years from 1977 to 1987, the two teams were 5–5–1 against one another. Moreover, not only was the record dead even for that period, the games were close, too.

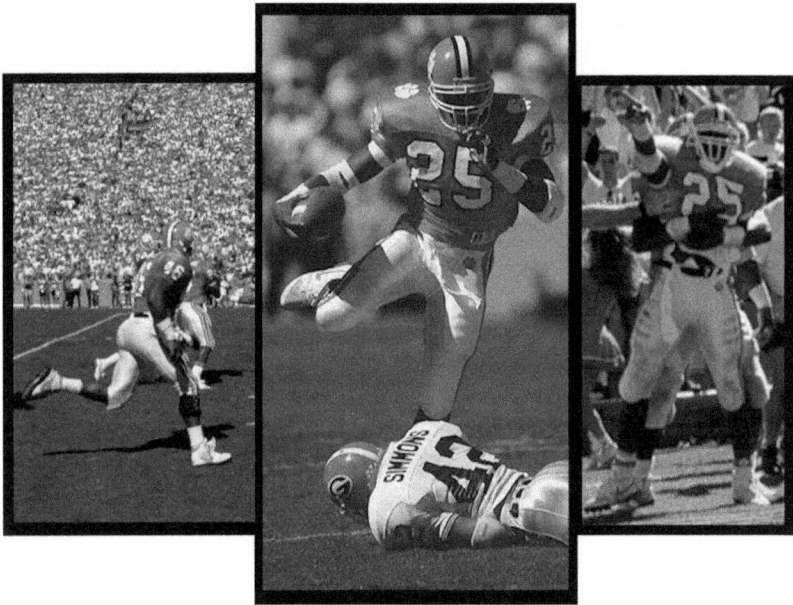

Freshman running back Ronald Williams had a breakout day against Georgia, rushing for 134 yards and two touchdowns, including one on a 51-yard run in the first quarter.

That stretch of Clemson-Georgia showdowns ended with margins of one, 12, five, four, 10, six, zero, three, seven, three, and one points, respectively. The combined scores of those 11 affairs came to 171 points for the Classic City Canines and 159 for the Fort Hill Felines, for an average final score of 16–15.

The 1986 contest was the only one of those in which either team scored more than 26 points against the other and, in eight of the 11 outings, even the *winning* (or, in one case, tying) team was held to 20 or fewer ticks on the scoreboard. During the nine seasons in which Vince Dooley and Danny Ford butted heads on the football field, each team won four times and the rival squads tied once, with Georgia narrowly outscoring Clemson by a cumulative 153–152 margin between 1979 and 1987.

It was into that context of low-scoring, closely-contested games that the Tigers dropped the 34-3 bombshell that shook up the series. Clemson had not scored so many points against Georgia since 1914; in the interim, the Country Gentlemen had been held in the single digits nine times and shut out entirely on 13 other occasions.

The 31-point margin of victory was the South Carolinians' fourth-largest ever over the Bulldogs, trailing only the 34-point manhandling of 1900, the 35-point steamrolling of 1905, and the 36-point throttling of 1902. The magnitude of the beatdown could have been even worse, in light of the fact that the Tigers earned first downs at the Red and Black's 11, 12, and 16 yard lines on a trio of drives that ended in Jungaleer field goals.

It was the first time in 75 years and 39 series meetings that Clemson had beaten Georgia by more than 19 points. Not only did the Country Gentlemen own a three-game winning streak over the Red and Black for the first time since the Roosevelt administration—*Teddy* Roosevelt, that is—they had won the game in undeniably decisive fashion for the first time in more than a third of a century. Ken Hatfield was not exaggerating when he claimed after the game, "This was Clemson football at its best."

The rest of the two teams' respective seasons merely confirmed the reality of the gap between them that had been exposed in their lopsided meeting. Clemson dropped a two-point decision in Atlanta against a 15th-ranked Yellow Jacket squad that would go on to share the national title with Colorado. The Jungaleers outrushed the Engineers by more than 200 yards, ran 40 more offensive plays than the Ramblin' Wreck, and retained custody of the pigskin for more than 38 minutes but fell to the Golden Tornado when a 61-yard field goal attempt by the Tigers came up short.

Clemson ended the season on a tear, beginning with a road win over an N.C. State club headed for an All-American Bowl triumph. A victory over Wake Forest gave the Tigers the 500th win in their gridiron history and the Fort Hill Felines limited Mack Brown's Tar Heels to 38 rushing yards in North Carolina's loss to the Jungaleers. Hatfield's team finished out the regular season with a home win over South Carolina.

The Orange and Purple's nine-win regular season (in which the Tigers' only two losses were to teams that posted a collective 19–4–1 record) earned them a trip to Tampa for their first Hall of Fame Bowl appearance on New Year's Day. DeChane Cameron earned MVP honors in the course of rushing for 76 yards and throwing for 141 in a 30–0 victory over John Mackovic's Illinois Fighting Illini.

The bowl win gave the Clemson senior class its record-setting 40th career victory and marked the largest margin ever by which the Tigers had won a postseason tilt. The Country Gentlemen's 10-2 record matched that posted by each of Ford's last three squads and, by guiding the Orange and Purple to a No. 9 ranking in the final AP poll, Ken Hatfield became the first ACC coach to take a team to a top 10 finish in his rookie season.

Not every head coach involved in the Clemson-Georgia show-down had similar success at replacing a legend, though. Ray Goff's 6–6 season in his first autumn on the job gave Georgia its first non-winning record since 1977 and the Dogs were in for an even worse fate in 1990. In 1914, the Red and Black's 35–13 loss to the Fort Hill Felines served as a galvanizing force for the Athenians, who righted the ship in the squad's last two outings.

This time, however, the Bulldogs' crushing loss at Death Valley sent them into a tailspin. A 28–12 home loss to Gator Bowl-bound Ole Miss followed. Even though a 39–28 victory over a Vanderbilt outfit headed for a second consecutive 1–10 campaign improved the Red and Black's record to 4–3, the worst was yet to come for Goff's squad.

A two-point loss to Kentucky in a night game in Lexington dropped the Bulldogs back to .500 heading into an open date. The bye week didn't help, as the Classic City Canines fell to Florida, Peach Bowl-bound Auburn, and Georgia Tech by a grand total of 111–40. The Athenians' last three opponents all ended the season ranked in the top 20 in the AP poll.

The seven losses were the most by a Georgia squad since 1961 and, for the first time in five years, the Red and Black went winless against the Gators, the Plainsmen, and the Yellow Jackets. The Bulldogs did not receive a bowl bid for the first time since 1979. Goff's career record now stood at 10–13.

Both teams had hoped for big things when longtime coaching leg-ends left the sidelines, but the Tigers' 1990 rout of the Bulldogs made it perfectly plain which of the two schools was enjoying the smooth-er transition. For all the turmoil swirling around the program at the time of Danny Ford's departure, Ken Hatfield's Fort Hill Felines hadn't missed a beat, but the Classic City Canines had taken a tumble, de-spite having had a one- year head start in making the change, as Ray Goff's first couple of Georgia clubs produced results much more akin to Johnny Griffith's than to Vince Dooley's.

In spite of the two teams' 7-7-1 record versus one another over the last 15 series meetings, an impartial observer doubtless would have predicted a coming run of Clemson dominance in the rivalry during the decade that had begun with a game every bit as one- sided as the final margin suggested. Such a forecast, however, would have proven flawed because of its failure to account for several unforeseeable factors, including the rocky relations between the head coach and the fan base at one campus and the arrival of a pro-style passing attack and the quarterback capable of leading it at the other.

Together, these ingredients would steer the series in a direction decidedly different from the one the 1990 clash hinted was the more likely, as the upper hand in the rivalry began unexpectedly to shift from the Palmetto State back to the Peach State. That reality, however, would not change the fact of Clemson's performance against an over-matched Georgia squad in Death Valley that day. Truly, the Tigers had won a victory for the ages.

1991

Dogs Win with D, Zeier

The two teams' respective rankings aside, it was a typical situation for a Clemson-Georgia game: the contest was tied at a field goal per side with under a minute remaining in the first half.

The Bulldogs, who were also the underdogs, had possession of the ball in their own territory. On first down, scatback Garrison Hearst had coughed up the oval at the end of a four-yard run, but a facemask penalty against the Tigers had allowed the Athenians to keep custody of the pigskin.

Under the circumstances, second-string quarterback Eric Royce Zeier, playing in his fifth game as a true freshman, surely would kneel out the clock and send the game to halftime with the Red and Black improbably tied with an opponent ranked in the top 10—the sort of opponent Georgia had never beaten in the Ray Goff era—on a warm evening in Athens before 85,434 fans. Goff and his offensive coordinator, Wayne McDuffie, had other ideas, though.

At his coaches' instruction, Zeier took the snap from center and dropped back to pass as the seconds ticked away. Facing the No. 1 defense in the country, which was allowing only 4.7 points per game, Zeier unleashed a bomb 60 yards downfield to split end Arthur Marshall, who was starting his first game since breaking his leg in the previous season's opening outing. (In the autumn's first four contests, the split end spot had been manned by future University of Georgia athletic director Damon Evans.)

Marshall made a spectacular catch at the Tigers' eight yard line. On the next play, Clemson cornerback Eric Geter had Georgia flanker Andre Hastings in man coverage. Although the Bulldogs had averaged an SEC-worst 130.65 passing yards per game the year before, the addition of McDuffie and quarterback coach Steve Ensminger to Goff's staff had brought such previously foreign concepts as the shotgun to the Georgia offense.

The flanker ran a fade pattern. Zeier, who would finish the night with 249 passing yards and a pair of TD tosses, put the ball into the air and Hastings, who caught five passes for 54 yards and two scores, went up to get it. The two connected for the first touchdown of the game with just 13 seconds remaining until halftime.

Momentum donned a red jersey and the Dogs headed to the locker room with a 10–3 advantage thanks to a three-play scoring drive requiring fewer than 30 seconds of clock time. Jungaleer skipper Ken Hatfield later conceded, "The touchdown right before half just broke our backs."

It wasn't supposed to be this way. Hatfield's second Clemson squad arrived in Athens sporting a 3–0 record and a No. 6 AP ranking. The Tigers were winners of eight straight games dating back to the previous season's 10–2 campaign, which featured a 31-point thrashing of a hapless Georgia squad that limped to its first seven-loss season in 30 years.

In a trio of home dates during the month of September, the South Carolinians had blanked Appalachian State in a 34–0 shutout, waxed Temple by a 37–7 final margin, and gutted out a win over defending co-national champion Georgia Tech by a 9–7 score to deal the Yellow Jackets their first ACC loss in ten league games.

The Bulldogs, in the meantime, had dubbed their season "Operation Turnaround" and begun by routing Western Carolina in the opener, trouncing the Catamounts by 48 points while holding an opponent scoreless for the first time in nearly a decade. In his debut as the backup to senior quarterback Greg Talley, Zeier had connected on 15 of his 22 attempts for 172 yards and a pair of touchdowns.

Georgia followed that up with a 21-point win over LSU between the hedges. Although new Louisiana State head coach Curley Hallman would guide the Bayou Bengals to their third straight losing season, the conference win was a confidence builder heading into Tuscaloosa, where the Red and Black had never won.

The euphoria ended before 70,000 fans and a regional television audience on ABC as Blockbuster Bowl-bound Alabama won a defen-

Bulldog flanker Andre Hastings's eight-yard touchdown reception just before halftime changed the momentum in the 1991 Clemson-Georgia game.

sive struggle, 10–0. There followed a lackluster effort in Athens against Cal State-Fullerton in a game that was tied at 14 late in the second period and ended with an unconvincing 27–14 Georgia victory.

The two teams were set to collide on a national ESPN telecast on October 5 in the first night game played in Sanford Stadium since 1985. Despite the fact that the unranked Bulldogs had the benefit of home field advantage, the oddsmakers decreed that the Country Gentlemen were a seven-point favorite. Certainly, the Clemson players sounded confident of victory when speaking of a Georgia squad that had never beaten the Tigers in the fifth game of a season that followed a losing record the year before.

After helping hold Georgia Tech to 282 yards of total offense one week earlier, Orange-and-Purple linebacker Levon Kirkland commented, "I think we have proven that we can get pressure on any quarterback in the country." Clemson middle guard Rob Bodine concurred, boasting: "If the offense can get us three points, that should be enough for the job." That statement did not appear overly bold after Cal State-Fullerton, which had the worst defense in the country in 1990, recorded three sacks of Georgia quarterbacks between the hedges.

The seemingly insurmountable obstacle confronting the Dogs did not diminish Ray Goff's confidence, however. "It's a new game and a new day," he declared on the Monday before the contest. "Any time you perceive a game will be an easy game," he added, "your players are going to struggle." Their faith perhaps bolstered by Goff's belief in his team, the writers of The Red and Black—and one in particular—felt free to engage in a war of words with the South Carolinians.

Mike Floyd, a sportswriter for the Georgia student newspaper, published a column on the Tuesday sports page which asked, "What does Clemson have?" While conceding that "Clemson was one of the nation's most successful teams during the 1980s, and its eight Top-20 finishes in the past 10 years is a grand achievement," Floyd peered back into the Tigers' past and found the Country Gentlemen lacking in national tradition. Argued the *Red and Black* columnist:

"Take a look at the top 20 bowl teams of all time. No Clemson. Gaze at a list of the 40 winningest programs in the history of college football. Still no Clemson. How about a list of the 30 best teams in regards to winning percentage? Gee, there must be a mistake, because Clemson can't be found there either."

Floyd's column, which was scheduled to appear in the following Friday's weekly edition of the Clemson student newspaper, *The Tiger,* got a head start on making the rounds in the Palmetto State, as numerous radio stations in the Greenville and Spartanburg areas read the column on the air. This prompted members of the Orange-and-Purple faithful to call in to local drive-time radio shows to voice their displeasure with the sentiments shared by Mike Floyd, whose father, John, was a Spartanburg resident.

After the elder Floyd reportedly received threatening telephone calls on Thursday afternoon—one of which warned him to "watch his house tonight"—his son remarked, "I may have been a little hard on their town, but it was obviously in jest. But what I said about their national tradition—facts are facts. They don't have one."

Not to be outdone in the blistering exchange, *Tiger* sports editor Geoff Wilson fired back with a column of his own. "In the last 10 years," he noted, "while Clemson has been busy churning out top-notch football, the only thing the University of Georgia has been known and recognized for is music." Pointing to the Bulldogs' dismal 1990 campaign and Ray Goff's 13–14 career ledger, Wilson observed: "There is no more probation at Clemson; the program has gone uphill since its end. There never was any probation at Georgia;

the program has gone downhill fast." *The Tiger* sports editor then concluded:

"Tradition is nice. The South under Reconstruction spoke of tradition—after it had lost. It seems most of the people who speak of tradition no longer have it. Look at recent history—in football, that's all that matters...[L]ast time I checked, the scoreboard read Clemson 34, Georgia 3. Take a good look at the scoreboard this Saturday night, Georgia fans: It will only read as a 0–0 tie for so long."

Thus was the stage set for the latest installment of an increasingly heated rivalry. Wilson proved prescient in at least one respect, as the scoreboard showed a scoreless deadlock for merely one minute and 45 seconds before Bulldog place-kicker Kanon Parkman connected on a 44-yard field goal to give the home team an early lead.

Georgia took the opening kickoff and moved 32 yards in seven plays. Most of that real estate was covered by a 22-yard completion from Talley to Marshall on third and eight to carry the Athenians inside the South Carolinians' 25 yard line. Parkman, a freshman, had taken over the field goal-kicking duties against Cal State-Fullerton and his first-quarter three-pointer against the Tigers was just his third collegiate attempt and his first of longer than 26 yards.

Clemson attempted to answer on the last play of the first quarter, on which tailback Ronald Williams bolted 54 yards through the center of the Georgia D. The big play threatened to give the visitors a huge boost, much as Williams's 51-yard touchdown run against the Dogs the year before had done, but safety Mike Jones ran him down from behind and stripped the ball from the Orange-and-Purple running back.

The Athenians' Willie Jennings, who had been moved from defensive tackle to nose guard during spring drills, reclaimed possession for the Classic City Canines by recovering the loose ball at the Red and Black's 27 yard line. One year earlier, Georgia's only points against the Jungaleers had come after Jennings scooped up a fumble at the home team's 27 yard line in Death Valley, and now the Bulldog defensive lineman had repeated that feat at the home team's 27 yard line in Sanford Stadium. It was one of five turnovers forced by the Georgia defense, which snagged a trio of interceptions (including a first-quarter pick by cornerback Chuck Carswell) and pounced on the ball two of the four times the Tigers put the pigskin on the ground.

Determined to bend but not break, the Bulldogs conceded everything to the opposition except points. Clemson quarterback DeChane Cameron matched Zeier pass for pass, hooking up on 19 of his 38 throws and amassing 246 yards through the air...just nine fewer feet than the Athenians' freshman signal caller tallied. The Tigers led in first downs (16–15), rushing yards (149–77), and return yards (29–16), whereas the Red and Black punted nine times to the Orange and Purple's five (although the home team's cause was aided by the fact that Bulldog punter Scot Armstrong twice penned Clemson inside its own five yard line).

The Country Gentlemen had a 100-yard rusher (Williams, who reached the century mark on 13 carries) and almost had a 100-yard receiver in Larry Ryans, who had five grabs for 95 yards and the visiting club's lone touchdown. Nevertheless, the Bulldogs won the battle of the big plays, ending the first period with Jones's forced fumble and wrapping up the half with Zeier's long strike to Marshall, whose half-dozen receptions accounted for 128 of Georgia's 283 aerial yards.

Zeier took over for Talley in the opening period and the freshman quarterback was sacked late in the second stanza by linebacker Wayne Simmons. The football came loose and Kirkland pounced upon the pigskin to jump-start a Tiger drive covering 23 yards in six snaps and slightly more than two minutes. When Clemson's Nelson Welch split the uprights on a 27-yard field goal with 45 seconds remaining until halftime, a 3–3 deadlock at intermission appeared certain.

Goff and Zeier had other ideas, however, and, with the winds having shifted distinctly in the Bulldogs' favor, the home team picked up where it left off in the third quarter. With not quite nine minutes to play in the period, Parkman answered Welch's three-pointer with a 27-yarder of his own to extend the Georgia lead to 13–3. The Bulldog freshman's successful field goal try capped off a 71-yard march highlighted by Zeier's 57- yard strike to running back Mack Strong.

Although Parkman would miss a 46-yard attempt later in the third quarter, Welch made good on a try from 29 yards out with just under two minutes remaining in the frame to shave the Athenians' lead back down to seven points. The Jungaleer score came at the end of a four-minute drive traversing almost 60 yards in 10 snaps, but the Fort Hill Felines proved incapable of punching it into the end zone.

Ken Hatfield was at a loss to explain why his team had been unable to close the deal on offense. "I don't know why we stalled," the Clemson coach offered after the game. Georgia linebacker Dwayne Simmons gave an explanation following the Red-and-Black victory, however. Simmons credited the Country Gentlemen's pregame "trash talk comments" with getting his "adrenaline flowing." The senior linebacker advised the rival Tigers, "Don't write a check if you're going to bounce it."

Georgia had scored the first points of the game with 13:15 remaining in the first quar ter, and, with 13:15 remaining in the contest, Hastings caught a seven-yard touchdown strike from Zeier to open up a 14-point lead, Georgia's largest of the night. The scoring drive had been set up by Marshall's return of the kickoff following Welch's second field goal.

The senior split end brought the ball out to midfield and the Dogs took nearly three and a half minutes to move the remaining 48 yards separating them from the end zone. Zeier completed a pair of third-down passes on the 11-play march, including a 12-yard hookup with Marshall that moved the chains on third and nine from the Georgia 35.

The score remained unchanged until Cameron connected with Ryans from 18 yards away to cut the Clemson deficit to 20–12. The South Carolinians had flown down the field in four snaps, picking up 66 yards in 44 seconds to notch their first touchdown with 4:29 showing on the scoreboard. The ensuing two-point try fell incomplete, so the Tigers continued to trail by eight.

The Fort Hill Felines got the ball back but turned the ball over on downs deep in their own territory after an unsuccessful pass attempt on fourth down. The Bulldogs took over inside the Clemson 15 yard line and took less than a minute to tack on another score. Hearst, who led all Georgia rushers with 41 yards on 20 carries, closed out the contest with a one-yard touchdown run with 79 seconds remaining in the fourth quarter. Kickoff and PAT specialist Todd Peterson then booted his third extra point of the evening to ice the game for the Bulldogs and make the final margin 27–12.

Despite being outweighed by the Clemson defensive front by almost 20 pounds per man, the Red-and-Black offensive line provided excellent protection, giving starter Greg Talley and SEC co-offensive player of the week Eric Zeier ample time to throw without allowing either quarterback to be sacked. On the other side of the ball, Dwayne Simmons earned conference defensive player of the week honors on the strength of 13 tackles, a pair of pass breakups, and a sack.

The win was Georgia's first over a top 10 team since the Bulldogs' upset victory over Auburn on the Plains in the infamous "between the hoses" game of 1986. Mike Floyd, no doubt relishing the opportunity to have the last laugh, reported in the following Monday's edition of *The Red and Black:* "The Bulldogs terminated Clemson's eight-game overall winning streak, dashed its national title hopes and handed the Tigers their worst defeat since they dropped a 30–14 decision to Georgia Tech in 1989."

Floyd was not alone in his delight at the outcome. Stephanie Goff had wept openly as the final seconds ticked away and her husband, the Georgia head coach, remarked afterward: "This feels awfully good. It's a great day. The Braves won and we won." The day not only had seen the Atlanta Braves clinch the National League West championship for the first of their 14 consecutive division titles, but longtime Bulldog rivals Auburn and Georgia Tech also had lost to Southern Miss and N.C. State, respectively.

Levon Kirkland acknowledged that Eric Zeier had been more mobile than the Clemson linebacker had anticipated after the standout freshman signal caller had become the first Red-and-Black QB to top 200 passing yards in a single outing since the final game of the Vince Dooley era. Arthur Marshall, noting that "Clemson had talked a lot of trash about our offense," admitted in the aftermath of the contest: "We just wanted to come out and take it to them. This was the most emotional game I've ever played in."

The victory earned the Dogs their first national ranking (No. 22 in both polls) since the end of the 1988 season. A week later, with Zeier now ensconced as the starter, the Red and Black handed 23rd-ranked Ole Miss a 37–17 hammering in Oxford to claim their first road victory in two years. A shocking upset in Nashville dealt the Classic City Canines their first loss to Vanderbilt in 18 years—since Ray Goff was the quarterback of the Georgia freshman team, in fact—but the Bulldogs rebounded to drop 49 points on Kentucky in a homecoming win.

Although the Athenians failed to compete in Jacksonville with a Florida Gator squad bound for its first official conference crown and a Sugar Bowl berth under second-year coach Steve Spurrier, the Dogs' 45–13 setback by the St. John's River did not discourage them. Georgia rebounded by beating Auburn at home and Aloha Bowl-bound Georgia Tech on the road to claim a spot in the Independence Bowl opposite Arkansas for the Razorbacks' final game before departing the Southwest Conference for the greener pastures of the SEC.

The usual suspects were on display in Shreveport, where Eric Zeier connected with Arthur Marshall and Andre Hastings for two first-quarter touchdowns and Kanon Park man added a second-quarter field goal to give Georgia a 17–0 lead. Despite a second-half rally, Arkansas came up short as the Dogs beat the Hogs by a 24–15 final margin to earn a final Associated Press poll ranking of 17th on the strength of a 1991 season in which the Red and Black defeated six of the seven teams to which Georgia had lost the year before, including all three sets of Tigers: Auburn, LSU, and Clemson.

Despite having come up short between the hedges, the South Carolinians bounced back to have a solid season of their own. Following a 20-all tie with a Virginia outfit headed for a Gator Bowl bid and an open date on the ensuing Saturday, the Country Gentlemen came out clad in purple jerseys for the first time since the 1930s to face an

N.C. State club sporting a 6–0 record and a No. 12 national ranking.

The Tigers gambled early in the game, faking a field goal to score their first touchdown on a three-yard run by fullback Rudy Harris. In a game in which freshman Nelson Welch booted a school-record five field goals, Clemson prevailed over the Peach Bowl-bound Wolfpack by a 29–19 score. Wins over Wake Forest and North Carolina by a combined margin of 49–16 followed, setting the stage for the Fort Hill Felines to clinch their twelfth Atlantic Coast Conference championship in the season's final game in Death Valley.

DeChane Cameron completed 13 of his 23 pass attempts for 213 yards in Clemson's 40–7 win over Maryland and the Tiger QB was even better a week later, when the Orange and Purple claimed the state championship with a 41–23 win at South Carolina. Cameron accounted for 322 yards of total offense, gaining 116 of them with his legs and the remaining 206 with his arm. For just the fifth time in school history, the Tigers had a 200- yard passer, a 100-yard rusher, and a 100-yard receiver (Terry Smith) in the same game.

Clemson closed out the regular season in Tokyo, where the Orange and Purple scored 26 fourth-quarter points to pull out a 33–21 victory over Duke in the Coca-Cola Bowl to give Ken Hatfield his 100th win as a college head coach. The Tigers' 9–1–1 finish earned them a No. 13 AP ranking and a Citrus Bowl berth.

Facing the 14th-ranked California Golden Bears in Orlando, the Fort Hill Felines found themselves battling a Pac-10 team enjoying its best season in more than four decades. The squad from Berkeley had lost just two games that fall, a seven-point setback to a Washington club that would capture the national championship in the coaches' poll and a 38–21 loss at Stanford in a rivalry game with a Cardinal team that would win eight of its last nine regular-season outings.

The Tigers, winners of six straight, could not overcome the passing of Cal quarterback Mike Pawlawski, whose 21-for-32, 230-yard per-

formance paced a 37–13 Bears victory to send the Orange and Purple tumbling to a No. 18 final ranking, just behind the Bulldog club
that had dealt Clemson its only other setback of the season. Whatever
squabbles had divided the teams from Lake Hartwell and the Classic
City in the week prior to their showdown, there could be little doubt
that, with both teams finishing in the top 20, Clemson had continued
the uphill trend of its recent history and Georgia had reasserted its
dormant national tradition.

1994

West's First Season Goes South

Three years had passed since Clemson and Georgia last squared off on the gridiron, but what a tumultuous three years they had been. In a two-month span early in 1993, terrorists had undertaken to bomb the World Trade Center in New York City and a 51-day-long standoff between federal agents and David Koresh's Branch Davidians in Waco, Tex., had ended in tragedy with the deaths of nearly 100 people. In the political realm, Arkansas governor Bill Clinton had unseated the incumbent president, George H.W. Bush, in the same year (1992) that the newly-chosen commander-in-chief 's state university had jumped from the Southwest Conference to the Southeastern Conference.

The Razorbacks joined the SEC at the same time as the Bulldogs' and the Tigers' longstanding rivals, the South Carolina Gamecocks. The addition of two new teams boosted the league's membership to an even dozen, allowing the SEC to split into two divisions and set aside the first Saturday in December for the Eastern and Western champions to meet in a conference title game.

The geographic split down the center of the SEC had Georgia competing against Florida, Kentucky, South Carolina, Tennessee, and Vanderbilt in the Eastern Division while Arkansas joined Alabama, Auburn, LSU, Mississippi, and Mississippi State in the Western Division. Meanwhile, the ACC also was getting into the conference expansion business, welcoming longtime independent juggernaut Florida State into the league in 1992, as well.

Quarterback Eric Zeier, who had performed so well against the Country Gentlemen as a true freshman in 1991 that he had started all 35 of the intervening games between consecutive Clemson-Georgia series meetings, was now a senior looking to shatter every passing mark in the Red-and-Black record book. As for the Orange and Purple, they came into Sanford Stadium on October 8 led by a new head coach.

Ken Hatfield had been an odd hire for Clemson from the time he was announced as the Tigers' 22nd head football coach in January 1990, just three days following the resignation of local legend Danny Ford. The Arkansas alum had never meshed well with the Tiger faithful and he did not endear himself to the Fort Hill fans when, in his first ACC outing, he led the Orange and Purple to a 20–7 loss at Virginia. The defeat not only left Hatfield 0–1 in conference play, it marked Clemson's first loss to the Cavaliers ever.

The Tiger coach's first two seasons at the helm produced 19 victories, an ACC championship, and back-to-back New Year's Day bowl berths, but the relationship remained an uneasy one, so a 5–6 record in 1992— Clemson's first losing record since 1976—put Hatfield on the hot seat.

An 8–3 regular-season record the following fall did little to improve the coach's circumstances. Although the Tigers were bound for a December 31 date with Kentucky in the Peach Bowl, they had been manhandled and shut out in a pair of road outings against eventual national champion Florida State (57–0) and Gator Bowl-bound North Carolina (24–0).

Making matters much worse was a midseason setback suffered in Death Valley... to Wake Forest. The loss marked the Demon Deacons' second straight victory over the Country Gentlemen and their first win by the shores of Lake Hartwell since 1961. Wake would go on to complete a 2–9 season in 1993, with the Deacs' only other victory being a home win over Division I-AA Appalachian State.

As evidenced by reduced IPTAY donations and a drop in attendance of almost 10,000 fans per game, the natives were getting restless. Hatfield, who was signed to a five-year deal when he was first hired, asked for a one-year contract extension, and, for the second straight season, his request was denied. The relationship between the coach and the school soured, and, on November 24, 1993, Clemson and Hatfield announced that they would part ways. As the coach put it, "This is not a termination. This is not a resignation. This is a separation."

Many considered that description fitting. *Tiger* staff writer Terry Manning observed that the relationship between Ken Hatfield and the

Fort Hill faithful "was like a bad marriage—the question was not if it would come to an end but when." The former Clemson skipper wound up at Rice, where he would coach for the next 12 years. Hatfield joined John Heisman and Jess Neely among the previous Jungaleer coaches to have guided the Owls after leaving the Palmetto State.

Five days after Hatfield's departure was announced, 39-year-old native Georgian Tommy West was introduced as his successor. Hired after a single season's experience as a head coach (a 4–7 campaign at UT-Chattanooga), he nevertheless was a popular choice because of his long association with the program under Ford. West had been a Clemson assistant from 1982 to 1989, during which period he had been a part of 69 victories, six top 20 finishes, five bowl appearances, and four ACC crowns for the Tigers.

To say the hire was well received would be an enormous understatement. Several Clemson trustees praised the move, using the word "family" in hailing West's return to the shores of Lake Hartwell. The attitude of many Tiger donors was summed up by the booster who handed a $1,000.00 check to IPTAY executive director George Bennett and said, "I'm back in." The new coach met with the players, who cheered and chanted, "We're back! We're back!" 84-year-old Frank Howard declared: "I think he'll be a good one." *The Tiger* noted that "he even looks like Danny Ford."

Upon becoming just the second coach ever to take over a team for a bowl game at the end of a season in which he had not served as an assistant at that school, West began his guidance of the Orange and Purple with a bang when quarterback Patrick Sapp's touchdown pass to wide receiver Terry Smith with 20 seconds remaining on the clock lifted the Country Gentlemen to a one-point win over Kentucky in the first bowl game played in the Georgia Dome.

Not since 1958 had Clemson scored a game-winning TD with so little time remaining and not since Tiger offensive line coach Danny Ford was promoted to replace Charley Pell prior to the 1978 Gator Bowl had a new coach for the Fort Hill Felines kicked off his career with a postseason victory. That win had been a memorable one—the Jungaleers had captured their first win over a Big Ten team in the 17–15 triumph—and West unquestionably benefited from drawing early comparisons to his old boss. "I'm not Danny Ford," the new head coach had assured the Clemson family when he was hired, "but I learned a lot from him."

The young head coach's regular-season debut on September 3, 1994, was therefore an eagerly-anticipated affair, all the more so because the pregame festivities included the induction of legendary Clemson football coach Frank Howard, two-time team captain (and quarterback of the 1978 Gator Bowl championship squad) Steve Fuller, and Banks Mc-Fadden (the starting tailback from the school's first bowl team in 1939) into the Ring of Honor.

The Tigers' opponent was Furman, a Division I-AA team whose coach, Bobby Johnson, was a 1973 Clemson alumnus, a former Jungaleer defensive back, the previous year's defensive coordinator for the Fort Hill Felines, and one of four finalists who had been in contention to replace Ken Hatfield. The Paladins fell to the Orange and Purple by a 27–6 margin and Tommy West improved his record at Fort Hill to 2–0. The going thereafter got a bit rougher.

One week later, the Tigers ended up on the short end of a 29–12 score in a home game against N.C. State. The Peach Bowl-bound Wolfpack, like Furman, was coached by a former Clemson player in second-year skipper Mike O'Cain. There followed a road trip to Charlottesville for the 1,000[th] conference football game in ACC history. Despite a trio of takeaways by Clemson free safety Andre Carter, a Virginia club destined for the Independence Bowl emerged victorious by a 9–6 final margin to give the Cavaliers their second victory over the Country Gentlemen in a five-year span.

Tommy West's first season opener as the Tigers' head coach was highlighted by the induction of Steve Fuller, Frank Howard, and Banks McFadden into Clemson's Ring of Honor.

After an open date, the South Carolinians righted the ship with an October 1 shutout of Maryland which left the Tigers sitting at 2–2 as they lit out for the Peach State, where West had begun his Clemson coaching career with such promise a little over nine months earlier. Awaiting them there was a Georgia squad that had troubles of its own.

Bulldog head coach Ray Goff, whose dismal 1990 season had been epitomized by the 34–3 loss in Death Valley that sent the squad spiraling down to a 4–7 finish, had turned his team's fortunes around with a 9–3 campaign in 1991 highlighted by a 27–12 win over the Jungaleers. A 10–2 record capped off by a New Year's Day bowl win had followed in 1992, but the early departures of key players Andre Hastings and Garrison Hearst had doomed the Dogs the following fall.

The Red and Black limped to a 5–6 finish in 1993 after suffering through the first 0–4 SEC start in school history. The season marked the third autumn with six or more losses in Goff's first five years on the job and gave the Classic City Canines their second losing record in a four-year period after having finished below .500 just once between 1964 and 1989.

Looking to implement another turnaround in 1994, the Bulldogs opened at home against Carquest Bowl-bound South Carolina and immediately made a statement that neither the Palmetto State Poultry nor the rest of the SEC could have overlooked. Well, not quite immediately…it actually was not until the *second* play of the game that Zeier let loose a 77-yard bomb to split end Hason Graham, who hauled in the touchdown pass with only 45 seconds having elapsed in the contest. Behind the Georgia quarterback's 31-for-51, 485-yard, three-touchdown performance, the Bulldogs went on to win 24–21.

A week later, four Georgia fumbles and a 212-yard, four-touchdown rushing effort by Volunteer running back James Stewart caused the Dogs to fall to Tennessee by a 41–23 margin. The Vols ended the season with a Gator Bowl win. The Red and Black took out their frustrations on hapless Northeast Louisiana in a game in which Zeier attempted just 10 passes. Nevertheless, three of his eight completions went for touchdowns against the Indians as Georgia cruised to a 70–6 victory in the course of scoring the most points put up by any Red-and-Black squad since the team's 76–0 victory over The Citadel in 1958.

Larry Bowie's emergence against Ole Miss on September 24 got the Red and Black back on the winning track in SEC play, as the Georgia junior rushed for 77 yards and caught passes for 68 more in his first start of the season in the scatback spot after having gotten the nod in the three previous outings as the Bulldogs' first-string running back. The resulting 17–14 win allowed the Athenians to improve to 2–1 in SEC play, but a golden opportunity slipped through the Classic City Canines' fingers the following Satur day night, when Georgia traveled to Alabama and took a 21–10 lead into the locker room at the end of the first half.

Crimson Tide quarterback Jay Barker came alive after the break, throwing for 276 yards and two touchdowns in the second half. Zeier answered Barker's effort, hooking up with running back Marisa Simpson for a touchdown late in the third period in the play on which the Georgia signal caller unseated Florida's Shane Matthews as the leading passer in SEC history. However, a 49–yard touchdown strike by Barker early in the fourth quarter cut the visitors' lead to 28–26, and, with just over a minute remaining in the game, Bama's Michael Proctor banged home a 32–yard field goal to secure a one-point win for the Tide, who would finish the year with a 12–1 record, a Citrus Bowl victory, and a top five ranking.

Accordingly, it was expected that the Georgia squad that took the field against the Tigers in Sanford Stadium for a regionally-televised contest at 12:08 the following Saturday afternoon would be a deflated unit. Many thought the Dogs would have difficulty rebounding from a heartbreaking defeat to face the team ranked first in the ACC (and ninth in the nation) in scoring defense. As it turned out, nothing could have been farther from the truth.

The game was a study in contrasting styles, as the Bulldogs launched 41 passes into the air while the Tigers ran the ball 55 times. The Classic City Canines completed 24 aerials, the same number the Fort Hill Felines attempted. Clemson's continued commitment to the ground game seemed somewhat curious, in light of the commanding lead Georgia built up on the scoreboard, but the Orange and Purple's reservations about mounting an aerial attack appeared well-founded after visiting quarterback Louis Solomon was picked off by Red-and-Black free safety Corey Johnson on the Country Gentlemen's first possession.

By the time Solomon launched his initial ill-fated aerial, though, the home team already had gotten on the board. Georgia flanker Brice Hunter began the contest with a 38-yard return of the opening kickoff, and, after Eric Zeier absorbed a hit from Tiger bandit Darnell Stephens on the first play from scrimmage, the Bulldogs' senior signal caller found Hunter for a 39-yard completion on the next snap. The six-play drive ended with place-kicker Kanon Parkman booting a 35-yard field goal 88 seconds into the contest.

Over the course of the afternoon, Parkman combined four field goals and four extra points to break Kevin Butler's school record for points scored in a game by a kicker. But ler's was not the only record that would fall on a day that Zeier moved past John Elway and six others on the all-time NCAA career passing list, but two marks just missed being set in Sanford Stadium.

Clemson place-kicker Nelson Welch arrived in Athens one field goal shy of tying Obed Ariri's and Chris Gardocki's shared school mark, but his only three-point try between the hedges came on a 49-yard attempt which Welch missed. Likewise, Zeier needed 25 completions to set a new SEC standard but came up just short by connecting on 24 of his 40 attempts against the Country Gentlemen.

After the Dogs had taken a 3–0 lead, the Orange and Purple went on the march for the first time. Solomon, together with freshman fullback Raymond Priester and sophomore tailback Antwuan Wyatt, guided a drive that yielded a pair of first downs before the first pass attempted by the Tigers' starting quarterback was intercepted. Solomon would end his afternoon with one completion in five attempts for negative passing yardage.

Later in the first quarter, the Red and Black moved 78 yards in four snaps and 82 seconds. Zeier hit split end Jeff Thomas in stride for a 44-yard pickup immediately before Hunter went over the middle and the Georgia quarterback found the Bulldog flanker in the seam of the Clemson zone. Hunter hauled in the 21-yard touchdown pass for the record-setting fourteenth TD reception of his career that gave Georgia a 10–0 advantage.

The Athenians went back on the march in the closing minutes of the opening period. Zeier's running and passing accounted for 47 of the 75 yards the Classic City Canines covered in a 10-play series that saw the Georgia quarterback hooking up with his intended receiver on his last four first-quarter passes. Less than a minute into the second stanza, Parkman capped off the drive by hitting a 34-yarder to extend the Dogs' lead to 13 points.

The game was shaping up well for the Red and Black, but the floodgates would beg in to open as a result of the Country Gentlemen's ensuing possession. Since Corey Johnson had snagged his second career interception to end Clemson's first drive of the contest, the Tigers had been forced to punt the ball away on their next two offensive series, setting the tone for what was to be an eight-punt day for the Orange and Purple.

Clemson started from its own 21 yard line. Solomon was flushed from the pocket on the second play of the drive and forced to throw an ill-advised pass that ended up in the arms of Georgia cornerback Robert Edwards, who now had his second career pick to set alongside Johnson's. The interception gave the ball back to the Bulldog offense on the opponent's 27 yard line...oddly enough, the same stripe at which the Athenians' Willie Jennings had recovered Jungaleer fumbles in each of the previous two series meetings.

Just 18 minutes into the game, Louis Solomon had thrown a pair of passes to unintended receivers wearing red jerseys. By intermission, the Georgians would have more yards off of two Clemson interceptions (10) than the Orange and Purple would have off of two Tiger completions (8). Four plays after Solomon's second pick, it got worse for the visiting South Carolinians.

The Dogs needed just 83 ticks of the game clock to punch the pigskin into the end zone. Zeier escaped a Clemson blitz with a spin move and completed a screen pass to Hason Graham. The senior split end went in untouched for the 16-yard touchdown reception that made it 20–0 with 12 minutes remaining until intermission.

Another Tiger punt followed and, when the South Carolinians got the ball back, a fumble by Wyatt was recovered by Georgia linebacker Randall Godfrey just 14 yards from the Jungaleer goal line. The Clemson tailback's miscue marked the first fumble lost by the Orange and Purple that season.

While the Dogs managed to advance the oval only six feet from the point at which Godfrey pounced upon it, the 49-second possession enabled Parkman to tack on his third three-pointer from 29 yards out to give the Classic City Canines a 23–0 edge with one second more than seven minutes left before the break.

Before an assemblage of 86,117 that represented the largest crowd ever to see the Clemson Tigers play, the Georgia Bulldogs had scored on four of their first five possessions against a Jungaleer defense that had allowed a total of just 44 points in the autumn's first four outings. Eric Zeier had been red-hot and Louis Solomon had been ice-cold, so much so that Tommy West had taken his prize pupil out of the box.

Nealon Greene, a true freshman quarterback from Yonkers, N.Y., thus far had spent the season on the sidelines, but, in the second quarter, the first-year Clemson head coach removed the promising underclassman's redshirt and sent him into the game. For the most part, Greene's initial action in the hostile environment consisted of handing off to his teammates in the offensive backfield, but West explained that he was "trying to find somebody to spark our football team right now."

An otherwise flawless first half for the Red and Black was marred only by a third-down scramble by Zeier late in the second quarter. With less than a minute to go before intermission, the quarterback's attempt to pick up a first down led him to try leaping over Tiger cornerback Dexter McCleon. The sophomore defensive back's helmet collided with Zeier's knee and a hush fell over Sanford Stadium when the Bulldog signal caller came up limping.

The home crowd's fears proved unfounded, however, as Zeier returned in the second half and picked up where he left off the quarter before. He completed two of his first three passes in the third period, the second of which (a 14-yard hookup with Graham) made Zeier the Southeastern Conference's all-time leader in total offense. The Georgia QB finished the day by throwing for 328 yards and a pair of TDs. It was Zeier's 13th career game in which he amassed at least 300 passing yards.

The Fort Hill Felines did not make it easy on him, though. During the break, Clemson had made the decision to switch from the three-man defensive line the Tigers had used in the first half to a four-man forward wall in the final two quarters. The result was that the Orange and Purple forced two fumbles and a punt on the Bulldogs' first four second-half possessions.

Accordingly, the score remained unchanged until three and a half minutes remained in the third period. The Red and Black took more than four minutes to traverse 70 yards in 10 plays. Zeier was sacked, but he shook it off in time to connect with flanker Juan Daniels for a 28-yard gain to the visitors' seven yard line. The drive ended with scatback Hines Ward taking the ball in from two yards out for a touchdown.

With a 30–0 lead and 15 minutes left to play, Ray Goff began pulling his starters from the game. Eric Zeier did not play in the fourth quarter and his backup, redshirt freshman Mike Bobo, attempted only one pass in relief. The South Carolinians' second- string signal caller, however, was put to more effective use, and Nealon Greene's efforts in the second half enabled the Fort Hill Felines finally to get on the board and avoid being shut out by a Georgia squad for the first time since 1978.

Greene guided the Tigers on a 48-yard march taking almost six and a half minutes. The series began inside the final two minutes of the third quarter, when Clemson earned its initial first down of the second half, and the true freshman QB completed four out of five aerials in the 15-play drive. Greene sustained the Country Gentlemen's possession with a fourth-down sneak, and, after the Dogs incurred a pass interference penalty in the end zone on a subsequent fourth down, Wyatt partially atoned for his earlier miscue by scoring on a six-yard run to put up Clemson's first points of the game with just under 11 minutes left in the contest.

Georgia answered on its next possession, taking a little over two minutes to go 46 yards. Scatback Bill Montgomery provided two scampers of 21 yards apiece to gain the ground that allowed Parkman to kick a 35-yard field goal inside of the eight-and-a-half- minute mark. Shortly thereafter, the Bulldogs went 59 yards in almost two and a half minutes to close out the home team's scoring. The six-play drive once more saw a Red-and-Black player break off a pair of 21-yard runs, with Marisa Simpson doing the honors this time. Simpson's one-yard touchdown run with 4:31 showing on the scoreboard gave the home team a 33-point lead.

The Tigers refused to allow that margin to stand. Greene led an 81-yard drive on which the South Carolinians again converted two fourth downs. The freshman QB ran for the first down on one and a 12-yard pass to flanker Kenya Crooks picked up the other. Crooks, a fellow frosh of Greene's who (like Georgia's Brice Hunter) wore the number 88, caught three passes on the Orange and Purple's final scoring drive. By the end of the afternoon, his eight catches for 66 yards set a freshman receiving record.

Crooks was not the only Clemson underclassman who was impressive between the hedges. The Tigers' last points were put on the board at the end of a possession featuring two receptions by rookie wide receiver Tony Horne and a 15-yard scamper on which running back Lamont Pegues escaped four would-be tacklers. Crooks's six-yard TD catch with 19 seconds showing on the game clock made the final score 40–14. The Bulldogs' 26-point margin of victory was Georgia's largest over Clemson since Ray Goff's senior season in 1976.

The visitors' option offense was held in check, as a pass-happy Red-and-Black attack still managed to outgain the South Carolinians on the ground (155–151). The return yards all but offset one another— Georgia led, 134–133—and the Tigers picked up 17 first downs to the

Bulldogs' 20. Astonishingly, the Jungaleers had custody of the football for almost 80 snaps and over 36 minutes while limiting the Dogs to just two third-down conversions.

Tommy West was able to draw encouragement from those figures, as well as from the fact that Nealon Greene led a couple of scoring drives while completing 13 of 19 passes for 102 yards without an interception. Two-thirds of the Tigers' total offense was tallied by freshmen from West's first recruiting class. The Clemson coach noted that, "[a] t one time…we had a freshman quarterback, a freshman halfback, a freshman fullback, and two freshman receivers in the game at the same time."

One week after conceding 493 yards of total offense to Alabama, the Georgia D gave up only 252 yards to Clemson. Following the contest, Godfrey made it clear that this was no accident. "A lot of people thought they were going to run on us like Tennessee," the Georgia linebacker told the press. "That bothered us. After the Tennessee game a lot of people said we couldn't stop the run, but lately I think we have been doing a pretty good job on it. We are coming together, but we have to improve in a few areas to gain respect."

As encouraging as it appeared at the time, the Clemson victory proved not to be a harbinger of better things to come for the Bulldogs. One week later, on a day on which Zeier offset his three touchdown passes with a trio of interceptions, the Red and Black were stunned by Vanderbilt at homecoming as the Commodores amassed 416 rushing yards on the way to the 43–30 upset that gave Vandy its first win between the hedges since 1961.

A second straight shocker appeared to be in the making in Lexington the following Saturday, as an errant pass by Zeier was picked off and returned 61 yards for Kentucky's go-ahead touchdown. Georgia's senior signal caller made up for the miscue by completing a 28-yard TD toss to Graham to put the Red and Black out in front for good in a 34–30 contest in which there were seven lead changes.

The only difference between the Bulldogs' 1994 meeting with Florida and those that had preceded it during the Steve Spurrier era was the venue; with the Gator Bowl in the process of being replaced by the stadium which was to accommodate Jacksonville's new NFL expansion franchise, Georgia had agreed to a two-year home-and-home arrangement with the Saurians and, on their first trip to Gainesville since 1931, the Classic City Canines were thumped to the tune of 52–14 by a Sugar Bowl-bound Gator squad.

Although the season ended on the upswing with an inexplicable tie at Auburn to snap the Plainsmen's 20-game winning streak and a 48-10 throttling of Georgia Tech between the hedges, the Bulldogs' 6-4-1 ledger was deemed inadequate to earn the Red and Black a postseason invitation. Many among the Georgia faithful were rankled by the fact that South Carolina was awarded a bowl bid, in as much as the Gamecocks had a worse record (6–5) and had lost to the Dogs head-to-head.

Part of what put the Palmetto State Poultry over the top undoubtedly was a 33–7 season-ending win over Clemson at Memorial Stadium. That setback finished a substan dard season for West's Tigers, who followed up their defeat in Athens with road losses to a Duke club bound for its first January bowl game since the 1960 season and to a Florida State squad steamrolling its way to an eighth straight season of double-digit victories.

The three-game losing streak dropped the Orange and Purple's record to 2–5. Some part of the season was salvaged with three straight wins over Wake Forest, North Carolina, and Georgia Tech. Louis Solomon ran for 159 yards in the 24–8 victory over Wake, setting a new school record for rushing yards in a game by a quarterback.

Even though there was little pride to be taken in the achievement of outdueling conference opponents who would finish with records of 3–8 and 1–10 (as the Demon Deacons and the Yellow Jackets, respectively, did), the Tiger D rose up against the 12th-ranked Tar Heels in Chapel Hill, limiting UNC to just 11 yards on the ground while Nelson Welch used five field goals and an extra point to become the Orange and Purple's all-time scoring leader in the 28–17 upset over Sun Bowl-bound North Carolina.

With bowl eligibility in the balance, Clemson came up short at home in the final game against in-state rival South Carolina. Even though Nealon Greene had ended the autumn as the Fort Hill Felines' leading passer in spite of the freshman quarterback's having started only five games, the Tigers also were left without a postseason berth.

1994 marked the first season since 1972 in which neither Clemson nor Georgia went to a bowl game, but, as somber as that reality may have left partisans both in the Classic City and alongside Lake Hartwell, there was another unsettling undercurrent to the rivalry, for, on both sides of the border, it was widely known that the following year's clash between the Bulldogs and the Tigers was the last scheduled series meeting between the two schools. Although both teams' fans hoped for more successful seasons in 1995, neither set of boosters was pleased by the knowledge that the rivalry might well be one game away from coming to an end.

1995

Kirtsey Takes a Bow

When the two teams met for what was at the time their final scheduled series meeting, Clemson and Georgia fans alike found themselves feeling increasingly dissatisfied, and for exactly the same reason: a well-liked longtime assistant with unimpeachable ties to the program had been promoted to the post of head coach, and both the Orange and Purple's Tommy West and the Red and Black's Ray Goff appeared to many of their teams' partisans to be in over their heads.

West, a former assistant under Danny Ford, had been victorious straight out of the gate when he guided the Tigers to a win in the 1993 Peach Bowl, but his first full season at the helm in Fort Hill had soured the following fall, when his club stumbled to its second 5–6 finish in a three-year period. When West became the first Clemson coach to miss out on a bowl game in his rookie campaign since Red Parker in 1973, the honeymoon came to an abrupt end.

Five games into his second season, West was continuing to struggle. The Tigers had opened the autumn with a 55–9 smashing of Division I-AA Western Carolina, only to fall to Florida State seven days later. The Seminoles won their 26th straight ACC contest since joining the league in 1992, claiming the Tribe's fourth consecutive conference win over Clemson by a 45–26 margin—in Death Valley, no less—*en route* to a 10-win season and an Orange Bowl berth opposite Notre Dame.

After a victory on the road over a Wake Forest team that would go winless in Atlantic Coast Conference play, the Tigers returned home to host Virginia. The Wahoos had beaten the Country Gentlemen in Charlottesville the year before, which was rough enough; Clemson had held a 29–0 series lead over the Cavaliers following Ford's final season in 1989, but the Orange and Purple had gone 2–2–1 against the Hoos in the 1990s, with both losses coming on the road.

West's stature in the Clemson community was not improved by Virginia's 22–3 victory over the Fort Hill Felines on September 23, a date which marked the Cavs' first win ever in Death Valley. A 43–22 road win seven days later against an N.C. State squad bound for a 3–8 finish did little to salve the Tiger faithful after the South Carolinians' loss to the team from the Old Dominion, which would go on to share the ACC crown with FSU.

Meanwhile, Goff, a former Georgia quarterback and assistant under Vince Dooley, occupied an even hotter seat in Athens. After a disheartening 6–4–1 season the year before left the Bulldogs home for the holidays for a second straight season for the first time since the early 1960s, Dooley, as the school's athletic director, had issued a declaration that Goff would have to show "significant improvement" to retain his job after 1995.

The season that would decide the Bulldog coach's fate began between the hedges against South Carolina. The Georgia fan base was divided, but Goff's vocal detractors had issued an ultimatum: "If you can't beat the poultry, go back to Moultrie." The Colquitt County native survived his first test, as the visiting Gamecocks' 14–7 halftime lead evaporated after intermission when junior Robert Edwards, a converted cornerback who had been moved to scatback in the final week of spring practice, set a school record by scoring five touchdowns in his first game in the offensive backfield.

The 42–23 shellacking of South Carolina earned a national ESPN audience for the Classic City Canines' next outing against Tennessee in Knoxville. In the third quarter, Edwards scored his second TD of the evening to pull the Bulldogs within three points of the Volunteers and quarterback Mike Bobo connected with split end Juan Daniels for the go-ahead score later in the period.

Unfortunately, the third quarter also saw Edwards forced from the game with a season-ending fracture to his left foot and Georgia went on to lose by a field goal to the Big Orange. The Vols ended the autumn with an 11–1 record, a Citrus Bowl victory, and a top three final ranking in both major polls.

A 40–13 pounding of New Mexico State followed before the Red and Black were on the road again, this time bound for Oxford and a date with Ole Miss. The injury bug once more leapt up to bite the Bulldogs in the hindquarters, as a fractured knee suffered by Bobo in the second quarter cost the Classic City Canines their starting signal caller and doomed the Dogs to an 18–10 setback against the Rebels.

The question mark at quarterback came no closer to being resolved at home against Alabama on September 30, as six Georgia turnovers transformed a defensive struggle into a rout and the Crimson Tide returned home with a 31–0 victory. Sporting a 2–3 record and with their season (and their coach's job) hanging by a thread, the Bulldogs packed their bags one more time and headed up I-85 to Clemson.

They did so with their offensive backfield in a state of flux. After Bobo was lost for the season in the game against Ole Miss, scatback Hines Ward had gotten the start under center against Bama. Ward had played quarterback in high school, but his effort after only a week's worth of practice at the position failed to produce so much as a single scoring drive. Third-string quarterback Brian Smith came on in relief of Ward against the Red Elephants and even his anemic stat line (9 of 29 for 60 yards, no touchdowns, and two interceptions) was enough to win him the starting job against Clemson.

The scatback position was even more uncertain. Ward had taken over for Edwards against New Mexico State, rushing the ball 18 times for 65 yards and a score. The following week, Selma Calloway had stepped into the position against the Rebels, but the game's leading rusher, Larry Bowie, tallied 61 yards on 10 carries to earn the starting job against Alabama. He performed capably in that role, rushing 24 times for 94 yards, but a groin pull took Bowie out of the lineup in the third quarter.

Accordingly, against the Tigers, Georgia was forced to field a fifth different starting scatback in as many outings. The duties of the position next devolved upon Torin Kirtsey, a true freshman out of Jacksonville, Fla., who, despite being listed at only 180 pounds, had rushed for nearly 2,750 yards in his final two years of high school.

Many in the Palmetto State already were familiar with Kirtsey, in spite of the fact that he was a native Floridian. The first-year collegian had verbally committed to South Carolina be fore signing with the Dogs, causing *The Greenville News*'s Tom Layton to call him "Georgia's turncoat Gamecock." Even so, though, the true freshman (who was making his first career start) had not yet become a household name, as evidenced by the fact that the News's Dan Foster mistakenly referred to the scatback as "Kirksey" five times in his postgame column.

Like Edwards in the first game of the season, Kirtsey was destined to provide a career performance in his first-string debut. Although he did so against a Clemson defensive line depleted by injuries, he also did so in the presence of an impassioned home crowd of 83,500 who were on hand to commence the "centennial celebration" commemorating 100 years of Tiger football in a night game at Death Valley on October 7.

The Orange and Purple donned special "turn back the clock" uniforms for the occasion, taking the field clad in replicas of the uniforms worn by the 1939 Tigers, the first Clemson team to attend a bowl game. The outfits consisted of dark blue pants, orange jerseys emblazoned with dark blue numerals, and blue helmets bearing a pair of criss-crossing orange stripes. (Since the final scheduled rivalry showdown was not being televised, the Clemson athletic administration sent one of the throwback uniforms to ESPN for analyst Craig James to model on "College Gameday.") For the first time in more than a quarter- century, the Fort Hill Felines took the field wearing football suits without a paw on them.

Tommy West, who said beforehand that he wanted "to take the run away" from the Dogs and indicated an intention to focus on the "exceptional player" Hines Ward, expected an electric atmosphere by the shores of Lake Hartwell. "The Georgia game is always a big, big week at Clemson," the Tiger coach explained. Noting that the timing of the game and the centennial celebration would heighten the energy level, West observed: "Then you make it the last game of the series...I think it will be probably as exciting a day as there has been at Clemson leading up to the game." The lineup of pregame festivities, including the Tiger walk at 4:45 that afternoon, rivaled that preceding the 1932 Clemson-Georgia tilt.

The Bulldogs came in as six-point underdogs and, after neither offense proved productive on its opening possession, the Country Gentlemen launched a 73-yard drive on their second series. Aside from a single swing pass netting a couple of yards, the 16-play march was entirely on the ground, with tailback Raymond Priester and fullback Emory Smith together tallying 56 yards along the way.

One of Smith's runs out of the Tigers' "Wham Right" formation came on a fourth-down scamper that moved the chains to the visitors' 32 yard line. The junior fullback went the opposite way out of the same formation at the end of the drive, running behind Clemson left guard Will Young and escaping Bulldog bandit end Frank Watts's would-be tackle on the one-foot dive into the end zone that got the Tigers on the board first with 2:39 remaining in the first quarter.

Place-kicker Jeff Sauve's ensuing extra point try was good enough to give Clemson a 7–0 lead. The scoring drive had taken up almost eight minutes of clock time and a Jungaleer offense that had averaged over 400 yards against eventual ACC co-champions Florida State and Virginia appeared to be well on its way to another outstanding outing. However, after picking up 71 rushing yards on their second possession, the Tigers would garner only 108 more in the remainder of the game. Following that first-quarter score, Clemson would be limited to just seven first downs.

The Red and Black came into Death Valley ranked eighth nationally against the run and a second-quarter defensive adjustment enabled the Athenians to prevent the hometown ballcarriers from skirting the edges of the line. Meanwhile, the Dogs began moving the ball on the Orange-and-Purple D on the strength of Kirtsey's 38-carry evening. Georgia forced Clemson to punt from its own end zone and the freshman back went on a 23-yard jaunt on the first snap of the ensuing

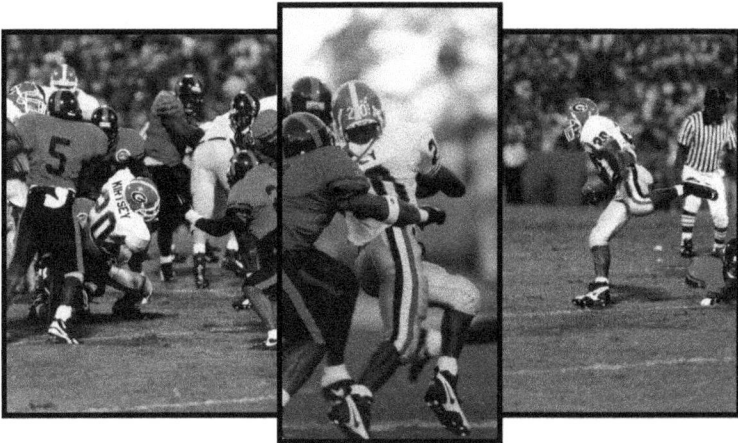

Freshman scatback Torin Kirtsey spoiled the celebration of Clemson's football centennial by rushing for 195 yards in his first collegiate start.

series. On 21 first-down plays in the second and third quarters, the Bulldogs averaged over eight yards per snap.

The next four plays netted 24 yards and the three-minute drive ended when Selma Calloway broke middle linebacker Andye McCrorey's tackle on a six-yard touchdown run with a little under nine minutes remaining in the second period. Fifth-year senior place-kicker Kanon Parkman, attempting his first PAT since the end of the first half in Oxford two weeks earlier, knotted the score.

The 7-all deadlock lasted fewer than four minutes. On the first snap of a Tiger drive traversing 41 yards in eight plays, Clemson quarterback Nealon Greene completed a 22-yard pass to his roommate, split end Tony Horne. Once the Jungaleers reached the Georgia 30, Sauve booted his longest field goal of the first half of the season. The senior kicker's 47-yarder put the home team out in front with five seconds fewer than five minutes left until intermission.

The visiting Athenians used up 289 of the remaining 295 seconds on their next series, taking 12 plays to move 72 yards. Although Georgia faced only one third down in the course of the march, a sack threatened to take the Bulldogs out of field goal range before redshirt freshman fullback Dave Williams went 19 yards on a draw play. Parkman split the uprights with six seconds showing on the scoreboard and the contest proceeded to halftime tied at 10 points per side.

A fast first half taking just 61 minutes of real time and featuring 48 running plays had played out remarkably evenly. Each team had four possessions in the opening two quarters, which produced a deadlock at the break. After a halftime show highlighted by a fireworks display over Lake Hartwell, however, the Georgia defense stifled the Clemson offense.

The Jungaleers tallied half as many yards of total offense following intermission as the Bulldogs gained in that same span. As had been the case in Athens the year before, the Country Gentlemen did not earn their initial first down of the second half until the penultimate play of the third quarter. Even with that 13-yard scramble by Greene tacked on at the end of the period, the Tigers managed to gain only 33 yards in the first 15 minutes following intermission. Clemson had custody of the pigskin just twice in the last 13 minutes of the contest and the home team failed to make it into Georgia territory either time.

While the Orange and Purple were being held scoreless over the course of the third quarter, the Classic City Canines were surging into a lead the home team would prove incapable of overcoming. Kirtsey, whom both *The Greenville News* and *The Tiger* compared to Florida State's Warrick Dunn, made big gains using misdirection by finding the creases on the back sides of plays. The freshman, who routinely broke tackles and proved difficult to bring down, racked up 91 rushing yards in the third stanza alone.

Georgia received the opening kickoff and, on the Red and Black's first drive following the break, Kirtsey led the way. The Athenians' initial march of the second half ended in a field goal attempt, but Clemson came through with a block. It would not be the last stop by the hometown special teams.

A trio of Tiger seniors (middle guard Carlos Curry, strong safety Brian Dawkins, and free safety Leomont Evans) each had a hand in blocking two Bulldog field goal attempts and an extra point. Seven potential Georgia points were kept off of the board by their efforts and another possible score by the visitors was prevented when the Classic City Canines lost a fumble after reaching the Clemson six yard line in the third stanza.

The night belonged to Kirtsey, whose churning legs kept the Red-and-Black attack clicking, but Brian Smith made a critical play from the quarterback spot late in the quarter to give Georgia its first lead of the game. Smith, a Palmetto State native whose brother came to the game from two states away to see him play, guided a 49-yard drive that threatened to stall at the Clemson 29 yard line, where the visitors faced third and seven.

Playing with poise behind a Georgia line that allowed him to be sacked just once over the course of the contest, Smith stayed cool under pressure as his offensive front picked up the oncoming Clemson blitz and took advantage of the man coverage he saw downfield. Juan Daniels, running a fly pattern down the left side, had gotten the better of Leomont Evans.

Evans, who had been named the ACC defensive back of the week following the N.C. State game and whose 18 tackles against Georgia were the most ever recorded by a Clemson defensive back, admitted his error afterwards. Confessed Evans: "I thought he was running an out-route. I took my eyes off him and I looked at the quarterback. It was just a lack of discipline. It was man-to-man and I just didn't check my man."

Evans's eyes returned to Daniels in time to see the Georgia receiver snag Smith's pass at the 10 yard line and continue untouched into the end zone for the Bulldogs' first touchdown toss in nearly nine quarters of play. Parkman's extra point try was batted down, keeping the visiting club's advantage at 16–10.

Nevertheless, as Tommy West later acknowledged, the Smith-to-Daniels TD pass swung the momentum in favor of the Dogs. Later in the quarter, Kirtsey opened a drive with a 38-yard gain on a first-down run, and, four plays later, Parkman knocked home a 42-yard three-pointer. With 40 seconds to play in the third period, the Georgia lead had been extended to nine points.

Early in the final stanza, Clemson moved swiftly down the field, using just six plays and only 107 seconds to go 60 yards. Emory Smith covered exactly half of those yards on the last two snaps of the series, using a 24-yard scamper to set the stage for a six-yard touchdown run. The Bulldogs held a two-point edge with nearly 14 minutes still to play.

The junior fullback's TD run ended the scoring but not the fireworks (of the on-field variety). The Athenians did not find the end zone again, but Brian Smith moved the visitors out to midfield with a 37-yard completion to flanker Brice Hunter inside the eight-minute mark as part of an overall effort that allowed the Dogs to retain possession of the football for more than 34 minutes.

The Tigers' final drive ended with Nealon Greene being run out of bounds three yards short of the marker on a fourth-down scamper and the Red and Black escaped with a 19–17 victory. Georgia had come into Death Valley sporting an all-time 6–6–2 mark in Memorial Stadium yet departed with the Bulldogs' 17th consecutive non-conference triumph.

Both coaches came away justifiably proud of how their teams had performed in what evidently was the final installment of the longstanding rivalry. "We are crushed that we lost the football game," said Tommy West, "but I was extremely proud of the effort." Ray Goff stated simply:

"I'm as proud of our football team as I was of any football team I've ever been associated with."

The Bulldogs had played without injured strong-side linebacker Randall Godfrey, who had come out of the Bama game with a strained hamstring. In the absence of his teammate, middle linebacker Whit Marshall stepped up his game, tallying 15 tackles in pacing Georgia's effort to slow down the Clemson offense. The Country Gentlemen also had sustained losses on defense, as lineman Bernard Randolph suffered a broken leg in the second half against the Dogs.

The Tigers were forced to punt the ball six times and they picked up just 12 first downs, moving the chains 10 fewer times than did the Dogs. Greene, who connected on only six of his 14 pass attempts, netted 51 yards through the air and failed to hook up with any of his receivers for a scoring strike.

The Fort Hill Felines fared rather better on the ground than over the top—four of the home team's aerials had come on the Tigers' final desperate drive—yet Georgia gained more yards on the ground (251) than Clemson amassed in total offense (235). The Country Gentlemen's total rushing yardage as a team (184) was less than Torin Kirtsey collected all on his own (195). Emory Smith's 12 carries yielded a scant 60 yards.

Kirtsey somehow managed to score two fewer TDs than Smith, whose nine touchdowns in the campaign's first six games matched the number of scores Emory's older brother, Emmitt, had tallied for the Dallas Cowboys that autumn. Nevertheless, the rookie scatback outrushed his Clemson counterpart by 135 yards and his relentlessness prevented the Bulldog assault from stalling. Kirtsey picked up nine of Georgia's 22 first downs.

Kirtsey later admitted, "I really don't see myself as the kind of guy who can carry the ball 37 or 38 times in a game. As a matter of fact, I didn't even know that I had carried the ball that many times before somebody told me." Irrespective of whether Kirtsey ever saw himself in that light, his numbers against the Tigers put him in select company. No back had ever before collected so many carries in Memorial Stadium and Clemson had not allowed so many rushing yards to an opposing ballcarrier since 1984.

Furthermore, Kirtsey's 195-yard effort was the best by a Georgia freshman since Rodney Hampton's 227-yard day against Ole Miss in 1987 and the best by any Bulldog back, regardless of class standing, since Garrison Hearst went for 246 yards against Vanderbilt in 1992. Most impressive of all was the fact that Kirtsey's 38 carries matched a mark set by Herschel Walker against the Commodores in 1982 and not equaled in the interim.

Kirtsey continued to shine as the season continued. The undersized Bulldog scatback had carried the ball just 37 times for 111 yards in the campaign's first five games *combined*, but he ended the year as the Classic City Canines' leading rusher in spite of making just three starts. Five of Georgia's 15 rushing touchdowns in 1995 were scored by Kirtsey.

Next to those numbers, Brian Smith's quiet competence in going 13 of 22 for 156 yards and a touchdown against the Orange and Purple amounted almost to an afterthought. Smith, like Kirtsey, made his first career start against Clemson, a school that had not offered the Georgia quarterback a scholarship when Smith was the signal caller at Spartanburg High School and Ken Hatfield was the coach at Fort Hill. Ray Goff originally had intended to spell Smith by inserting Hines Ward under center, but the starter performed well enough that the Bulldog skipper elected not to substitute the player Tommy West had most feared facing.

Clemson and Georgia each emerged from their clash in Death Valley at 3–3 and both there after went on winning streaks. The Bulldogs beat Vanderbilt and Kentucky in the next two weeks, with the triumph over the Wildcats giving the Athenians the 600th victory in school history. While this gave the Classic City Canines their first three-game winning streak since the middle of the 1993 campaign, the Red and Black faltered in home games against Florida and Auburn.

The Fiesta Bowl-bound Gators, playing their first game in Athens in 63 years, scored the last of their seven touchdowns on the day with just over a minute remaining in the game to become the first Georgia opponent ever to score 52 points in Sanford Stadium. In the Red and Black's final home game before the removal of the historic hedges for the 1996 summer Olympics, a squad of invading Plainsmen headed for the Hall of Fame Bowl escaped the Classic City with a 37–31 victory to leave the Dogs at 5–5 for the year.

Those setbacks dropped Goff's career records against the Classic City Canines' orange-and-blue-clad rivals to 1–6 versus Florida and 2–4–1 versus Auburn. Vince Dooley had seen enough to know that the requisite "significant improvement" would not come to pass, so it was announced before the season-ender against Georgia Tech that the head coach would not return for an eighth season at the helm of his *alma mater*'s football program.

Goff's players won one for their deposed coach at Grant Field, overcoming a 17–7 deficit two minutes into the fourth quarter to score a Torin Kirtsey touchdown, a Hines- Ward-to-Brice-Hunter two-point conversion, and a wobbly 34-yard Kanon Parkman field goal in the final nine minutes to claim a fifth straight series win over the Yellow Jackets and punch their return ticket to Atlanta for a December 30 date with Virginia in the Peach Bowl.

Due partly to two first-quarter interceptions and a blocked punt, the Cavaliers led 27–17 after 45 minutes, but a Parkman field goal early in the fourth quarter pulled the Bulldogs to within a single score. That seven-point deficit remained unchanged until a fumble by the Wahoos' Walt Derey was scooped up by defensive tackle Jason Ferguson and returned 10 yards for the tying touchdown with 69 seconds showing on the clock.

Seemingly bound for what would have been the first overtime game in school history under newly-instituted NCAA rules, the Red and Black watched their hopes vanish as Parkman's ensuing kickoff, pushed back due to a celebration penalty, was brought back 83 yards by Virginian Demetrius Allen for the decisive score in the final minute to send Ray Goff out a loser in his last game.

Clemson's run of good luck following the Tigers' loss to Georgia proved more lasting, as the Country Gentlemen rebounded from their third setback in their first six games by going on a tear through their last five regular-season outings, beating conference foes Maryland, Georgia Tech, North Carolina, and Duke in succession before polishing off their slate with a win over South Carolina in Columbia. Only one of those five victories was by a margin of fewer than 17 points and several of them featured noteworthy milestones for the Tigers.

Against the Terrapins, Clemson ended the first half with a successful "Hail Mary"on the last play before intermission. Tony Horne tipped quarterback Louis Solomon's pass into flanker Antwuan Wyatt's grasp to pave the way to the South Carolinians' third straight shutout of Maryland. The Tigers donned orange pants for the showdown with the Carquest Bowl-bound Tar Heels, a squad that had won at least eight games in each of the three previous seasons. The contest was hallmarked by the play of defensive backs Andy Ford and Peter Ford, each of whom picked off UNC passes to become the first twin brothers in ACC history to record interceptions in the same game.

Raymond Priester's 263-yard day against the Blue Devils surpassed the previous school record for rushing yards in a single game and Brian Dawkins's three first-quarter interceptions in a driving rain against Duke likewise set a new Clemson mark for picks in a period. Finally, the Country Gentlemen capped off their season with a 21-point fourth quarter against the Gamecocks to claim their fourth consecutive victory in Williams-Brice Stadium.

The Fort Hill Felines' 8–3 record earned them their first New Year's Day bowl berth since Clemson's 1991 ACC championship season and

Tommy West's troops headed to Jacksonville for a Gator Bowl date with Syracuse in Torin Kirtsey's hometown. Paul Pasqualoni's Orangemen came into the game with an identical 8–3 ledger, but the Big East squad was reeling from league losses at Virginia Tech (31–7) and Miami (35–24) in two of the team's last four regularly-scheduled outings.

Nevertheless, in a contest dubbed "the *other* Orange Bowl" because of the two teams' shared signature color, Syracuse handed Clemson a 41–0 whitewashing to deal the Tigers the worst postseason defeat in their history. The loss dropped Tommy West's career ledger with the Orange and Purple to 14–10, ending an autumn of disappointment that soon turned into a winter of sorrow.

On January 26, 1996, beloved Clemson coach, athletic administrator, and ambassador Frank Howard passed away exactly 13 years to the day after the death of Bear Bryant. Howard, a 1989 Hall of Fame inductee, was buried on campus atop Fort Hill, in the cemetery that also held the remains of University presidents Robert F. Poole and Walter Merritt Riggs. Just as the Baron's old nemesis, Wally Butts, had been interred in Athens in the shadow of Sanford Stadium, so too was Howard laid to rest in a spot adjacent to the arena he had built for the Tigers to call their home.

As badly as 1995 had ended and 1996 had begun for Clemson, though, Tommy West at least had another year with his club to look forward to the following fall. For Ray Goff, the quarterback and permanent captain of the 1976 Georgia team that had won the SEC championship and beaten the Tigers in Death Valley by the selfsame 41–0 margin by which Clemson had just fallen in the Gator Bowl, there was no next year, for the Bulldog coach's career was done after a 46–34–1 seven-year run.

Alas, there was no "next year" for Clemson's and Georgia's 98-year-old gridiron rivalry, either. The series was being suspended indefinitely after a reliably regular run (24 games in 26 seasons from 1962 to 1987) had given way to only intermittent meetings (four games in eight years between 1988 and 1995). Thanks to league expansions affecting both schools, the longstanding rivalry was falling by the wayside.

Ray Goff, for one, did not seem sad to see the series end. "After tonight," said Goff, "it doesn't hurt my feelings at all." The Georgia coach may have been echoing a sentiment expressed by Danny Ford after the rivalry's last nailbiter in 1987, but he otherwise seemed alone in his point of view. His Clemson counterpart, Tommy West, reflected the perspective of the majority when describing the contest as "a throwback type of game" and "the toughest, most hard-nosed game we played in a while." However, West acknowledged that, due to the toughness of the ACC and the SEC, it probably was too much to ask the two teams to continue squaring off against one another.

The fans wanted more, though. On the day before the game, *The Tiger* had proclaimed in a headline "[t]he end of an era" and the student newspaper's sports editor had declared: "Clemson's true rivals over the past 15 years haven't been those posers over in the capital—they've been the boys from Athens." In the October 16 *Red and Black*, a Georgia columnist agreed, arguing:

"We shouldn't lightly sacrifice such a storied series as the Georgia-Clemson border war. We've been playing Clemson seven years longer than we've been playing Florida. Georgia and Clemson have met on the gridiron 60 times, exactly as many times as Alabama and Auburn will have faced one another after this year's Iron Bowl...Only our rivalries against Florida, Auburn, and Georgia Tech have been more important to Georgia's football history, and the Clemson fans I met at Frank Howard Field earlier this month showed a good deal more class and hospitality than our other great rivals have shown us on the road."

At the time of the 60th meeting between the two squads, the Clemson and Georgia athletic associations had no plans to schedule subsequent series meetings. The historic rivalry appeared to have been consigned to history.

2002

Shocked!

It was a banner evening between the hedges. A lengthy period fraught with change (including the transition to a new millennium) had passed since Clemson and Georgia last met on the gridiron, but an intervening shift in circumstances permitted the old foes to knock helmets yet again. It was the debut not only of a new fall, but also of numerous players, none of whom would have a larger impact than the home team's second-string quarterback.

Following a seven-year layoff between series games, the Bulldogs and the Tigers resumed their rivalry on August 31, 2002, in the season opener for both teams. The schools had suspended play following the 1995 contest due to increasingly daunting conference schedules; beginning in 1992, Clemson had to contend with the Florida State Seminoles as a perennial league opponent, and the SEC's split into two divisions that same year meant that Georgia would be forced to face the Tennessee Volunteers each autumn. When the two universities' respective in-state non-conference rivals, South Carolina and Georgia Tech, were added to the mix as well, little room remained on either team's slate for another challenging contestant.

A quirk of the calendar made possible the resumption of the interrupted Clemson- Georgia series. Because there were 14 Saturdays between the earliest permitted playing date and the final weekend of November in 2002 and 2003, teams were allowed to schedule a 12th regular season contest in each of those years. Many schools used the opportunity to arrange early intersectional matchups with cross-country opponents, but the Bulldogs and the Tigers took advantage of the additional game by setting up home-and-away meetings to start those seasons.

In the interim since the last series confrontation, however, much had changed in the Palmetto and Peach States. Clemson coach Tommy West and Georgia coach Ray Goff lost their status as favorite sons after too many league losses, with Goff being the first to be shown the door. Although he could claim a 3–1 mark against Clemson, Goff managed ledgers of only 0–5 against Tennessee, 1–6 against Florida, and 2–4–1 against Auburn. In his final three seasons, Goff had gone a middling 17–16–1.

After a messy negotiated resignation, he was replaced (or so it first appeared) by Kansas coach Glen Mason. Just days after Bulldogs athletic director Vince Dooley introduced his new head football coach at a press conference in Athens, Mason changed his mind as his Jayhawks prepared to take the field to face the UCLA Bruins in the Aloha Bowl on Christmas Day. Although caught by surprise, Dooley was not without a backup plan and, before sundown, he had tapped Jim Donnan, the former Oklahoma offensive coordinator and current head coach at Division I-AA Marshall, for the job.

West survived in Death Valley a little longer, lasting until the end of the 1998 season before being relieved of his responsibilities. After being given a mulligan for a losing record in his initial autumn, West partially redeemed himself with an 8–3 regular season in 1995. The Country Gentlemen's subsequent Gator Bowl loss left a bad taste in many Tiger fans' mouths, however, and West's job security was not improved by consecutive 7–5 efforts in the next two years, each of which was capped off by a narrow Peach Bowl loss to another set of Tigers from the SEC: LSU in 1996 and Auburn in 1997.

The 1998 campaign was the last straw for West. Following a 33–0 whitewashing of Division I-AA Furman, the Orange and Purple proceeded to lose eight of their next nine outings, winning a lone home game over a Maryland squad whose only victims that autumn would be James Madison, Temple, and Duke. The victory over the Terrapins was all that prevented the Tigers from going winless in ACC action.

Despite ending the season on a high note with a victory over South Carolina that stranded the Gamecocks at 1–10, the Tigers' stumble to a 3–8 finish to close out Clemson's worst ledger since

1975 spelled the end for Tommy West after a five-year span during which the Country Gentlemen won 31 games while losing 28.

Tommy Bowden, son of legendary FSU coach Bobby Bowden, was hired away from Tulane after leading the Green Wave to an undefeated regular season, a Conference USA championship, and a Liberty Bowl berth. The younger Bowden had taken over a program in New Orleans that hadn't won more than three games in a season since 1990 and hadn't posted a winning record in more than a decade and a half. He guided Tulane to a 7–4 record in his first autumn and an 11–0 mark the following year.

True to Clemson tradition, Bowden brought with him ties to the Yellowhammer State. The new Tiger skipper had been born in Birmingham, had spent three seasons as the wide receivers coach at Alabama, and had served seven years as the running backs coach and offensive coordinator at Auburn.

Bowden's departure from the Big Easy helped bring about Donnan's downfall in Athens, as Georgia offensive line coach and longtime Donnan assistant Chris Scelfo soon made the trek from the Classic City to the Crescent City as Bowden's successor. Without Scelfo, Donnan's next two Bulldog squads faltered, including a talent-laden 2000 team which was favored by many to win the SEC East yet stumbled to a disappointing 8–4 record, signaling the end to Donnan's tumultuous five-year tenure between the hedges.

Despite winning two-thirds of his games to post a 40–19 record which included four straight bowl victories, Donnan came up short against the Bulldogs' four major rivals: Donnan's Dogs were 2–3 against Auburn, 1–4 against Florida, 2–3 against Georgia Tech, and 1–4 against Tennessee. Donnan was the first Georgia head coach with a multi-year tenure since Pop Warner in 1895 and 1896 to have ended his career in Athens without ever facing the Clemson Tigers.

Enter Mark Richt, who had been the quarterbacks coach and offensive coordinator at Florida State since 1990. In the course of his service in Tallahassee, Richt had been a part of nine Seminole victories over Clemson. Just 40 years old at the time he was hired by Georgia, the Bobby Bowden protégé brought a quiet confidence to bear in steadying the ship in the Classic City.

Although Richt's first Georgia squad posted the same 8–4 record as Donnan's last Bulldog club, wins over Tennessee in Knoxville and Georgia Tech in Atlanta left the Red-and-Black faithful hopeful heading into a 2002 campaign in which the Dogs were a preseason top 10 team.

The Tigers had question marks, so the uncertainty which reigned following the departure of quarterback Woodrow Dantzler (who had led the Orange and Purple in passing and in rushing in each of the two previous seasons) left Clemson unranked and picked to finish behind Florida State and Maryland in the Atlantic Coast Conference standings.

The renewal of the rivalry took place in an ESPN-televised night game in Sanford Stadium. The Jungaleers were opening on the road against a ranked opponent for the sixth time in their history, and the Orange and Purple were looking for their first win in such a situation since upending No. 12 North Carolina in 1959. It was the first Clemson-Georgia game in seven years, and the first season opener between the two teams in two decades, and they made the most of it.

Following a pregame ceremony honoring Richard Appleby, Horace King, and the other three players who integrated the Bulldog football team in 1971, the outing got underway. The visiting Tigers were guided by first-time starter Willie Simmons under center. Simmons, who had graduated with two years of eligibility left, opened the game by directing a seven-play drive that netted 23 yards and took up over four minutes of clock time before the Country Gentlemen were forced to trot out Athens native Wynn Kopp for the purpose of punting.

With 2001 SEC freshman of the year David Greene directing the offense on the Bulldogs' ensuing drive, the Red and Black ran only three plays before Jonathan Kilgo was sent in to boot the ball away. One day earlier, the Clemson student newspaper had offered a prediction: "If Greene gets rattled early, don't be surprised to see the Tigers edge the Bulldogs." The forecast failed adequately to reckon with the home team's backup quarterback.

For the moment, though, the game belonged to the punters. Kopp (who had transferred to Clemson from Georgia after spending the 1998 and 1999 seasons as the Classic City Canines' starting punter) and Kilgo dueled to a standstill over the course of the evening, with the Bulldog-turned-Tiger averaging 37.3 yards on eight punts (with a long of 47) and the Red-and-Black punter averaging 37.2 yards on six punts (with a long of 48).

The South Carolinians got the ball back and began to move, mounting a 56-yard drive that appeared destined to end in the first points of the game. However, Georgia free safety Kentrell Curry tipped a Simmons pass and the batted ball found its way into the hands of Bulldog cornerback Decory Bryant, whose first interception gave the Dogs posession at their own 20 yard line.

Aided by a pair of personal foul penalties against the Country Gentlemen, Greene led the home team on a nine-play march that lasted over four minutes and covered 80 yards, culminating in a four-yard touchdown pass to split end Damien Gary that gave Georgia a 7–0 lead with less than a minute remaining in the first quarter.

The Tigers managed to pick up a dozen yards on their ensuing possession before Kopp punted the ball back to the Bulldogs, but the Red and Black did not retain custody of the pigskin for long. After two plays netted only two yards, Greene threw an interception on third down and the Orange and Purple took advantage of the turnover as fully as their hosts had done at the end of the preceding period.

Tiger linebacker Kelvin Morris picked off Greene's pass and returned it 17 yards. The Fort Hill Felines covered the remaining 30 yards in just four plays, taking less than 30 sec onds to tie the game on a short touchdown run by senior running back Bernard Rambert. Rambert, like Simmons, was a first-year starter, having spent the previous seasons of his collegiate career backing up Travis Zachery.

The tailback who accounted for Clemson's first points of the contest had started just three games in his first three years on campus, but he had performed capably in those outings, averaging 5.8 yards per carry as a first-teamer, as opposed to just 3.9 yards per rush when coming in off the bench. With Zachery suspended for the preceding year's Humanitarian Bowl, Rambert had gotten the nod and had answered the call to the tune of 101 rushing yards and 77 receiving yards. In the first game of his final autumn of eligibility, Rambert would carry the ball 10 times against the Dogs, garnering only 35 yards yet putting the Tigers on the board.

Although the 86,520-strong Sanford Stadium crowd had been fired up for the season-opening test against a longstanding rival, the reversal of the Bulldogs' fortunes did not escape the home fans' notice. Just over three and a half minutes into the contest's second stanza, the score was tied and, while both defensive fronts had been succes ful at getting pressure on the opposing signal caller, Clemson had gone on four drives collectively covering 121 yards, whereas Georgia had managed just 89 combined yards in the Dogs' first three possessions. Whatever sense of dread had begun to settle over those in attendance, though, was about to be dissipated even more quickly than it had descended.

Georgia quarterback David Greene opened the scoring with a first-quarter touchdown pass, but he finished the evening with only 12 completions for 67 yards.

The Tigers kicked off, but an offsides penalty forced the Country Gentlemen to tee it up anew. Bulldog return man Fred Gibson capitalized on this second chance, taking the kick and firing up the crowd once more with a 91-yard sprint to paydirt. Place-kicker Billy Bennett, who had been the subject of preseason doubts about his accuracy, drove home his second extra point of the evening to make it 14–7 inside of 11 minutes to play in the first half.

Simmons continued to feel the heat when the Orange and Purple resumed possession. Although first-half injuries would deprive the home team of the services of defensive end Nic Clemons and linebacker Tony Gilbert, the Dogs maintained pressure on the Clemson quarterback, with defensive end Will Thompson recording two of the Red and Black's four sacks of Simmons.

After three Tiger plays resulted in a loss of 12 yards, Kopp again came in to punt. The Clemson specialist dropped the snap and sent the ball off the side of his foot. The shanked spheroid sailed only 17 yards and

Bulldog free safety Thomas Davis brought it back nine yards to give Georgia excellent field position at the visitors' 15 yard line.

Richt, who had watched his starting quarterback struggle in the face of a daunting Clemson pass rush that often got the better of a Red-and-Black offensive line on which three true freshmen were given playing time, elected to add a new wrinkle to the Bulldogs' offensive package. For the ensuing series, Greene remained on the sideline and redshirt freshman backup D.J. Shockley lined up under center for the first snaps of his college career.

Donald Eugene Shockley had been a four-sport athlete at North Clayton High School, competing in baseball, basketball, and track and field in addition to turning in a sufficiently solid performance on the gridiron to earn *Parade* All-American honors as what at least one recruiting service called the best prep quarterback in the country. Despite Greene's outstanding performance as a redshirt freshman the year before, Shockley had come on strong enough in the spring to push the starter for playing time and Richt, along with Georgia quarterbacks coach Mike Bobo, had found it necessary to balance the needs of the Athenians' two accomplished signal callers.

Shockley was sent into the game in a good situation and he took advantage of his inaugural opportunity. The heralded backup ran three plays, calling his own number on two of them, and the drive ended with a nine-yard touchdown run on a quarterback keeper. With just over eight minutes remaining in the first half, Bennett extended the Athenians' advantage to 21–7.

After Shockley's successful debut electrified the crowd anew, the game briefly settled into a defensive struggle that showcased Kopp's and Kilgo's skills. The next four possessions yielded as many punts: Clemson's ensuing two drives covered barely three minutes and together netted only 12 yards, whereas Georgia's pair of possessions during that same span yielded 14 yards and lasted only four minutes.

With halftime fast approaching, Simmons led the Tigers on a 64-yard march in just 76 seconds. Simmons was beset by misfortune a good deal of the night; in addition to being harassed by the Georgia defensive front, the Clemson quarterback repeatedly was victimized by such standouts in the Bulldog secondary as Bryant (who added a trio of pass deflections to his first-quarter pick).

When his receivers beat the coverage provided by a young secondary, Simmons saw well-thrown balls dropped repeatedly by the Tigers' wide receivers. Airese Currie missed making a grab at the Georgia 20 and Derrick Hamilton dropped a pass in the end zone. Nevertheless, Simmons overcame adversity to rack up 165 aerial yards on 17 completions, well outpacing Red-and-Black starter Greene, who finished the evening having gone 12 of 21 for a paltry 67 yards.

The final Clemson drive of the second quarter, though, saw the Orange-and-Purple quarterback begin to get into a rhythm with his wide receivers. First Tony Elliott brought in a 20-yard reception at the home team's 23 yard line on third down. Later, on the ninth play of the possession, Simmons connected with Kevin Youngblood, who had been slated to replace NFL first-round draft pick Rod Gardner a year before, only to lose the entirety of the 2001 campaign to a broken leg suffered in preseason practice. In his first game back, Youngblood hauled in six catches for 66 yards, including the 21-yard touchdown reception that cut the Country Gentlemen's deficit to seven points with a scant eight seconds remaining until halftime. Clemson kicked off and Greene knelt out the clock to take the contest to intermission.

Whatever problems had plagued the Georgia offense in the first half escalated early in the third quarter. A five-minute drive to start the second half was nearly snuffed out when a muffed center-quarterback exchange forced Greene to fall on his own fumble. One play later, tailback Musa Smith couldn't hang onto a pitch from Greene and the loose ball was picked up by Tiger defensive end Bryant McNeal, who advanced the recovered fumble 55 yards for the tying touchdown with just under 10 minutes remaining in the period.

Matters went from bad to worse for the Bulldogs on the ensuing kickoff, which was dropped by Gibson for the third consecutive Georgia fumble on as many plays. (Those would be the Red and Black's only three fumbles of the game. Although the Country Gentlemen put the ball on the ground six times over the course of the contest, the visitors retained possession on each of them.)

Clemson once again pounced on the loose ball but the Bulldog defense asserted itself, allowing the Fort Hill Felines to pick up only a lone yard on their next three plays. The South Carolinians' Aaron Hunt, who had matched Bennett kick-for-kick on a trio of successful point after tries, came on to attempt a field goal. The 37-yard try struck the goalpost and Hunt's failure to split the uprights kept the score snarled at 21-all.

The Athenians went three and out on their next possession, punting the ball back to the Orange and Purple. Clemson again mounted a lengthy drive, chewing up nearly five minutes of clock while covering

76 yards of real estate in 10 plays to punch in the go-ahead score. Running back Yusef Kelly broke multiple tackles on the 19-yard scamper that set up his subsequent two-yard touchdown run. This time, Hunt's aim was true and the Tigers held a 28–21 advantage between the hedges with two minutes and change remaining in the period.

Still the Georgia offense could not get anything going, as three plays netted a mere two yards before the Dogs were forced to give the ball back once more. The Red-and-Black defense rose up again, moving the Tiger offense backwards until the Country Gentlemen were compelled to surrender possession after three plays lost them 16 yards.

Damien Gary returned the punt 40 yards to the visitors' 31 yard line. With the Classic City Canines in good field position and needing a spark, Richt sent Shockley back into the game and the second-string signal caller responded with another three-play touchdown drive. Flanker Terrence Edwards beat cornerback Brian Mance on a quick slant and Shockley's 24-yard strike to Robert Edwards's younger brother in the end zone knotted the score at 28, breathed new life into a struggling Georgia attack, and gave the senior receiver the school record with 20 career TD catches.

The Bulldog D continued to play tenaciously and ferociously, pushing the Fort Hill Felines back five yards on their ensuing possession. Kopp put his foot into the pigskin for the seventh time and the Red and Black began to mount some offense, covering 23 yards in a half-dozen plays before punting the ball away again after almost three minutes had bled away on the scoreboard.

This time, the Tigers at least managed to make some forward progress; specifically, the Country Gentlemen gained a combined two yards on their next trio of plays for the Orange and Purple's third straight three-and-out. With half of the fourth quarter remain ing to be played, Greene guided the Dogs 19 yards downfield in six snaps. Musa Smith's six-yard run to the Jungaleers' 26 yard line set up a 43-yard field goal attempt by Bennett. The Georgia junior banged it home to reclaim the lead for the Red and Black.

Now trailing 31–28 with barely five minutes of clock time remaining, the South Carolinians retook the field with urgency and mounted a 33-yard drive that ran off over three and a half minutes. Seeking to redeem himself for his earlier miss, Hunt came on to try a 46-yard three-pointer to tie the game anew. A year before, the Tiger place-kicker had missed just two field goal attempts all season, going 10 of 12 over the course of the 2001 campaign and splitting the uprights five times in five tries from 40 or more yards.

Bowden had every reason to be confident in Hunt. Unlike Bennett, the Clemson kicker had been consistent in preseason scrimmages, regularly hitting three-point tries of 40 yards or longer. In the Country Gentlemen's spring game, Hunt had connected on a 52-yarder. However, it was the maligned Bennett who came through in the clutch and the reliable Hunt who fell short, as the second Tiger field goal attempt of the game failed to find its intended target. Aaron Hunt's fourth-quarter try in Sanford Stadium matched exactly the distance of David Treadwell's 1986 game-winner in the Classic City.

With 103 seconds yet to be played, the Georgia offense trotted back out onto the field nursing a three-point lead. The line of scrimmage was the Bulldog 29 yard line. After gaining nine yards on their next three plays, the Red and Black faced fourth and inches at their own 38 with 40 seconds left. Mark Richt faced a decision and he later explained his decision in this way: "My initial gut reaction was to punt it, but we had two time outs. I just felt confident that we could get what I thought was about 10 inches."

Although the Classic City Canines were 62 yards shy of the opposite end zone, they ran a play ordinarily reserved for goal line situations. The ball went to Smith, who had been the Bulldogs' leading rusher (105 yards on 23 carries) and leading receiver (16 yards on four catches) of the night. Extending the ball as though attempting to break the plane for a touchdown, the Georgia running back dived over the top for the first down that allowed the Dogs to run out the clock to secure the three-point victory in a wild renewal of a storied rivalry.

The game was every bit as close as the score indicated. Although the Tigers came up short between the hedges, Clemson held the edge in time of possession (30:41–29:19), passing yards (165–117), first downs (19–14), and total plays (71–64). The 28 points scored by the Orange and Purple would be the most allowed by the Bulldogs in a 2002 season in which the Red and Black set a new school record for victories (13) and held 10 of their 14 opponents to 20 or fewer points.

The Country Gentlemen picked up the requisite yardage on third down at a greater clip (41%) than their hosts (31%), but the conversion percentage that mattered most was the Athenians' 100 per cent fourth-down pickup rate. By reversing the 31–28 margin by which the Jungaleers had bested the Bulldogs between the hedges 16 years previously, the 2002 contest matched the 1986 showdown as the highest-scoring game in series history.

The Tigers turned their 233 yards of total offense into 28 points for the highest tally the South Carolinians had ever posted in a loss to the Dogs. A late field goal had determined the outcome, as had been the case four times in five years between 1983 and 1987, and, after three straight double-digit decisions by an average margin of 24 points in the early 1990s, the border war had produced back-to-back nailbiters of the sort to which Clemson and Georgia fans had become accustomed during the rivalry's heyday.

Vince Dooley, the head coach who had presided over that period for the Red and Black, said after the contest: "It's a great Clemson-Georgia football game. It just kind of fell in line with so many of the great ones." Tommy Bowden, on the other hand, saw the glass as half-empty, observing that the Tigers had been the better team in two phases of the contest but remarking, "If I had a special teams coach, this would have been his last game."

Despite the home team's anemic display of offense—Georgia was limited to just 203 yards of total offense, over half of which was the handiwork of Musa Smith—the Red and Black managed to score their

Bulldog backup D.J. Shockley stole the show in the 2002 season opener, running for one touchdown and passing for another.

second- highest point total against the Orange and Purple in the last 16 meetings be tween the two. Noting the spark given to the Bulldog attack by Shockley's insertion into the lineup, Richt remarked, "Yeah, I think we'll see D.J. play more."

In the minds of some Georgia partisans, Shockley's heroics also sparked a quarterback controversy, or ought to have. Tiger defensive coordinator John Lovett stated, "The thing that was different about them was their other quarterback. He is a little different tempo." The second- string quarterback would do nothing to fuel the debate, however; all Shockley said afterwards was, "What- ever comes out of it does."

There could be little doubt, though, that the backup QB had acquitted himself effectively, both as a runner and as a passer (3 of 4 for 50 yards and a TD). Shockley very likely had saved the day for the Dogs and paved the way to Georgia's 19th win over Clemson in Sanford Stadium, the Classic City Canines' 40th series victory over the Tigers overall, and the Red and Black's 650th win since taking the gridiron for the first time in 1892.

It appeared initially that the August 31 setback in Athens had done nothing to dampen the Tigers' prospects for 2002, as the Fort Hill Felines went on an undefeated run during September. The Orange and Purple returned home to beat by 20 points the selfsame Louisiana Tech squad the South Carolinians had encountered in the previous year's Humanitarian Bowl, following up that victory by beating both a Georgia Tech team that came into the contest riding a three-game winning streak and a Ball State club bound for its first non-losing season since 1996.

Conference road losses to FSU in Tallahassee and to Virginia in Charlottesville in early October dropped the Country Gentlemen to 3–3. No sooner had the Tigers climbed back above .500 with a win over Wake Forest than Clemson turned right around and fell to 4–4 five days later in a Thursday night outing in which a Gator Bowl-bound N.C. State squad led by Philip Rivers and T.A. McLendon pounded the Orange and Purple 38–6 in Death Valley. That outcome ran the Wolfpack's record to 9–0 and vaulted Chuck Amato's squad into the top 10 in both major polls.

A close shave against Duke in Durham did little to assuage the fears of fans of the Fort Hill Felines, as the Blue Devils were well on their way to a third straight season of going 0–8 in ACC play. The Tigers' 34–31 win in Wallace Wade Stadium was followed by a 42–12 walloping of North Carolina. The Tar Heels had fallen far and fast after winning the Peach Bowl the year before and UNC would finish the year at 3–9, with their lone league win coming against rival Duke.

Maryland came to Memorial Stadium on November 16 and Ralph Friedgen's revived Terrapins beat Clemson by 18 points en route to a top 15 finish and a Peach Bowl win. In their final regular-season outing (and their eighth home game of the autumn), the Tigers sneaked by South Carolina by a touchdown, claiming a 27–20 victory over a Gamecock team that had faded down the stretch, losing its last five outings to finish 5–7.

The Orange and Purple's 7–5 ledger was enough to earn Tommy Bowden's squad a Tangerine Bowl berth opposite Mike Leach's Texas Tech Red Raiders, who had just completed only the team's second eight-win regular season since 1989. The explosive offense from Lubbock had produced scoring outbursts of 42 points or more eight times during its last 11 outings, riddling Big 12 scoreboards to the tune of 42 points against Texas, 48 points at Texas A&M, 49 points against Oklahoma State, 52 points against Missouri, and 62 points against Baylor.

That pattern continued in Orlando two days before Christmas, as Clemson came into Citrus Bowl Stadium and managed only a second-quarter safety along the way to a 34–2 halftime deficit. Texas Tech's Kliff Kingsbury earned MVP honors in the course of a 32-of-43 day in which the Lone Star State gunslinger threw for 375 yards and three touchdowns in the 55–15 rout that left Clemson at 7–6. The Orange and Purple had lost five or more games eight times in an 11-season span after having lost more than two games in an individual autumn just four times in the 14 campaigns between 1978 and 1991.

The favored Bulldogs' narrow victory over the Tigers was the first of several close shaves for the Red and Black. In the first half of the season, Georgia won lopsided victories against overmatched New Mexico State and Division I-AA Northwestern State but had to hold on to survive scares from South Carolina (13–7), Alabama (27–25), and Tennessee (18–13). After the wins at Columbia and Tuscaloosa, as well as the Bulldogs' third straight conquest of the Volunteers, Georgia found itself at 6–0 and ranked No. 5 in the land.

At the midpoint of the season, a Bulldog D which had been surrendering early leads began to dominate in the second half. Led by linebackers Tony Gilbert and Boss Bailey and defensive end David Pollack, the defense held Vanderbilt to a lone touchdown after intermission and blanked Kentucky in the final two quarters. The Dogs carried an 8–0 record to Jacksonville for the annual showdown with the Gators, who were coached by someone other than Steve Spurrier for the first time since 1989. In a game hallmarked by offensive miscues such as dropped passes, personal foul penalties, and an inability to convert on third down, Georgia lost a heartbreaker to Florida, 20–13. It was Georgia's 12th loss to the Gators in the previous 13 series meetings.

With their hopes of an undefeated season shattered, the Bulldogs refocused in time to hand Ole Miss a 31–17 setback in which the Rebels were held scoreless in the second half. Next up was Auburn, in a game which would determine whether Georgia or Florida captured the Eastern Division championship. The Tigers took a 14–3 first-half lead into the locker room and led 21–10 late in the third quarter, but the Bulldogs cut the War Eagle lead to 21–17 on a Jon Stinchcomb fumble recovery in the end zone. Then, on fourth and 15 from the Auburn 19 yard line, David Greene connected with wide receiver Michael Johnson, in for the injured Terrence Edwards, for the game-deciding touchdown with just 85 seconds remaining.

The Dogs followed up their division-clinching performance in the Loveliest Village with a 51–7 dismantling of Georgia Tech between the hedges. The most lopsided Georgia win in the history of the in-state rivalry capped off an 11–1 regular season for the Red and Black. One week later, on Saturday, December 7, 2002, a date which will live in Bulldog lore, Georgia ended its 20-year championship drought with a convincing 30–3 throttling of the Western Division-winning Arkansas Razorbacks.

The showdown with the Hogs in the Georgia Dome was over almost before it started, as a blocked punt by Decory Bryant three minutes into the first quarter set up a two-yard touchdown run by Musa Smith on the Bulldogs' first play from scrimmage. The Red and Black never looked back, jumping out to a 23–0 halftime lead and cruising to victory.

The win in the SEC championship game propelled the fourth-ranked Bulldogs into the Sugar Bowl, where they were to face Richt's former team, Florida State. Against his old mentor, Bobby Bowden, Richt oversaw a 26–13 Georgia effort in the Superdome as Musa Smith earned MVP honors with 145 rushing yards and Billy Bennett set a school record with four bowl-game field goals. Georgia's only touchdown pass of the game came from D.J. Shockley, who had continued to impress as a backup QB getting regular playing time under center.

With the win in New Orleans, the Dogs finished the season ranked third in the final Associated Press poll. It did not escape the notice of many observant Georgia fans that their successful season had been the third autumn since 1905 in which the Red and Black opened the campaign against Clemson. In each of those three seasons (1946, 1982, and 2002), the Bulldogs finished the year as a top-five team and the Southeastern Conference champions.

2003
(Throw) Up, (Fourth) Down, and (Shut) Out in Death Valley

After the temporarily dormant Clemson-Georgia series had been not only revived but reinvigorated in the previous season's opening outing, much was expected of the two teams' return engagement by the shores of Lake Hartwell on August 30, 2003. Although the combatants failed to deliver a repeat of the prior year's excitement, it was not for the reason initially expected.

The defending SEC champion Bulldogs had a boatload of problems heading into the autumn following their first conference title in two decades. The rotating quarterback combination of David Greene and D.J. Shockley would have to operate behind a completely new offensive line composed entirely of underclassmen, while several defensive starters (including rover Greg Blue, free safety Kentrell Curry, defensive end Will Thompson, and nose tackle Ken Veal) were sidelined by injuries. Georgia coach Mark Richt had suspended eight other players, including three defensive backs, and, arguably, only a loophole in NCAA regulations had kept him from having to suspend even more after several Bulldogs had given the program a black eye in the offseason by selling their SEC championship rings.

As Richt's worries about his team had multiplied, so had his fan base's expectations been raised. In this, the coaches and the sportswriters were complicit, as those two groups had ranked Georgia ninth and 11th in their respective preseason polls. Clemson, still sting ing from the 40-point postseason whipping administered to the Tigers in the

2002 Tangerine Bowl, was not to be found in the top 25, although at least three familiar preseason publications (Athlon, Lindy's, and *The Sporting News*) identified the Fort Hill Felines' receiving corps as one of the 10 best in college football heading into Dabo Swinney's first season as the Jungaleers' wide receivers coach.

The Tigers were motivated by the lack of national respect shown to a Clemson club that returned eight starters on offense and brought back four of its top six linebackers and six of its top seven defensive ends. "Clemson has had this game circled on their schedules for a year," wrote Andrew Gibbons in the Fort Hill student newspaper on the eve of the season opener. "[W]hile Georgia probably won[']t look past the Tigers, they probably don't realize how bad we want this game."

The contest, held on a sweltering IPTAY Day in recently-renovated Memorial Stadium, got underway at noon with 83,000 fans and a national ABC television audience watching the first game ever played at Fort Hill during the month of August. The Tigers caught a break at the outset, as the opening kickoff by Billy Bennett—his first such attempt as the Bulldogs' new kickoff specialist—sailed out of bounds to give the Orange and Purple good field position for their opening drive. For the South Carolinians, it was largely downhill from there.

For starters, Tiger center Tommy Sharpe was sick at his stomach. The former walk-on from Albany, Ga., had overcome his relatively small stature (6'0" and 270 pounds, up 15 pounds from the year before) to win a scholarship and a starting spot on the offensive line. After making it onto the field for 22 plays as a backup in Athens the year before, Sharpe was ready to take on the Bulldogs as a first-teamer. "Growing up a Georgia fan in South Georgia," he said before the contest, "you want to give them your best shot."

Sharpe, like former Jungaleer center Tony Berryhill in the 1981 Tulane game, vomited while in his stance over the pigskin. As Bart Wright of *The Greenville News* noted in a newspaper column the following year, Sharpe was "renowned in the Clemson locker room for his propensity to blow chunks when he gets especially excited." Wright wrote as much after the Country Gentlemen's 2004 victory over Wake Forest, in which Sharpe rushed to the sidelines after the Orange and Purple's tying score in the fourth quarter and promptly lost his lunch.

On this occasion, Sharpe barfed *on the ball* before hiking it to quarterback Charlie Whitehurst, who received the snap to become the first sophomore since Nealon Greene in 1995 to start a season opener under center for the Tigers. The underclassman QB had started the final five games of the Fort Hill Felines' 2002 campaign, throwing for an ACC- best 420 yards against Duke in his first outing with the first string. Whitehurst threw four touchdown strikes at North Carolina and closed out the regular season by connecting on 27 of his 38 pass attempts against South Carolina.

Whitehurst, the son of an NFL signal caller, would go on to amass a school-record 3,561 passing yards in 2003…but, quite understandably, the sophomore quarterback was unable to hold onto the pigskin in its unpleasant condition after Sharpe's bout with ner vous nausea. ("Don't worry, Charlie," wrote columnist Matt Williams in the following week's edition of *The Tiger*, "I would have dropped it, too.") Nevertheless, after recovering his own fumble at the Clemson 36, Whitehurst engineered a four-minute, eight-play drive that covered 24 yards before the Tigers were compelled to punt the ball away to the visitors.

The Bulldogs took over at their own 20 and, on the Red and Black's first offensive snap, quarterback David Greene handed off to tailback Tony Milton, who went around the right side for a 16-yard pickup. After the next two plays netted eight yards, Georgia lined up with flanker Fred Gibson split to the near side as the lone receiver in the formation on third and two at the Athenians' 44 yard line.

Gibson, a preseason second-team All-American, ran a post route. He was up against cornerback Justin Miller, who had been tapped as a contender for the Jim Thorpe Award (given to the country's top defensive back) in the preseason. The previous autumn, Miller had earned unanimous freshman All-American honors after a rookie campaign in which he had chalked up an ACC-leading eight interceptions and tied a school record with 17 passes defended.

The Georgia coaches had noticed, however, that Miller had a tendency to charge forward against the receiver on short-yardage snaps. Accordingly, Gibson faked toward the sideline, cut back inside, and got behind the Tiger defensive back in the middle of the field. Greene found the wide-open receiver for a 56-yard hookup that put the Classic City Canines up by seven points. Just over nine minutes remained in the first quarter.

Clemson's ensuing possession ended when Whitehurst fumbled Sharpe's snap (this time, evidently, without any vomit being involved) and Georgia defensive tackle Marcus Jackson recovered the ball near midfield. Aided by a Gibson reception on which the Red and Black's leading receiver broke a tackle to pick up a first down, the Bulldogs took the turnover and moved the ball 27 yards in eight plays.

Georgia flanker Fred Gibson beat Clemson cornerback Justin Miller to bring in the 56-yard touchdown pass that started the scoring in 2003.

It did not appear at first that the drive was going anywhere, though. Greene was sacked for a five-yard loss on the initial snap of the series and Tiger defensive end J.J. Howard halted Milton behind the line of scrimmage one play later. Instead of facing third and 17 at midfield, however, the Dogs found themselves with a first down inside the Clemson 35 on account of a facemask flag thrown against Howard.

At the end of the four-minute possession, Bennett kicked a 34-yard field goal with just under two minutes to go in the period. The score gave the Georgia place-kicker his 280th, 281st, and 282nd career points to move him into a third-place tie with Kanon Parkman on the all-time school scoring list. It also called to mind the concern expressed by Andrew Gibbons in *The Tiger* the day before: "The Bulldogs played in many big games last year including the SEC Championship and the Sugar Bowl. The Tigers have not won a 'big game' in a while, and might not know how to bounce back from an early game momentum swing."

That fear proved well founded. Trailing by 10, the Jungaleers received the kickoff and proved unable to do much with it. Although the

Dogs' defense was depleted by inju ries and suspensions, cornerback (and converted running back) Bruce Thornton stopped Whitehurst for no gain on second down and cornerback (and converted running back) Kenny Bailey hurried the host squad's signal caller into a third-down incompletion.

Due to that defensive effort and a 10-yard penalty for an illegal block on the initial return, the Country Gentlemen not only were held to three yards on three plays, they actually ended up seven yards shy of where they originally took possession. This forced the second of six Clemson punts on the afternoon.

Shockley entered the game under center and handed off to Milton, whose 11-yard burst put the Red and Black in Tiger territory and gave the visitors a first down. On the first play of the second quarter, Shockley tacked on 10 yards of his own on a quarterback keeper. An 11-yard pass to split end Damien Gary and a pair of Ronnie Powell rushes totaling eight yards gave the Classic City Canines a short third down at the Clemson 15 yard line, but linebacker LeRoy Hill pressured Shockley into tossing an incomplete pass.

Georgia had marched 42 yards on eight snaps in the possession, chewing up nearly three minutes of playing time before being forced to line up for Bennett's second field goal attempt of the contest. When the three-point try was botched because of a high snap, Bennett took the ball and scrambled. The Bulldog place-kicker soon crossed paths with Tiger linebacker Lionel Richardson, who outweighed Bennett by 35 pounds. Their collision ended as the laws of physics dictated it would, with Richardson dragging him down just shy of the first-down marker.

Clemson could not capitalize on the Red-and-Black miscue, however. Two plays later, linebacker Arnold Harrison forced a fumble by wide receiver Derrick Hamilton, stripping the ball loose and sending it into the waiting arms of rover Sean Jones. After the Orange and Purple fumbled the pigskin away, the Bulldogs moved the ball five yards in the opposite direction yet were stymied when a would-be touchdown pass glanced off of split end Michael Johnson's hands in the end zone.

The Athenians then attempted again the field goal that had gone so poorly a minute and a half earlier. This time, Bennett divided the uprights from 30 yards away to grab sole possession of the third spot on the Georgia career points list with 285. Only Kevin Butler (353) and Herschel Walker (314) had scored more in a Bulldog uniform than Bennett, who was not yet done for the day.

The 13-point deficit lit a fire under the home team, as the Orange and Purple proceeded to mount their longest drive of the day. Following a 31-yard kickoff return by Justin Miller (whose 35.1-yard return average as a freshman in 2002 had led the ACC), a Georgia personal foul penalty moved the Tigers across midfield and Whitehurst's next two passes carried Clemson to the visitors' 12 yard line. Running back Chad Jasmin rushed for two yards then hauled in a pass for five more. An Airese Currie reception on third down brought the South Carolinians three feet nearer to their objective.

Having thus covered 58 yards in two minutes, the Fort Hill Felines found themselves facing fourth down on the Georgia four yard line. Rather than send his place-kicker onto the field, Clemson coach Tommy Bowden opted instead to try picking up the two yards his team needed to make it first and goal…or, better yet, to punch it into the end zone to make it a one-score contest.

The Jungaleer skipper knew how high the stakes were for his team and for his future. In an interview published in *The Tiger* the day before the game, Bowden had called the Georgia game "the biggest home opener" of his tenure and promised: "We have worked hard on our running game." The Tigers had lined up in the I formation on the first play of the afternoon and the Bulldogs had responded by stacking the box to stop the ground game.

There was little doubt which team had gotten the better of the exchange. Clemson's first drive featured just three running plays that picked up only two yards. The Orange and Purple rushed four times on their second series, gaining no ground in the process and ending with a fumbled snap. Later in the game, the Jungaleers tried unsuccessfully to draw the Dogs offsides rather than run a play in a short-yardage situation. The Tigers tallied a mere 21 *feet* of rushing yardage in the first half. On fourth and two inside the visitors' five yard line, power football went out the window.

Bowden, who called every offensive play for the Fort Hill Felines, instead borrowed a page from his father's book and attempted some trickery. The South Carolinians ran a flea flicker, with Whitehurst pitching the ball to tailback Duane Coleman and heading for the corner of the end zone as an intended receiver. Georgia defensive end Robert Geathers broke up Coleman's pass and the Bulldogs took over on downs.

The Red and Black proceeded to flip the field, moving 51 yards in almost six minutes on a pair of Greene-to-Gibson hookups of 17 and

22 yards, respectively. However, Hill hurried the Georgia quarterback into throwing an incompletion in the direction of his star receiver on second down, enabling defensive end Vontrell Jamison to sack Greene at the Clemson 40 on the following play.

The Dogs punted the ball back to their hosts and again the Tigers went on the march from their own 21 yard line. Whitehurst did most of the work on the drive, putting the ball in the air eight times in nine plays in the course of the possession. He opened with a nine-yard completion to wide receiver Currie and followed that with a 19-yard connection with Hamilton three plays later. That got the Orange and Purple to midfield and a subsequent pass interference penalty against the Athenians advanced the Fort Hill Felines another 15 yards.

Due to the constant hounding of the Bulldog pass rush, Whitehurst's last five tosses fell incomplete, so the 44-yard drive served to set up another three-point try. On a day that simply was not destined to belong to the Country Gentlemen, Lou Groza Award candidate Aaron Hunt came up short on his 52-yard field goal attempt. Despite having made good on 27 of his previous 34 three-point tries heading into his senior season, Hunt ended his career against the Red and Black with three missed field goals to show for his efforts.

The score remained 13-0 at intermission after the Dogs ran out the clock. In spite of the missed field goal, the Orange and Purple had to feel much like Georgia quarterback Preston Jones had felt at the break 13 years before. As had been the case in 1990, the trailing team had been shut out in the first half yet found itself down only by 13 points, some of which were gift-wrapped for the squad that held the halftime lead due to miscues by the opposition. Clemson was still in the game.

Certainly, Mark Richt believed this to be the case. "I don't know how long it was 13-0," the Bulldog head coach remarked afterwards. "All it took was one touchdown and they were one play away from taking the lead." The Tigers' last two drives had been their longest of the afternoon, and both very nearly ended in scores. Many of the fans in the stands had voiced their displeasure with Tommy Bowden's fourth-down play call in the red zone, but the Country Gentlemen were not out of it, and (unlike the Red and Black 13 years earlier) they had the benefit of playing at home.

The third quarter opened with a long kickoff by Clemson freshman Jad Dean—Fred Gibson fell down while attempting to retrieve the pigskin in the back of the end zone— followed by a long drive by the visitors. Milton and Powell were the work horses as the Georgia tailback tandem racked up yardage on the ground during an initial possession that consumed nearly half of the period. Although Greene also contributed completions of 23 yards to split end Reggie Brown and of 21 yards to tight end (and Palmetto State native) Ben Watson, his pass to tight end Robert Brannon for no gain on fourth down killed a 14-play, 77-yard march that ended three yards shy of the end zone. The Tigers now had their chance.

Given new life, Whitehurst and his teammates took the field needing to move the ball as effectively as they had at the end of the first half. This they failed to do. Over the course of the contest, the Clemson ground game never materialized, as the Orange and Purple lost more yards on penalties (45) than they gained on running plays (35). Meanwhile, the Tiger signal caller was harried and hurried whenever he dropped back to pass.

The Country Gentlemen's first three offensive snaps of the second half netted them only one yard when a five-yard Chad Jasmin run was followed by a four-yard Robert Geathers sack of Charlie Whitehurst. The South Carolinians booted the ball back to the Classic City Canines and Damien Gary returned punter (and Peach State native) Cole Chason's 40-yard punt to the home team's 32 yard stripe. For the second straight season, a Gary return near the Clemson 30 would set up a second-half score led by Georgia's second-string quarterback.

The Bulldogs advanced the pigskin a mere seven yards under D.J. Shockley's direction yet still put themselves in position for Billy Bennett to hammer home the 42-yard field goal that extended the visitors' lead to 16 ticks on the scoreboard inside the five-minute mark of the third period. The drive marked the Athenians' third four-play scoring march of the afternoon. Another Clemson three-and-out followed in spite of Justin Miller's 33- yard return to set up the Orange and Purple at their own 45 yard line.

Now it was the Tigers' turn to rise to the occasion defensively. Hill and Richardson converged on Shockley, forcing the first of two consecutive incomplete passes hurled in the direction of Watson. Having been limited to a three-play, one-minute possession that gained just two yards, the Classic City Canines had no choice but to punt.

All was not lost for the South Carolinians, who still could tie the game with two touchdowns and a pair of two-point conversions. Whitehurst directed the Orange and Purple downfield, taking his team on a 15-play march that ate up nearly eight minutes and carried the Country Gentlemen into the red zone once more.

A 13-yard pass from Whitehurst to wide receiver Kevin Young-blood on third down moved the chains and carried the Tigers onto the Red and Black's side of the field. Back- to-back six-yard rushes by Coleman picked up another first down and brought the Fort Hill Felines to the Bulldog 26 to close out the third quarter.

After a loss of four yards on third down at the outset of the fourth period, Whitehurst used his legs to pick up 11 yards on fourth down and Coleman pounded the ball for five yards on the next snap. An off-sides penalty on the defense and an ensuing false start flag against the offense set up first and goal inside the Georgia 10 yard line.

Bulldog defensive end David Pollack blew up the option play on which Whitehurst was sacked for a seven-yard loss. Youngblood hauled in a five-yard reception, but Clemson's 45-yard drive ended un-ceremoniously when Pollack picked off a Whitehurst screen pass to keep the home team off the board and reclaim possession for the Red and Black. After snagging the ball, Pollack rumbled 24 yards before being brought down at the Georgia 40, so he even gave his offensive teammates good field position from which to start.

The shutout-preserving grab gave Pollack, the 2002 SEC player of the year who eventually would become the Bulldogs' second (after Herschel Walker) three-time consensus All-American, his third career interception. His first collegiate pick had also come in the Palmetto State, when Pollack batted down a Corey Jenkins pass attempt in the end zone and held onto it for the game-winning touch- down against the Gamecocks in Columbia the year before.

The Bulldogs now had the chance to salt the game away and they made the most of their opportunity. Greene guided the team 60 yards downfield in six plays, taking exactly three minutes to direct a touch-down drive that included a 39-yard grab by Michael Johnson and cul-minated in a three-yard run on a quarterback keeper. After Greene broke the plane, Bennett split the uprights to give the Red and Black a commanding 23-0 advantage.

The Tigers ran three plays for no gain and punted the ball away after having held it for just 27 seconds. Shockley was under center for the ensuing drive and, once again, the hero of the previous year's Clemson-Georgia showdown was not to be outdone.

Greene had led the visiting team on a six-play drive taking three minutes, covering 60 yards, and ending in a three-yard touchdown run by the Georgia signal caller? Shock ley saw that performance and raised the stakes, taking the Dogs on a six-play drive of his own. This

Bulldog defensive end David Pollack intercepted a pass by Clemson quarterback Charlie Whitehurst deep in Georgi terri- tory to preserve the shutout at Memorial Stadium.

time, sparked by first-down rushes of 24 and 12 yards by tailback Michael   Cooper, the Athenians went 61 yards in two minutes and 44 seconds, and the possession concluded with a 29-yard touchdown run by Shockley himself. Bennett's PAT was his 12th point of the day and the 290th of his career.

The score that made it 30-0 came with just under three minutes remaining in the game, so there was nothing else to do but let the contest play out as it had all afternoon. Clemson's freshman quarterback, Chansi Stuckey, ran three plays before the Tigers punted and Georgia ran out the clock. The victory marked the 20th time that the Bulldogs had held the Tigers scoreless in 62 series meetings, but 13 of the previous 19 shutouts had come before World War II.

Now, keeping an opponent off of the scoreboard entirely in a Clemson-Georgia game was something of a rarity, as neither team had blanked the other since 1978. No Mark Richt-coached team had ever before posted a shutout and no Tommy Bowden-coached team (either at Clemson or, before that, at Tulane) had ever before been held to a goose egg. It was the first time the Dogs had shut out an opponent in a season opener on the road since 1954. The Red and Black had evened their all-time record at Clemson at 9-9-2 in Bowden's 50th game as the Tigers' head coach.

In some respects, the contest was a mirror image of previous series meetings. For instance, the 1969 Georgia squad, fresh off of an SEC championship season in which the Athenians had lost only one game and had been ranked fourth in the final coaches' poll in that Sugar Bowl season, had played its first away outing of the autumn in Death Valley, where the Red and Black posted a 30-0 victory. Now, the 2003 Georgia squad, fresh off of an SEC championship season in which the Athenians had lost only one game and had been ranked third in the final coaches' poll in that Sugar Bowl season, had duplicated its effort 34 years later.

Likewise, the 2003 score looked suspiciously similar to that posted by Clemson over Georgia exactly a century earlier, when the Jungaleers beat the Athenians by a 29-0 margin to begin John Heisman's last season at Fort Hill. Finally, in 2002, the Tigers had come to Sanford Stadium and limited the Bulldogs to 14 first downs and 203 yards of offense. One year later, the Red and Black traveled to Memorial Stadium and held the Orange and Purple to 14 first downs (three of which came by penalty) and 199 yards of offense...just two more total yards than the Classic City Canines had managed rushing yards.

The Athenians had made clear their preference for the running game, keeping the ball on the ground 46 times in 70 snaps, including 23 rushes on 29 first-down plays. The Bulldogs ran on three of their four fourth-down tries (one of which, admittedly, was inadvertent on Billy Bennett's part) and, even on second and long, Georgia called more running plays (7) than pass plays (6). The Tigers, by contrast, ran the ball 22 times in 61 offensive plays, with a first-down ratio of 14 passes to 10 rushes.

The most remarkable aspect of the Red-and-Black running tally was the way in which the visitors gained their 197 yards on the ground. While the Tigers eked out only 35 rushing yards as a unit, four different Bulldogs ran for 45 yards or more. Starting tailback Tony Milton carried the ball 14 times for 53 yards before exiting the game with a knee bruise. Tailback Ronnie Powell led the team with 54 yards and Michael Cooper tacked on 45 more, with D.J. Shockley adding 45 of his own. Perhaps due to the presence of such a wealth of talent in the offensive backfield, 2003 would be only the second season since 1972 in which no individual Bulldog had 100 yards rushing in any game.

Charlie Whitehurst performed admirably, completing 19 of his 33 passes for 151 yards, but Clemson's leading receiver, All-ACC track star Airese Currie, caught seven balls for a combined 56 yards, equaling the gain by Fred Gibson on his first-quarter touchdown reception alone. The figures favored the Bulldogs in every facet of the game, as Georgia held the ball for 33:45, had three takeaways yet no giveaways, and managed to hold an edge in third- down conversion percentage (38%, as opposed to the Tigers' 29%) comparable to the ad vantage Clemson had enjoyed in that same category in the preceding fall's opening outing.

After the game, the home team seemed more than a little shell-shocked. Duane Coleman, who led the Country Gentlemen's rushing effort with 12 carries for 29 yards in his first college game, said, "We worked on the running game all spring, and I had hoped it was going to be a big part of the game today. Unfortunately, it wasn't. I don't know what we can say about it."

Coleman's head coach agreed, as Tommy Bowden remarked: "I thought we would have performed better offensively…. It's discouraging." The area press concluded that, even though Hank Williams, Jr., had played a concert at Clemson the night of the First Friday parade just prior to the Georgia game, the Fort Hill Felines were not ready for some football. Bart Wright wrote in the next day's Greenville News that the Jungaleers "just got exposed." Wright minced no words when placing the head coach squarely on the hot seat: "Without a major turnaround in the next three months, Tommy Bowden will be out of a job."

Even so, much as they had done following their loss to Georgia the year before, the Ti gers ripped through their September slate with three victories and no additional losses, handling Furman, Middle Tennessee State, and Humanitarian Bowl-bound Georgia Tech by a combined 104-34 margin to demonstrate that the Country Gentlemen were better, both offensively and defensively, than they had appeared in Death Valley in their season opener.

In particular, the 39-3 road win over the Yellow Jackets at Grant Field gave the Jungaleers their biggest win over the Engineers in Atlanta in a century. Incidentally, queasy-stom ached Clemson center Tommy Sharpe reportedly threw up during the MTSU game, as well.

In the midst of that successful run through the season's first full calendar month, the Fort Hill faithful found themselves facing a tragic loss off the field. Longtime announcer Jim Phillips, the legendary "voice of the Tigers," passed away at age 69 on the Tuesday following the Jungaleers' triumph over the Paladins. Phillips's final Saturday in the broadcast booth marked the 401st Clemson football game he had called for loyal listeners throughout the Palmetto State and beyond.

The Orange and Purple proceeded to swap road setbacks and home wins between the first Saturday in October and the first Saturday in November, falling at Gator Bowl- bound Maryland by two touchdowns before beating Continental Tire Bowl-bound Virginia by a field goal, coming up short at Tangerine Bowl-bound N.C. State by a 17-15 margin then sinking North Carolina by eight, and taking a whipping in Winston-Salem from a Wake Forest squad that thumped the Tigers 45-17 yet bouncing back to defeat third-ranked Florida State by 16 points.

The latter two games represented a dramatic reversal of the Country Gentlemen's fortunes. The lopsided setback suffered against the Demon Deacons dropped the South Carolinians to 5-4, yet the Clemson head coach addressed his team in the locker room afterward and said, "I fully expect us to win next Saturday against Florida State." The Ti gers responded by holding the Seminoles out of the end zone for three periods as Charlie Whitehurst went 17 for 27 and connected with Derrick Hamilton on a 56-yard touch- down strike to snap an 11-game losing streak to the Tribe from Tallahassee.

The victory over FSU gave Tommy Bowden his first win over his famous father in the annual "Bowden Bowl" and began the "major turnaround" Bart Wright had proclaimed essential the day after the Dogs defeated the Jungaleers. After dealing the Orange Bowl-bound Seminoles their only loss of the season to a team other than the Miami Hurricanes, the Orange and Purple closed out the campaign on a winning streak.

A Duke squad that had won just two games overall (and none in ACC play) over the previous three seasons had shown (relative) signs of life under new head coach Ted Roof, whose initial Blue Devil squad came into Memorial Stadium sporting a 3-7 ledger and fresh from a baffling 41-17 conquest of a Georgia Tech team headed for a seven-win season and a convincing postseason victory.

The Fort Hill Felines made short work of the club from Durham, administering a 40-7 drubbing before turning in an even more dominant performance one week later. In a season-ending showdown with the Gamecocks in which Tommy Bowden's job likely was on the line, the Country Gentlemen blasted their in-state rivals in Columbia to the tune of 63-17.

The 63 ticks with which they riddled the scoreboard marked the most points ever scored by the Tigers in 101 series meetings with South Carolina, as well as being the most tallied by a Clemson club since the Orange and Purple's 1981 national championship season. Charlie Whitehurst completed all seven of his first-quarter pass attempts for 149 yards and three touchdowns and Chad Jasmin became the first Tiger in 85 years to score four rushing touchdowns against the Gamecocks.

The strong finish earned Bowden a new lease on his coaching life and landed Clemson a Peach Bowl date with sixth-ranked Tennessee. The Volunteers' Casey Clausen completed 31 of his 55 pass attempts for 384 yards and a pair of TDs to outperform the Tigers' Charlie Whitehurst (who was 22 of 40 for 246 yards and an interception), but the South Carolinians held Tennessee to just 38 rushing yards in the course of a 27-14 victory paced by Chad Jasmin's MVP-clinching 130-yard effort.

The Red and Black had been matter-of-fact about their victory in Death Valley. Georgia nose tackle Darrius Swain said after the game, "It was a great feeling. Fire up the bus, and let's go home." The Dogs went back to Sanford Stadium, where they cruised to a comfortable win over Middle Tennessee State (in a game in which Fred Gibson would suffer the hamstring injury that caused him to see only intermittent action for the next several outings) before following up their shutout of the Tigers in Memorial Stadium with a near-blanking of South Carolina between the hedges.

The Red and Black led the Gamecocks 24-0 with a minute to go in the contest, but, after the SEC squad from the Palmetto State scored a trash touchdown with 52 seconds remaining in the game, Damien Gary returned the ensuing onside kick attempt 44 yards for the TD that made the final margin 31-7.

Although the Dogs crossed their opponent's 40 yard line six times in the first half, three turnovers doomed the visitors as Georgia fell to 10th-ranked LSU in Baton Rouge by seven skinny points. The Athenians rebounded to hammer Alabama (in its first year under head coach Mike Shula), Tennessee, and Vanderbilt by a combined 105-45 score before escaping against UAB at homecoming by a Billy Bennett field goal.

In Jacksonville, the Bulldogs were sunk by a trio of field goals from the Outback Bowl- bound Gators' Matt Leach, the last of which broke a 13-all deadlock with 33 seconds left in the fourth quarter. Nevertheless, dominant Georgia performances over an Auburn outfit headed

for the Music City Bowl (in a game in which a thrilling 99-yard interception return by linebacker Odell Thurman cemented a 26-7 Red-
and-Black victory) and Kentucky (by a 30-10 final) clinched a share of
a second straight SEC East crown for the Dogs.

Following a 34-17 win over the Yellow Jackets at Grant Field, the
Classic City Canines returned to Atlanta for an SEC championship
game rematch with Louisiana State one week later. The Bayou Bengals
had improved steadily since September and the No. 3 Fighting Tigers
built up a 17-point second-quarter lead before cruising to a 34-13 victory and an eventual national championship.

The Bulldogs' season ended on a positive note in Orlando, where
the Red and Black were sent to face Purdue in the Capital One Bowl. In
Georgia's previous postseason pairing with the Boilermakers, the Big
Ten squad had stunned the Athenians with 25 unanswered points to
open the Outback Bowl on New Year's Day 2000 before subsequently
surrendering 28 unanswered points as the Dogs claimed an overtime
victory in the largest bowl comeback in college football history.

A similar pattern unfolded between the two teams on New Year's
Day 2004, when Georgia leapt out to an early 24-point advantage,
only to see Purdue explode for 17 points in the final period, including a 44-yard field goal to tie the contest in the final minute. The two
teams went to overtime once again and Bulldog tailback Kregg Lump-
kin (whose fourth-quarter fumble had allowed the Boilers to knot the
score) punched in the game-winning touchdown that gave the Athenians the 34-27 victory and prompted Mark Richt to exclaim after the
game, "I'll tell you what…that was fun!"

The Bulldogs' and the Tigers' respective postseason victories made
2003 the first year since 1988 in which Clemson and Georgia both won
bowl games. In the interim, the Country Gentlemen had lost six of
seven postseason engagements between 1995 and 2002. The Red and
Black ended up ranked seventh in the final AP poll, while the Orange
and Purple climbed to 22nd.

In as much as each squad had improved its ranking between the
preseason and post- season polls, neither Clemson nor Georgia could
doubt that the season was an overall suc- cess. Both teams suffered
some setbacks which were frustratingly narrow and others which were
embarrassingly lopsided—including, in the Tigers' case, the opening
contest against the Bulldogs—but one club demonstrated definite improvement and the other showed staying power after its best autumn
in ages.

Although the 12-game regular season had been made possible by the fortuitous way in which the fall Saturdays fell, the extra revenue generated by the additional game soon gave rise to a movement to make the change permanent. The ultimate success of that cause heightened the likelihood that major conference programs would schedule out-of- conference games with members of their own weight class, so it quickly became apparent that 2003 represented not the last gasp of the Clemson-Georgia rivalry, but the renewal of a series which may have been made more infrequent but was not yet on its last legs.

For fans on both sides of the state line who bled Bulldog red and Tiger orange, that reality was good news that offered legitimate hope for future tussles between the two old foes who had spent 106 years fighting like Cats and Dogs.

www.ingramcontent.com/pod-product-compliance
Lightning Source LLC
Chambersburg PA
CBHW051212090426
42742CB00021B/3421